Global Trends and Transformations in Culture, Business, and Technology

Global Trends and Transformations in Culture, Business, and Technology

Hamid Yeganeh

BUSINESS EXPERT PRESS

Leader in applied, concise business books

Global Trends and Transformations in Culture, Business, and Technology

Copyright © Business Expert Press, LLC, 2022.

Cover design by Charlene Kronstedt

Interior design by Exeter Premedia Services Private Ltd., Chennai, India

First published in 2022 by
Business Expert Press, LLC
222 East 46th Street, New York, NY 10017
www.businessexpertpress.com

ISBN-13: 978-1-63742-072-0 (paperback)
ISBN-13: 978-1-63742-073-7 (e-book)

Business Expert Press International Business Collection

First edition: 2022

10 9 8 7 6 5 4 3 2 1

Description

The current volume offers a concise and analytical portrait of the contemporary world. The author encompasses concepts and theories from multiple disciplines notably sociology, anthropology, business, and economics to examine major global trends and transformations of the modern world, their underlying causes, and their consequences. The volume is organized in two parts and 17 chapters. The first part examines global demographic trends, globalization, culture, emerging markets, global security, environmental degradation, large corporations, and economic inequality. The second part analyzes major transformations in health care, food, the sharing economy, Fourth Industrial Revolution, consumption, work and organization, innovation, and various technologies in areas such as automation, robotics, connectivity, quantum computing, and new materials.

This book is a valuable reference for business leaders, managers, students, and all those who are passionate about understanding the rapidly changing contemporary world.

Keywords

culture; inequality; emerging markets; environmental degradation; global demographics; large corporations; global health care; food; the sharing economy; innovation; automation; robotics; data; connectivity; quantum computing; materials

Contents

CHAPTER 1

Global Demographic Trends

An Incredible Growth of Human Population

Throughout most of human history, for thousands of years, the world population growth has been very slow. For instance, it is estimated that the world's population grew slowly from about 2.4 million people in 10,000 BCE to 295 million in 1,000 CE [1]. Only 200 years ago there were less than one billion human beings living on earth. Since the 18th century with the advent of industrial revolution and advances in medicine, agriculture, and sanitation, the world population has increased exponentially. Around the 1830s, the world population reached one billion for the first time. It took another century for the world population to hit two billion around the 1930s. The third billion was reached only 30 years later in the 1960s. Since then, the world population has grown very rapidly soaring to a colossal number of seven billion in 2011 (see Table 1.1 and Figure 1.1). In other words, the world population has witnessed an astonishing surge of 133 percent only in 50 years between 1960 and 2011. At the time of this writing (mid-2021), the world population is estimated at 7.9 billion, and it is expected to rise another 100 million by the end of the year. Accordingly, the world's population has increased by approximately one billion over the last 12 years.

The surge in population growth rates in the 1950s and 1960s was caused mainly by quick declines in death rates across the developing world [2–4]. According to the United Nations Population Division, the world's population is expected to grow to 8.5 billion in 2030 and further to 9.7 billion in 2050 and to 10.9 billion in 2100 [5]. If these predictions come true, the world's population will see an increase of seven billion in 100 years between 1956 and 2056 or an astonishing growth of almost 234 percent! To put it in perspective, 10 billion would be the equivalent of adding China and India's populations to the present world

Table 1.1 World population historical data

Year	Population	Yearly change (%)	Yearly change	Urban population (%)	Urban population
2020	7,794,798,739	1.05	81,330,639	56	4,378,993,944
2019	7,713,468,100	1.08	82,377,060	56	4,299,438,618
2018	7,631,091,040	1.10	83,232,115	55	4,219,817,318
2017	7,515,284,153	1.11	82,620,878	54.70	4,110,778,369
2016	7,432,663,275	1.13	83,191,176	54.30	4,034,193,153
2015	7,349,472,099	1.18	83,949,411	53.80	3,957,285,013
2010	6,929,725,043	1.23	82,017,839	51.50	3,571,272,167
2005	6,519,635,850	1.25	78,602,746	49.10	3,199,013,076
2000	6,126,622,121	1.33	78,299,807	46.60	2,856,131,072
1995	5,735,123,084	1.55	85,091,077	44.80	2,568,062,984
1990	5,309,667,699	1.82	91,425,426	43	2,285,030,904
1985	4,852,540,569	1.79	82,581,621	41.30	2,003,049,795
1980	4,439,632,465	1.80	75,646,647	39.40	1,749,539,272
1975	4,061,399,228	1.98	75,782,307	37.80	1,534,721,238
1970	3,682,487,691	2.08	71,998,514	36.70	1,350,280,789
1965	3,322,495,121	1.94	60,830,259	NA	NA
1960	3,018,343,828	1.82	52,005,861	33.80	1,019,494,911
1955	2,758,314,525	1.78	46,633,043	NA	NA

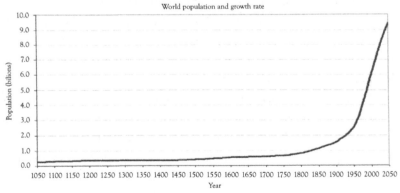

Figure 1.1 World population growth over time, 1050 to 2050

population [6]. Because of a very fast population growth between the 1950s and the 1970s, many countries encountered difficulty in implementing their development plans and introduced birth control and family planning programs. Subsequently, population growth rate fairly slowed down in the 1990s. Due to the birth control programs and contagious diseases such as AIDS/HIV, currently, the world population grows more slowly than in the 1970s and 1980s.

Historically, it is possible to identify three major phases in the world's population growth. The first phase was premodern era or the period before the 17th century when population growth was very slow due to a combination of factors including a shortage of food resources and lower levels of life expectancy. The second phase began in the 18th century with the industrial revolution and was marked by rising standards of living and improving health. The third phase started in the 1980s as the world's population growth rate, particularly in developed countries, started to slow down [1]. Despite the slackening growth, the world population will continue to grow in short term and midterm because the fertility rates in developing countries are still high and survival rates are expected to improve. Therefore, continued population growth until 2050 is almost certain.

In addition to the global population growth, we should pay attention to the distribution, the density, and the uneven patterns of growth across the world as these issues imply important consequences. At the present, 4.5 billion people or an equivalent of 60 percent of the world's population live in Asia making it the most populous continent. After Asia, Africa hosts 1.3 billion people or 16 percent of the world's population, while Europe with a population of 742 million and Latin America and the Caribbean with 646 million, respectively, contain 10 and 9 percent of the world's population. North America and Oceania with 361 million and 41 million, respectively, together contain only 5 percent of the world's population and enjoy a low degree of population density [5] (see Table 1.2). The two most populous countries of the world, namely China (1.45 billion) and India (1.35 billion), astonishingly account for almost 40 percent of the human population. Based on these observations, we understand that the world's population is distributed lopsidedly in such a way that the low-income Asian and African countries account for the largest populations and have the highest demographic densities. By contrast, the high-income countries of Europe and North America are scarcely populated and have the lowest level of demographic density. An important observation is that many of high-income countries have been

Table 1.2 Distribution of the world's population by region

No.	Region	Population 2020	Yearly change	Net change	Density (P/km²)	Migrants (net)	Fertility rate	Median age	World share
1	Asia	4,641,054,775	0.86%	39,683,577	150	−1,729,112	2.151942	32	59.50%
2	Africa	1,340,598,147	2.49%	32,533,952	45	−463,024	4.4383749	20	17.20%
3	Europe	747,636,026	0.06%	453,275	34	1,361,011	1.60964603	43	9.60%
4	Latin America	653,962,331	0.90%	5,841,374	32	−521,499	2.04466043	31	8.40%
5	North America	368,869,647	0.62%	2,268,683	20	1,196,400	1.75268862	39	4.70%
6	Oceania	42,677,813	1.31%	549,778	5	156,226	2.35700692	33	0.50%

Source: www.worldometers.info

witnessing very low fertility rates and high life expectancies for the past seven decades [7]. On the contrary, developing countries are still experiencing high fertility rates combined with improving life expectancy and declining infant mortality. It is important to note that the least developed countries have the highest fertility rates around 4.3 children per woman and the fastest growth rates estimated about 2.4 percent per year [5]. The general pattern is that the population growth rates across the world are inversely associated with the levels of socioeconomic development. The poorest and the least developed regions (mainly the sub-Saharan Africa and Indian subcontinent) have the highest population growth rates. Another important disparity between the rich and the poor countries resides in their median age levels, as they represent, respectively, older and younger populations. For instance, Europe with a median age of 42.5 years has the oldest population, while the median age in many developing countries is estimated around 20 years.

The Diverging Growth Rates: Sub-Saharan Africa and India Are the Fastest Growing Areas

The global population is expected to grow in the next five decades, but there are significant disparities across the world (see Figure 1.2). Those countries with lower median age levels are poised to have the highest population growth in coming years. Africa has the highest growth rate at 2.5 percent, while Europe has the lowest growth rate at 0.04 percent [6]. This high rate of population growth in Africa means that the African population is expected to double in the next 28 years. Based on similar projections, more than half of the global population growth in the next four decades will occur in Africa. Between now and 2100, the populations of many African countries are expected to increase at least three- to fourfold. The populations of extremely poor African countries such as Angola, Burundi, the Democratic Republic of the Congo, Malawi, Mali, Niger, Somalia, Uganda, the United Republic of Tanzania, and Zambia are projected to increase fivefold by 2100 [5]. Nigeria may surpass the United States to become the world's third populous country by 2050. Simply put, 1.3 billion people will be added only in Africa between now and 2050, while Asia and mainly India are responsible for an increase of

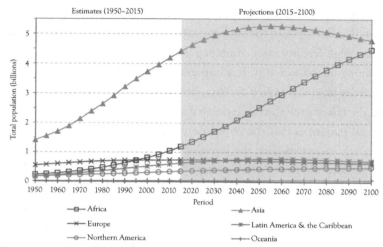

Figure 1.2 Population growth by region, 1950 to 2100

Source: United Nations, Department of Economic and Social Affairs, Population Division (2017). *World Population Prospects: The 2017 Revision.* New York: United Nations.

another billion people for the same period. Based on similar forecasts, the drastic population growth in Africa, unlike Asia, will continue even after 2050 [5]. Consequently, sub-Saharan Africa's share of global population is projected to grow to 25 percent by 2050 and 39 percent by 2100, while the share of the people residing in Asia will fall to 54 percent by 2050 and 44 percent by 2100.

China (approximately 1.4 billion) and India (approximately 1.3 billion), the two most populous countries of the world, respectively, account for 19 and 18 percent of the global population, but they are on radically different paths. Unlike China, the fertility rate in India has remained very high (see Table 1.3). As a result, India is supposed to overtake China as the world's most populous country by 2025. Consistent with the same estimates, India's population will reach 1.5 billion in 2030 and 1.7 billion in 2050, while the population of China is expected to remain constant until the 2030s and decrease slightly afterward [5]. Northern America, Latin America and the Caribbean, and Oceania are projected to experience smaller population growth levels, while Europe is expected to have a population decline by 2050. By 2050, the populations in six countries could exceed 300 million, including China, India, Indonesia, Nigeria,

Table 1.3 *Demographics of the 20 largest countries*

No.	Country	Population 2020	Yearly change	Net change	Density (P/km²)	Fertility rate	Median age	Urban population	World share
1	China	1,439,323,776	0.39%	5,540,090	153	1.7	38	61%	18.47%
2	India	1,380,004,385	0.99%	13,586,631	464	2.2	28	35%	17.70%
3	USA	331,002,651	0.59%	1,937,734	36	1.8	38	83%	4.25%
4	Indonesia	273,523,615	1.07%	2,898,047	151	2.3	30	56%	3.51%
5	Pakistan	220,892,340	2.00%	4,327,022	287	3.6	23	35%	2.83%
6	Brazil	212,559,417	0.72%	1,509,890	25	1.7	33	88%	2.73%
7	Nigeria	206,139,589	2.58%	5,175,990	226	5.4	18	52%	2.64%
8	Bangladesh	164,689,383	1.01%	1,643,222	1,265	2.1	28	39%	2.11%
9	Russia	145,934,462	0.04%	62,206	9	1.8	40	74%	1.87%
10	Mexico	128,932,753	1.06%	1,357,224	66	2.1	29	84%	1.65%
11	Japan	126,476,461	-0.30%	-383,840	347	1.4	48	92%	1.62%
12	Ethiopia	114,963,588	2.57%	2,884,858	115	4.3	19	21%	1.47%
13	Philippines	109,581,078	1.35%	1,464,463	368	2.6	26	47%	1.41%
14	Egypt	102,334,404	1.94%	1,946,331	103	3.3	25	43%	1.31%
15	Vietnam	97,338,579	0.91%	876,473	314	2.1	32	38%	1.25%
16	DR Congo	89,561,403	3.19%	2,770,836	40	6	17	46%	1.15%
17	Turkey	84,339,067	1.09%	909,452	110	2.1	32	76%	1.08%
18	Iran	83,992,949	1.30%	1,079,043	52	2.2	32	76%	1.08%
19	Germany	83,783,942	0.32%	266,897	240	1.6	46	76%	1.07%
20	Thailand	69,799,978	0.25%	174,396	137	1.5	40	51%	

Source: www.Worldometers.info.

Pakistan, and the United States. The population growth in the next decades will be so uneven that nine countries will be responsible for more than half of the world's population surge. These countries include the Democratic Republic of the Congo, Egypt, Ethiopia, India, Indonesia, Nigeria, Pakistan, the United Republic of Tanzania, and the United States of America. In this club, the only developed country is the United States, but the rest of the countries represent the developing or poor economies of Asia and Africa.

In sharp contrast to Africa and most parts of Asia, the populations of 48 countries and areas are expected to decline between 2020 and 2050. Many Eastern European countries including Bulgaria, Croatia, Hungary, Latvia, Lithuania, the Republic of Moldova, Romania, Russia, Serbia, Ukraine, and Japan may experience a sharp population drop of 15 percent or more by 2050 [5, 6]. According to *Financial Times*, Japan's population may decline as much as 31 percent by 2065 and 60 percent by 2115. This means that the population of Japan could plummet from 127 to 88 million by 2065 and to 51 million by 2115 [8]. The population decline in these countries is a result of lower fertility rates and higher median age levels over the course of the past four decades. By 2025, the largest relative reductions in population size are expected in Bulgaria, Latvia, Lithuania, and Ukraine [5].

Aging Populations: All Areas of the World Are Aging Fast, Except Africa

In most parts of the world including developing countries, we have been observing two important trends: the decline in fertility rates on the one hand and the rise in life expectancy on the other hand. The outcome of these two trends is the emergence of aging populations across the world. Currently, there are around 962 million people aged 60 or over in the world, comprising 13 percent of the global population and growing at a rate of about 3 percent per year [9]. It is projected that, by 2050, half of the global population will reside in countries where at least 20 percent of the inhabitants are aged 60 years or over [10]. The number of people aged 60 and above is expected to double between 2015 and 2050 from 960 million to 2.1 billion globally [5]. Almost 66 percent of this increase will occur in Asia, 13 percent in Africa, 11 percent in Latin America and the Caribbean, and the remaining 10 percent in other regions [5]. Similarly, the number of the oldest-old or people aged 80 or over may triple by 2050 and increase more than sevenfold by the end of the century. This means that the number of people aged 80 or over is projected to increase from 125 million in 2015 to 434 million in 2050 and to 1 billion in 2100 [5].

The pace of population aging is accelerating, but it is not uniform across the globe. Europe and many developed countries such as Japan have been aging for decades; however, the newly industrialized countries such as South Korea have entered the aging phase more recently. In 2015, elderly people comprised 22 percent of the population of high-income countries, 13 percent of upper middle-income countries, 8 percent of lower middle-income countries, and 5 percent of low-income countries [10]. Europe, with a median age of 42 years, has the oldest population, which is expected to reach 46 years by 2050. By contrast, the median age for much of developing countries is hovering around 20 years and may reach 26 years in 2050. Therefore, it is possible to project that the older populations in developed countries will grow in size, but at a much slower pace than those in newly developed countries of Asia and Latin America. In the next two decades, upper middle-income countries are expected to continue to experience a rapid growth in the number of old people. Several upper middle-income countries are projected to become as aged as many of today's high-income countries within the next 15 years. In many developing countries, population aging is taking place much more rapidly than it did in the countries that developed earlier. For example, it took 115 years for France, for the proportion of the population aged 60 years or over to increase from 7 to 14 percent [11]. In contrast, it is estimated that for Brazil it will take just 25 years for the percentage of older people to rise from 7 to 14 percent [10]. For that reason, today's developing countries must adapt much more quickly to the aging populations and their necessities. The impact of aging will be particularly noticeable in the case of Asian countries that account for large portions of the world population. For instance, by 2050, two-thirds of the world's older people will live in Asia (see Figure 1.3). As mentioned previously, China and India are on very different paths of demographic change because of their

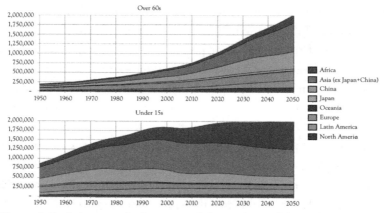

Figure 1.3 **Aging populations growth by region, 1950 to 2050**

dissimilar age structures and family planning policies. While China is already an aging country, India is still young. Latin American and African countries are expected to have younger populations until 2050 as they still have high fertility rates and lower median age levels. Unlike all other regions, Africa is and will remain the youngest region in the forthcoming decades.

A massive aging population could involve significant implications for the labor market, personal savings, and global productivity. For instance, in Europe and Japan, the social protection systems including health care and pension systems may encounter difficulty in managing their finances [12]. Because of aging populations, disabilities and noncommunicable illnesses such as cardiovascular diseases, cancer, diabetes, and dementia will be rampant, causing financial pressure on public health systems. On the other hand, because of aging populations, many countries may benefit from demographic dividend or a significant boost to their income per capita. As fertility rates decline, the burden of youth dependency reduces, the proportion of workers and savers in the population increases, and women are liberated from childbearing. In an aging society, the existing resources can be allocated to building infrastructure and investing in education and research and development [6]. Indeed, the global aging in most developing countries except in sub-Saharan Africa is expected to result in lower levels of poverty. Nevertheless, the global aging could slow the pace of economic development in emerging economies particularly in

China that will experience a massive shrinking of their workforce in near future. India unlike China will be immune to the effects of population aging, at least for the next two decades.

Urbanization: 2.5 Billion Will Be Urbanized by 2050

Because of the widespread socioeconomic development in the past six decades, the world has gone through a process of fast urbanization. The world's population is constantly becoming more urbanized as cities are attracting a large number of inhabitants. For the first time in 2007, the world's urban population surpassed the world's rural population. According to the World Bank reports, the share of the world's urban population has risen from 30 percent in 1950 to more than 55 percent in 2018. The ongoing urbanization in conjunction with the growth of the global population will add 2.5 billion people to the urban population by 2050, with nearly 90 percent of the increase concentrated in Asia and Africa [13]. By 2050, almost 68 percent of the world's population is projected to live in urban centers [14].

As of 2018, North America and Latin America were the most urbanized regions of the world with over 80 percent urban settlements [14]. In the same year, Europe's rate of urban settlement was close to 74 percent, while Africa and Asia were mostly rural with urban settlement rates of 40 and 48 percent, respectively [14]. In 2018, 16 countries still had low levels of urbanization of 20 percent and less, including Burundi, Ethiopia, Malawi, Niger, South Sudan and Uganda in Africa, and Nepal and Sri Lanka in Asia [14]. There are considerable disparities between developed and developing countries with regard to the urbanization process. For instance, most of the developed countries urbanized in the 1960s and 1970s as the urban share of their total populations rose from 47 percent in the 1960s to 60 percent in the early 1980s and plateauing subsequently. At present, more than 75 percent of the populations in developing countries still live in rural areas, suggesting that the sharpest increase in the urban centers will happen in such countries [15]. Based on the United Nations estimates, almost 2.5 billion people will be added to the global urban population by 2050. Of these 2.5 billion new urban dwellers, almost 90 percent will live in Africa and Asia. Only three countries, namely India, China, and Nigeria, are expected to account for more than one-third of global urban population growth [14]. Seven other countries, notably the Democratic Republic of the Congo, Ethiopia, the United Republic of Tanzania, Bangladesh, Indonesia, Pakistan, and the United States, will account for another 20 percent of the growth of the global urban population [14]. In some Asian countries such as China and Korea, urbanization accompanied economic development, but in many other countries, including Pakistan, Haiti, and the Democratic Republic of the Congo, urbanization happened in the absence of socioeconomic development and despite dysfunctional politics [16]. Indeed, a remarkable trend in the contemporary world is the rapid urbanization in developing and poor nations. For example, in the 1960s, most of the poor nations were rural with urbanization rates over less than 25 percent. In the recent years, the majority of poor countries have urbanized. According to the United Nations, the urbanization rate in developing countries increased from 18 percent in 1950 to 47 percent in 2011 [16].

The urbanization phenomenon has resulted in the emergence of the very large urban centers or "megacities" with more than 10 million inhabitants. By 2030, the world is projected to have 41 cities with more than 10 million inhabitants [14]. Currently, 29 megacities are home to 471 million people, an equivalent of 6 percent of the world's total population [6]. Furthermore, the number of cities with populations over 20 million is increasing fast. In this category, Tokyo (38 million), Delhi (26 million), Shanghai (23 million), Sao Paulo (21 million), Mumbai (21 million), and Mexico City (21 million) are ranked as the largest cities. Several decades ago, most of the world's largest cities were located in the developed countries, but currently, large urban centers are found or are being formed in the developing countries of Asia [14] (see Table 1.4). The megacities involve significant social and economic consequences as some of them like Tokyo (38 million) and Delhi (26 million) are more populous than sizeable countries such as Canada (37 million) and Australia (25 million). The proliferation of such large cities may put a strain on environmental resources including air, water, soil, and ecological systems [6].

Urbanization, particularly in the lower middle-income countries where the pace of urbanization is fastest, may cause substantial socioeconomic challenges. Nevertheless, urban centers can offer advantageous

Table 1.4 *The 30 largest cities*

Rank	City, country	Population	Rank	City, country	Population	Rank	City, country	Population
1	Tokyo-Yokohama, Japan	37,343,000	11	Sao Paulo, Brazil	20,365,000	21	Buenos Aires, Argentina	14,122,000
2	Jakarta, Indonesia	30,539,000	12	Mexico City, Mexico	20,063,000	22	Tehran, Iran	13,532,000
3	Delhi, India	24,998,000	13	Mumbai, India	17,712,000	23	Istanbul, Turkey	13,287,000
4	Manila, Philippines	24,123,000	14	Osaka, Kobe, Japan	17,444,000	24	Lagos, Nigeria	13,123,000
5	Seoul, South Korea	23,480,000	15	Moscow, Russia	16,170,000	25	Shenzhen, China	12,084,000
6	Shanghai, China	23,416,000	16	Dhaka, Bangladesh	15,669,000	26	Rio de Janeiro, Brazil	11,727,000
7	Karachi, Pakistan	22,123,000	17	Cairo, Egypt	15,600,000	27	Kinshasa, Congo	11,587,000
8	Beijing, China	21,009,000	18	Los Angeles, the United States	15,058,000	28	Tianjin, China	10,920,000
9	New York, the United States	20,630,000	19	Bangkok, Thailand	14,998,000	29	Paris, France	10,858,000
10	Guangzhou-Toshan, China	20,597,000	20	Kolkata, India	14,667,000	30	Lima, Peru	10,750,000

Source: www.Worldometers.info

services to a large number of people. For instance, health care, education, public transportation, housing, electricity, water, and sanitation are generally available to urban dwellers in a quite effective manner [14]. Populations move to large cities because they are the centers of trade, foreign direct investments, and economic development. Urban dwellers have a better access to larger and more diversified labor markets and enjoy healthier lives. The life expectancy in urban centers is generally higher, while the fertility rate is significantly lower. An important pattern is that as countries urbanize, their overall total fertility rates decline because the fertility rates in urban centers are much lower than those in rural areas [15].

Global Migration: Poverty, Instability, and High Birth Rates

Demographic trends and international migratory movements are closely correlated. Europe, Northern America, and Australia are net receivers of international migrants because they have lower fertility rates and higher median age levels. On the contrary, Africa, Asia, Latin America, and the Caribbean countries are net senders of international migrants because they have much higher fertility rates and lower median age levels. Between 2000 and 2015, 2.8 million people per year migrated to Europe, Northern America, and Oceania [5]. Europe and North America contain 15 percent of the global population but are home to more than half of the world's international migrants [6]. In addition to the diverging demographic trends between developed and developing countries, geopolitical turmoil, war, conflict, and instability in the Middle East and Asia will contribute to the increasing influx of populations from the poor to the rich countries in the next four decades. The demographic forces are the main drivers of international migration, but the economic factors also have important implications for the direction of migration is always from the less developed and low-income countries to the developed and high-income ones. In the next four decades, the United States, Canada, the United Kingdom, Australia, Germany, the Russian Federation, and Italy are expected to be the top receivers of international migrants [5, 13]. During the same period, sub-Saharan Africa, India, Bangladesh, China, Pakistan, and Mexico are expected to be the top sources of international migrants. In the current globalized world, skilled and educated migrants are privileged over unskilled and uneducated ones [17]. The international migration flows are affected by multiple constraints set in developed countries' laws. Therefore, in comparison with the historical large-scale migrations, the recent international migratory movements are more selective [17].

It is widely accepted that migration has negative effects on labor supply in developing countries as most of the emigrants come from the educated and skilled workforce [17]. Instead, the sending countries may benefit from the remittances that migrants send back to their countries of origin. Because of increasing economic development in emerging countries, the migration flows from South to North may change to a South-to-South migration pattern. Some emerging countries with high economic growth rates could attract a large number of migrant workers from low-income neighboring countries [18]. Climate change, desertification, destruction of farmland, resource scarcity, air and water pollution, terrorism, and regional conflicts may create new patterns of international migration among the Southern and low-income countries. For example, due to the Syrian conflict, about 3.2 million Syrians have fled their homeland and have migrated to Turkey. The flight of more than one million Syrians to Europe in 2015, perhaps one of the largest mass migrations in the recent history, shows that the patterns of international migration are becoming more complex and unpredictable.

Migration is becoming a key contributor to population growth in high-income countries, as the migrants from low-income countries often have higher birth rates than the host population. For example, the average fertility rates of migrants in Europe and the United States are significantly higher than the national averages [19]. Furthermore, by reducing median age levels, migration can indirectly influence the population size and age structure of receiving countries [15]. Migration increases the total dependency ratio of sender countries and reduces their share of working-age population. On the other hand, in receiving countries, migration increases the share of working population and reduces old-age dependency [15].

The Demographics of Faith and Religious Affiliations: The Revival of God

The differences in fertility rates and median age levels across the world are working to change the global religious composition. While many sociologists had predicted the end of religion in the 19th and 20th centuries, it seems that the world as a whole has become more religious in the past four decades. For instance, the share of religious people has grown from 82 percent in 1970 to 88 percent in 2010, and it is expected to increase to 90 percent in the next decade. Religiousness is growing mainly because of demographic trends as religious communities have higher fertility rates and procreate more than average. Globally, the number of religiously unaffiliated people, agnostics, and atheists was estimated about 1.1 billion in 2010 [20]. Atheists and other people who do not affiliate with any religion are expected to increase in absolute number particularly in the Western countries such as France, Germany, and the United States, but they will constitute a declining share of the world's population because of the twofold demographic disadvantages of low fertility rates and old-age structures. As a consequence, the share of religiously unaffiliated people is expected to decline from 16 percent in 2010 to 13 percent by 2050 [21].

Currently, Christianity and Islam with, respectively, 2.2 and 1.6 billion adherents are considered the first- and the second-largest religious affiliations and together account for almost half of the world's population [22] (see Table 1.5). Christianity is and will remain the largest religious group in the next four decades, but Islam is growing faster than any other major religion and is expected to overtake Christianity as the largest religious affiliation after 2050 [15]. According to the Pew Research projections, the adherents of Christianity are expected to grow, but their growth will be slower and they will constitute 35 percent of the global population by 2050 [15]. The Jewish population was estimated about 14 million in 2010 and is expected to reach 16.1 million worldwide by 2050. In the United States, the share of Christians will decline from 75 percent of the population in 2010 to 66 percent in 2050 and Muslims will be more numerous in the United States than the adherents of Judaism will. Unlike all other major religions, the number of Buddhist

Table 1.5 World major religions

Religious affiliation	Share of world population	Population
Christian Catholic 50%, Protestant 37%, Orthodox 12%, Other 1%	31%	2,173,180,000
Muslim Sunni 87%–90%, Shia 10%–13%	23%	1,598,510,000
No religion affiliation (atheists and agnostics)	16%	1,126,500,000
Hindu (94% of Hindus live in India)	15%	1,033,080,000
Buddhist (50% of Buddhists live in China)	7%	487,540,000
Folk religionist (faiths associated with a particular group, ethnicity, or tribe)	6%	405,120,000
Other religions (Baha'i, Taoism, Jainism, Shintoism, Sikhism, Tenrikyo, Wicca, Zoroastrianism)	1%	58,110,000
Jew (41% of Jews live in the United States, another 41% in Israel)	0.20%	13,850,000

Source: http://pewforum.org/2012.

adherents is expected to be constant because of low fertility rates and aging populations in countries such as China and Japan. At the same time, the Hindu population is estimated to surge from 1 to 1.4 billion by 2050 representing an increase of roughly 40 percent. There are important geographic disparities in the patterns of religious growth in the coming decades. For example, the religiously unaffiliated population will be concentrated in Europe and North America and will increase as a share of the population in these areas. On the other hand, most of the global growth in the number of Muslims and Christians is expected to happen in the low-income and sub-Saharan African countries characterized by low median ages and high fertility rates. Consistent with these estimates, more than 40 percent of the world's Christians will reside in sub-Saharan Africa by 2050. The rapid changes in religious identities may involve important implications for different spheres of life, including politics, the legal system, family, education, and technology [23, 24]. Furthermore, the growing disparities among the major religious affiliations may lead to cultural collisions, social or geopolitical tensions, conflicts, and political turmoil.

The Languages of Present and Future

Currently, there are almost 7,000 languages spoken across the world, but a large number of these languages have limited scopes and some are facing the risk of disappearance [25]. The linguistic diversity is under increasing pressure, as 50 to 90 percent of the world's languages are predicted to extinct by the end of 21st century [25]. Because of globalization and advances in telecommunication and transport, the world as a whole is becoming linguistically and culturally less diverse than ever. Currently, 15 languages dominate the global stage because they constitute the mother tongues of half of the world's population. At the top is Mandarin Chinese with almost one billion native speakers followed by Spanish, which is the second most common mother tongue of 500 million people. English is at the third place with over 450 million native speakers, and Hindi and Arabic are at the fourth and fifth places with almost 300 million native speakers. While the number of native speakers is an important criterion in determining the power of a language, other variables such as geography, economy, communication, knowledge, and diplomacy seem relevant in evaluating the present and future influence of a language. Relying on these criteria, the 10 most dominant languages may be ranked as English, Mandarin, French, Spanish, Arabic, Russian, German, Japanese, Portuguese, and Hindi (see Table 1.6). With an estimated 450 million native speakers, English is considered as the most important language. Indeed, English is the dominant language of the world's largest economy (the United States) and other large economies such as the United Kingdom, Canada, and Australia. English will remain the global lingua franca at least for the next three decades and its native speakers will reach 540 million by 2050. Mandarin is becoming an important language, not only because of a large size of its native speakers but also because of the growing Chinese economy that has become the world's second largest after the United States. While the number of French native speakers is close to 80 million, French is considered as the third influential language of the world because of its geopolitical impact on Africa and its importance in diplomacy and international affairs [1].

It is almost impossible to predict the future of languages, but the power of a language depends highly on the number of its native and

Table 1.6 *The most powerful languages*

Rank	Score	Language	Native (MM)	Geography	Economy	Communication	Knowledge and media	Diplomacy
1	0.889	English	446.0	1	1	1	1	1
2	0.411	Mandarin	960.0	6	2	2	3	6
3	0.337	French	80.00	2	6	5	5	1
4	0.329	Spanish	470.0	3	5	3	7	3
5	0.273	Arabic	295.0	4	9	6	18	4
6	0.244	Russian	150.0	5	12	10	9	5
7	0.191	German	92.5	8	3	7	4	8
8	0.133	Japanese	125.0	27	4	22	6	7
9	0.119	Portuguese	215.0	7	19	13	12	9
10	0.117	Hindi	310.0	13	16	8	2	10

foreign speakers. Accordingly, English will remain the most influential language of the world with close to 550 million native speakers at least by 2050. By 2050, there will not be any sizeable growth in the number of native speakers of Mandarin, French, Russian, German, and Japanese. Indeed, these languages belong to countries that because of their socio-economic conditions have very low birth rates and will not experience significant demographic increases. By contrast, the native speakers of languages such as Spanish, Arabic, Hindi, and Portuguese are supposed to have significant growths by 2050. According to a report by the British Council, Hindi, Bengali, Urdu, Indonesian, Spanish, Portuguese, Arabic, and Russian will be some important languages for doing business in the next three decades [26].

References

[1] Population Division. 2017. "World Urbanization Prospects: The 2017 Revision." United Nations, Department of Economic and Social Affairs.

[2] Lam, D., and M. Leibbrandt. 2013. "Global Demographic Trends and Their Implications for Employment." Background Research Paper Submitted to the High-Level Panel on the Post-2015 Development Agenda and Lee, R. 2003. "The Demographic Transition: Three Centuries of Fundamental Change." *The Journal of Economic Perspectives* 17, no. 4, pp. 167–190.

[3] Lam, D. 2011. "How the World Survived the Population Bomb: Lessons from 50 Years of Extraordinary Demographic History." *Demography* 48, no. 4, pp. 1231–1262.

[4] Bloom, D.E. 2016. "Demographic Upheaval." *Finance and Development* 53, no. 1, pp. 6–11.

[5] Parkes, R. 2015. "The European Union and the Geopolitics of Migration." UI Paper no. 1/2015.

[6] United Nations, Department of Economic and Social Affairs, Population Division. 2019. *World Population Prospects 2019: Highlights* (ST/ESA/SER.A/423).

[7] Japan's Population Set to Fall to 88m by 2065. https://ft.com/content/00df659e-1dcf-11e7-a454-ab04428977f9 (accessed June 18, 2017).

[8] Nations, U. 2013. "World Population Aging 2013." Department of Economic and Social Affairs PD.

[9] Lakner, C., D.G. Mahler, M. Negre, and E.B. Prydz. 2022. How much does reducing inequality matter for global poverty? *The Journal of Economic Inequality*, pp. 1–27.

[10] Kinsella, K.G., and Y.J. Gist. 1995. *Older Workers, Retirement, and Pensions: A Comparative International Chartbook (No. 95)*. US Department of Commerce, Economics and Statistics Administration, Bureau of the Census.

[11] European Commission, European Union. 2015. "European Strategy and Policy Analysis System." *Global Trends to 2030: Can the EU Meet the Challenges Ahead?*

[12] United Nations, Department of Economic and Social Affairs, Population Division. 2019. *World Urbanization Prospects 2018: Highlights* (ST/ESA/SER.A/421).

[13] Zmud, J., L. Ecola, P. Phleps, and I. Feige. 2013. *The Future of Mobility.* Santa Monica, CA: RAND Corporation.

[14] Winthrop, R., G. Bulloch, P. Bhatt, and A. Wood. 2015. "Development Goals in an Era of Demographic Change." Global Monitoring Report, 2016.

[15] Gunter, B.G., and R. Hoeven. 2004. "The Social Dimension of Globalization: A Review of the Literature." *International Labour Review* 143, nos. 1–2, pp. 7–43.

[16] Population Division. 2018. *World Urbanization Prospects: The 2018 Revision, Highlights* (ST/ESA/SER.A/352). United Nations, Department of Economic and Social Affairs.

[17] The United Nations, Department of Economics and Social Affairs. n.d. http://un.org/en/development/desa/population/publications/factsheets/index.shtml

[18] Andersson, G. 2004. "Childbearing After Migration: Fertility Patterns of Foreign-Born Women in Sweden." *International Migration Review* 38, no. 2, pp. 747–774.

[19] Hackett, C., P. Connor, M. Stonawski, V. Skirbekk, M. Potancokova, and G. Abel. 2015. *The Future of World Religions: Population Growth Projections, 2010–2050.* Washington, DC: Pew Research Center.

[20] Hackett, C., M. Stonawski, M. Potancokova, B.J. Grim, and V. Skirbekk. 2015. "The Future Size of Religiously Affiliated and Unaffiliated Populations." *Demographic Research* 32, p. 829.

[21] Johnson, T., G.A. Bellofatto, A.W. Hickman, B.A. Coon, P.F. Crossing, M. Krause, and J. Yen. 2013. *Christianity in its Global Context, 1970–2020: Society, Religion, and Mission.* Southampton, MA: Center for the Global Study of Christianity.

[22] Zuckerman, P. 2009. "Atheism, Secularity, and Well-Being: How the Findings of Social Science Counter Negative Stereotypes and Assumptions." *Sociology Compass* 3, no. 6, pp. 949–971. doi:10.1111/j.1751-9020.2009.00247.x

[23] Funk, C., and G. Smith. 2012. *"Nones" on the Rise: One-in-Five Adults have No Religious Affiliation.* Washington, DC: Pew Research Center.

[24] Romaine, S. 2015. "The Global Extinction of Languages and its Consequences for Cultural Diversity." In *Cultural and Linguistic Minorities in the Russian Federation and the European Union,* pp. 31–46. Springer International Publishing.

[25] Noack, R. 2015. The Future of Language. The *Washington Post.* https://washingtonpost.com/news/worldviews/wp/2015/09/24/the-future-of-language/?utm_term=.eec17bd2e40f (accessed August 20, 2017).

[26] Glaeser, E.L. 2014. "A World of Cities: The Causes and Consequences of Urbanization in Poorer Countries." *Journal of the European Economic Association* 12, no. 5, pp. 1154–1199.

CHAPTER 2

Globalization

Transformations and Consequences

Different Views on Globalization

Globalization can be defined as a process resulting in more interdependence and mutual awareness among economic, political, and social units of the world [1–4]. Globalization is a complex and multifaceted phenomenon that is associated with increasing cross-national movements of goods, services, capital, people, and information [1, 2]. Because of its complex nature, globalization is not consensual rather it is accompanied by intense conflicts among various social groups, states, and hegemonic powers [5]. As such, it constitutes an array of interconnections that transcend the borders of nation-states and local communities. Globalization creates conditions through which the events, decisions, and activities in one part of the world cause significant consequences in other parts [6]. It breaks the traditional relationships between territoriality and authority and moves authority from the state and local levels to the universal levels [7]. Consequently, globalization enables us to operate in a network society and interact with each other in real time on a planetary scale regardless of our temporal and spatial constraints.

The origin of globalization can be found in ancient times, but the modern usage of the terminology is associated with the rapid socio-technological transformations of the late 20th century [1, 2] (Table 2.1). Historically, the end of the Cold War coincided with the beginning of globalization, but it is not clear whether there is a causal relationship between these two phenomena [8]. We might speculate that the end of the Cold War and the subsequent detente between the United States and

Table 2.1 The multiple views on globalization, their meanings, features, and consequences

Perspective	Central idea	Features and consequences
Economic	A global marketplace for production, distribution, and consumption	Liberalization and deregulation of markets Privatization of assets Financial deregulation Cross-national production Integration of capital markets
Cultural	An increasing convergence in the world's cultural values	Homogenization of all cultural values Prevalence of modernization Acceptance of capitalism and liberal democracy
Socio-technological	A connection of the local communities together so they can function in a coherent planetary system	Unprecedented explosion of information, products, and services Reconciliation between the local and global
Business	Glocalization of business activities	Reproduction of international businesses on a regional or local basis
Sociological	A compression of temporal and spatial dimensions	Dialectical linkage of distant localities Reflexivity

the Soviet Union created better opportunities for international trade and exchange of ideas. From an economic standpoint, globalization is a significant shift toward an economic system that is no longer based on independent national economies but on a global marketplace for production, distribution, and consumption [9, 10]. Economic globalization is particularly characterized by a sequence of events including liberalization and deregulation of markets, privatization of assets, cross-national production, and the integration of capital markets [11].

From a cultural standpoint, globalization can be viewed as an increasing convergence in the world's cultural values leading to homogenization of all human societies, irrespective of their historical roots (Table 2.1). In the past five decades, almost all countries have been witnessing significant socioeconomic transformations marked by state centralization, urbanization, universal education, and higher levels of literacy. According to this view, globalization characterizes a prevalence of modernization, a homogenization of values around the principles of capitalism and liberal democracy, and an acceptance of American version of Enlightenment [12]. Furthermore, globalization can be seen as a social revolution driven by technological advances that eventually transform the globe into a single market [12]. According to Castells [13], globalization connects the local communities together so they can function in a coherent planetary system. In the recent decades, we are witnessing a paradigmatic shift in the way we think about a variety of social and economic relations [12]. An extensive shake-up of economic activities at the regional and local levels is happening, and an unprecedented explosion of information, products, and services is sweeping across the planet [12]. As a consequence of these transformations, the global is meeting the local and globalization is becoming glocalization, in other words, a mélange of local and global. From a business standpoint, large corporations are often considered multinational or transnational entities that adopt a "glocalization strategy" to reproduce their businesses on a regional or local basis. Thus, the glocalization strategy allows an international company to become accepted as a local organization while trying not to transfer control to the local subsidiaries.

From a sociological perspective, it is possible to suggest that globalization brings about a compression of temporal and spatial dimensions [14–16]. This implies that the inhabitants of the globalized world are becoming more and more aware of each other's presence and are communicating and interacting reciprocally. Consistent with this idea, Giddens emphasizes that globalization is an interactive and dialectical process that links distant localities in such a way that local happenings are shaped by events occurring many miles away and vice versa [15]. Globalization is often described as an unfinished, changeable, and intermittent phenomenon with many contradictory effects and implications [1, 17, 18].

Globalization and the Changing Role of Nation-States

Globalization denationalizes the markets, opens the door to international competition, and eventually pushes nation-states to react to international forces rather than to domestic population. Therefore, nation-states become increasingly responsive to the global community [19]. Economic integration empowers international organizations, so they can directly decide about the fiscal and monetary policies, trade, tariffs, environmental issues, and interest rates. Globalization restraints nation-states to tax, spend, and control their domestic affairs. Moreover, globalization, by facilitating the cross-border movements of labor and capital, loosens the government control and makes national borders less relevant. In addition to the strong supranational institutions, big businesses and powerful corporations put a lot of pressure on the ability of nation-states to function properly [1]. Nations and their citizens become hostages of supranational markets, international lenders, and investment banks. Globalization weakens the ability of nation-states to regulate what happens on their own land. Thus, it is plausible to suggest that by creating a constant tension between national and supranational forces, globalization and the ensuing economic integration undermine the traditional roles of nation-states. The advocates of globalization believe that the economic integration affects the nation-states, but does not destroy them. As a solution, they suggest that the nation-states should become more resilient and agile to benefit from the economic effects of globalization. Some go further and argue that nation-states should not fear globalization, as the global forces ultimately serve the interests of citizens. This argument advocates that globalization is a continuation of capitalist development; therefore, those nation-states that become more globalized are more likely to become prosperous and successful.

Regardless of the perspective that we adopt, it is obvious that globalization undermines the traditional functions of the nation-state, particularly in the case of smaller countries that do not have abundant financial resources and large populations. Furthermore, the large multinational corporations (MNCs) and many other global institutions such as the International Monetary Fund (IMF), the World Trade Organization (WTO), and the World Bank are not restrained by any democratic legitimacy or social accountability. The financial crises in Greece and Ireland showed that the smaller nation-states are incapable of exerting their sovereign rights during financial hardship or extended periods of distress, rather they become fully dependent on supranational institutions to avoid the risk of collapse.

The aforementioned discussion leads us to three important conclusions. First, the effects of globalization on nation-states are mainly inevitable because these effects are the direct consequences of temporal and spatial compression. Second, globalization and economic integration could serve the interests of nation-states. The more globalized nation-states are generally more successful, powerful, and prosperous. Therefore, global-ization might change the role of nation-states, but it does not necessarily undermine their power. Third, we can assume that in the game of global-ization, some nation-states could be winners as they gain power and influ-ence, while others could be losers as they continue to decline. In addition to these three conclusions, we should keep in mind that the changing role of nation-states offers an opportunity for the creation of a system of global governance where important issues such as environmental degra-dation, climate change, overpopulation, and international security can be effectively tackled.

A New Balance of Economic Power

Globalization of trade and production has led to a surge in the worldwide wealth over the past three decades. Despite the financial crisis of 2007 to 2008, the global trade has risen more than 50 percent in the last decade as more developing countries are embarked on international business [20]. Currently, the South–South commercial relations mark more than 30 percent of the global trade. In merchandise, the South–South trade is almost equal to North–North trade [21]. The cross-border value chains and operations are becoming so popular that a large fraction (almost 56 percent) of global trade is devoted to intermediate or unfinished products [22]. As globalization is easing the cross-national movements of capital, people, technology, and merchandise, a new balance of eco-nomic power is being formed. While the economists and trade theorists emphasize that trade is not a zero-sum game, it appears that there are some apparent winners and losers in the globalization game. In the early decades of the 20th century, only a couple of Western countries namely the United States, Britain, France, Germany, and the Netherlands dom-inated the arena of international trade [23]. In the past four decades, the dominance of the Western countries has been challenged by the rise of many southern countries, notably China, South Korea, South Africa, and India (Figure 2.1). For instance, the share of the United States of the world's output has fallen from 27.3 percent in the 1950s to 18 percent in 2008, while for the same period, the share of China of the world's output has risen drastically from 4.6 to 17.5 percent. China's growth is an essential feature of globalization. China grew from 5 percent of global gross domestic product (GDP) in 1978 to 17 percent in 2011 and may become the world's largest economy at some point within the next 15 years [24]. The shares of Japan and the European Union (EU) of the world GDP are expected to fall to 6 and 20 percent, respectively, while those of China, Association of South East Asian Nations (ASEAN), and Latin America are expected to rise to 15.3, 3.3, and 8.3 percent, respectively. The impact of globalization on the wealth of individuals in the southern countries is particularly noteworthy. For instance, in the past 30 years, GDP per capita in China has risen from a tiny $314 in 1990 to more than $6,000 in 2012 [25]. Even in Sub-Saharan Africa, the GDP per capita has climbed from $627 in 2004 to $1,349 in 2012. The growth of emerging economies, in particular, China and India, is radically changing the distribution of global economic power. Based on some projections, the Organization for Economic Co-operation and Development (OECD) countries may constitute a minority of the world economy by 2030. Globalization implies the increasing interdependence of the world's economies; therefore, it may rebalance the distribution of wealth across the world leading to the resurgence of China, India, and many other emerging countries with sizeable populations and resources. As Eastern and Southern countries are rising, they become more assertive and claim more space on the world stage vis-a-vis big global players at the top of the pyramid. The developed countries of Western Europe and North America are required to make severe and often painful structural adjustments that often lead to the popular discontent of their citizens. In the recent years, the right wing and populist movements are gaining momentum as they are taking advantage of the popular dissatisfaction with globalization and push their agenda in favor of more interventionist and protectionist economic policies. It seems that as Western countries are losing their traditional economic dominance and privileges, their domestic affairs are adversely affected.

Pressure on Wages, Employment, and Social Welfare

Globalization of production means that MNCs scatter their value chain activities across the world to maximize the location advantages

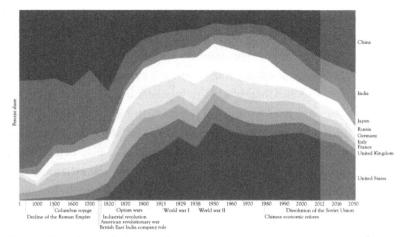

Figure 2.1 **A new balance of economic power: past, present, and future (based on share of combined GDP of nine countries)**

Sources: GDP data for years 1 to 2000: Angus Maddison, University of Groningen: 2016 IMF-projected GDP growth; 2050 PricewaterhouseCoopers-projected GDP growth.

including labor, natural resources, and technology. With the advent of new telecommunication technologies in the 1990s, there was a massive departure of manufacturing companies from the industrialized countries to the Asian developing countries. The sudden shift to low-cost countries caused massive unemployment and underemployment in the manufacturing sector in many industrialized countries and stressed the workers' compensation levels. Since then, American workers employed in the industries in direct competition with low-cost imports have seen job dislocation and sliding wage pressures [26]. At the same time, a significant drop in domestic revenues collected from lower tariffs and lower corporate taxes led many governments to cut on social protection programs, and thus strained unskilled or semiskilled workers even more. Under such budgetary pressures, many national governments in the western countries have cut their spending in social protection programs, including pension plans, unemployment, and child care [27]. European countries remained mainly reluctant to wage reduction, maintained their social protection programs, and emphasized equitable income distribution. Not surprisingly, under the pressure of the global forces, most of the European countries namely France, Spain, and Italy have lost their labor competitiveness and have shown higher unemployment levels in the recent years. Globalization in the United States has resulted in higher wage gaps, stagnant income, but relatively lower levels of unemployment than in Europe [28, 29]. The negative effects of outsourcing on the wage levels are particularly significant in the case of low-skilled manufacturing workers implying that they are the real losers of globalization. By contrast, the globalization of production does not cause negative implications for high-skilled workers as they are mainly immune to outsourcing and even may benefit from it [30]. The impacts of globalization in developing countries are very different. Indeed, a few emerging countries have essentially benefited from the globalization, but a large number of nations that do not have reliable political, legal, economic, and social institutions have been left behind and in some cases have lost their manufacturing and even their agricultural industries. Joseph Stiglitz, an American economist and a professor at Columbia University [31], suggests that globalization and the subsequent economic liberalization in developing countries that do not have adequate economic institutions may hurt both employment and productivity.

Living in an Age of Insecurity and Uncertainty

By making the national borders less relevant and by compressing time and space, globalization has created higher levels of economic, political, and technological risk. The sociologists Ulrich Beck and Anthony Giddens coined the term "risk society" to emphasize the risky nature of globalization era [32]. Similarly, Zygmunt Bauman uses the term "liquidity" to illustrate the uncertainty and riskiness of a globalized world. According to Beck, globalization is essentially an uncertain phenomenon that increases social insecurity: it undermines the territoriality and sovereignty of the nation-state, weakens its authority, and compromises economic stability by prioritizing the whims of financial markets and international speculators [32]. The risks associated with globalization and economic integration are various: unemployment and underemployment, food supply contamination, mass migration, identity crises, terrorism, fundamentalism, cultural and racial clashes, financial instability, market turmoil, currency war, cyberattacks, industrial espionage, computer snooping, compromised privacy, environmental degradation, health problems, and pandemics [28, 33]. For instance, the growth of international trade and movement of people may spread communicable diseases around the world. Globalization is believed to have very negative implications for the natural environment. As emerging countries strive to attract more foreign capital and production, they turn a blind eye on the environment. Under these circumstances, the MNCs of Western nations rush to set up production facilities in the emerging countries to take advantage of their lenient environmental regulations [34]. The neoliberal policies of a globalized economy facilitate the privatization and monetization of natural resources and mines, and thus provide big multinationals the opportunity to maximize their profits to the detriment of local communities. Globalization risks affect all the humanity, but the poor are particularly vulnerable, as they do not have sufficient resources to withstand the tumultuous times when markets collapse, economies contract, and jobs are lost.

Furthermore, since globalization increases exposure of people to foreign cultures, it can cause collisions among racially, culturally, or religiously distinct members of our societies. The movements of people across the globe lead to multicultural or heterogeneous societies whose members suffer from identity crisis. Globalization and its multiple technological artifacts create a standard universal culture that destroys the existing traditions, values, and patterns of communication and thus brings about new types of risk and uncertainty [34]. The effects of globalization on culture are paradoxical because it seeks to homogenize cultural values on the one hand, but it also increases awareness of cultural heterogeneity on the other hand. International marketing and communications pave the way for the mass import of various American materials including food, clothing, music, films, books, and television programs that ultimately change the traditional and religious cultural values in conservative societies [9]. As the traditional and religious groups feel threatened by the globalized values, they confront all manifestations of globalization particularly the American artifacts and symbols. In the extreme cases, the encounter between global cultural flows and inherited local identities leads to a bitter conflict between two opposite worldviews: "McWorld" and "Jihad" [9, 35].

The Decline of Interstate Wars and the Rise of Intrastate Conflicts

By creating interdependence among trade partners, globalization could deter the interstate military conflicts. After the Second World War, the number of interstate wars has dropped despite the fact that the number of states in the international community has tripled [36]. Obviously, the decline in the occurrence of interstate conflicts may be attributed to other factors including the deterrent effect of nuclear weapons and the success of many liberal democracies and free-market economies across the world. Nevertheless, the key role of globalization and economic exchange in establishing and maintaining peace cannot be denied. It has been suggested that countries with more extensive economic relations are likely to have higher opportunity costs from escalation to war. Such countries are more likely to reach resolution via diplomacy and negotiation. Simply put, if "war is the continuation of politics by other means" [37], the globalized states are less likely to choose it. The EU is the prime example of a globalized project that was designed to maintain peace and prosperity across Europe. That is why the 2012 Nobel Peace Prize was awarded to the EU for its contribution to the advancement of peace and reconciliation in Europe for the past six decades. The decline of direct and interstate conflicts has led to an increased incidence of other types of conflict such as proxy wars, intrastate flights, asymmetrical warfare, and terrorist attacks. The share of irregular fights is estimated at 80 percent of all conflicts. In the past 15 years, we have been witnessing the formation of multiple proxy wars, namely in Syria, Libya, Afghanistan, Ukraine, Yemen, and Iraq where opposing states prefer indirect war via proxy groups rather than full-fledged and classical confrontations. Taliban, Al-Qaeda, and the Islamic State of Iraq and Syria (ISIS) are the well-known examples of terrorist groups that have appeared in the past 15 years. These terrorist groups fight on the behalf of the states that do not want to enter an interstate war directly. Among them, ISIS exemplifies how a terrorist group can grow thanks to globalization and new technologies. Indeed, the ISIS has been extremely effective in utilizing the Internet and social media to hire new members, raise funds, organize terrorist operations, and disseminate its propaganda across the globe.

Time–Space Compression

Globalization changes the most fundamental divisions in our social relations including the distinctions between local and global, proximity and distance, domestic and foreign, and national and international. Because of the innovative telecommunication and transport technologies, global events take place nearly simultaneously anywhere and everywhere in the world [38]. Globalization allows the geographically distant events and actions to increasingly impact on the local conditions. By intensifying, multiplying, and accelerating social relations, globalization reduces the spatial and temporal distances [39]. This dual time–space compression is an essential feature of globalization that implies some important consequences.

According to Harvey, capitalism attempts to eliminate all spatial barriers and annihilate space through time [14] (Figure 2.2). The impetus to the annihilation of barriers results in a tempo-spatial compression, suggesting that the world is experienced socially and materially as a smaller place [40]. For instance, MNCs increasingly rely on new technologies of telecommunication to disperse their business activities across the world and take advantage of location endowments, such as cheap labor, abundant resources, sizeable markets, and fiscal rewards. Therefore, the large and even midsized businesses do not belong to a specific location or a nation anymore, rather they are becoming liquid entities that evolve beyond the limits of time and space. For them, the social space as a geographically recognizable location no longer exists.

Hence, globalization brings about deterritorialization process implying that various social activities occur regardless of the location of participants. Globalization transforms the social world by linking together and expanding human activities across regions and continents [2]. As a consequence of the tempo-spatial compression, economic production is accelerated through processes such as vertical disintegration and just-in-time delivery. The accelerated economic production in its turn leads to an acceleration of financial exchange and consumption [40, 41]. Especially, globalization is marked by a shift from an economy based on the manufacturing of industrial goods by low-skilled workers to one based on the creation of more ephemeral informational goods and services

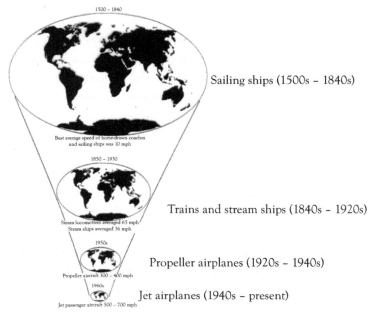

Sailing ships (1500s – 1840s)

Trains and stream ships (1840s – 1920s)

Propeller airplanes (1920s – 1940s)

Jet airplanes (1940s – present)

Figure 2.2 Time–space compression
Source: Harvey [14].

by knowledge workers [13, 42]. This "global informational capitalism" creates the different organizational forms that drastically change our relationship with our environment. The new information technologies make it necessary to reorganize businesses into global webs operating efficiently, abolishing constraints of space and time [42, 43]. The global workplace becomes a virtual place or a "nonspace" where the constraints of space, social organization, and local institutional arrangements are eliminated or weakened. In this globalized world, the geographical distance is dead and a new virtual social space has emerged that is controlled by capitalists, traders, and managers. They are using high-speed around-the-world and around-the-clock technologies in cyberspace to run their businesses. The global workplace is stripped off from its temporal and spatial contexts and becomes a universal space for communication and innovation among employees [16, 42, 43]. Inherent in the tempo-spatial compression is the increasing velocity of social activity that is driven by the proliferation of high-speed transportation, telecommunication, and information technologies in the past three decades after the 1970s. Indeed, the interconnectedness of social relations and the compression of time and space hinge upon the fast movement of people, information, capital, and merchandise across the world. According to Harvey, in a globalized society, capital moves at a pace faster than before, as the production, circulation, and exchange of capital happen at increasing speeds [14]. In the absence of a high social velocity, the compression of time and space seems impossible.

References

[1] Guillen, M.F. 2001. "Is Globalization Civilizing, Destructive or Feeble? A Critique of Five Key Debates in the Social Science Literature." *Annual Review of Sociology* 27, no. 1, pp. 235–260.

[2] Held, D., A. McGrew, D. Goldblatt, and J. Perraton. 1999. *Global Transformations.* Stanford, CA: Stanford University Press

[3] Petrella, R. 1996. "Globalization and Internationalization." *States Against Markets: The Limits of Globalization,* pp. 62–83.

[4] Steger, M.B. 2010. *Globalization,* 63. John Wiley & Sons, Ltd.

[5] Santos, B.D.S. 2002. "The Processes of Globalisation." *Revista Crítica de Ciencias Sociais and Eurozine,* pp. 1–48.

[6] McGrew, A. 1990. "A Global Society." In *Modernity and Its Futures,* eds. S. Hall, D. Held and A. McGrew.

[7] Cerny, P.G. 1997. "Paradoxes of the Competition State: The Dynamics of Political Globalization." *Government and Opposition* 32, no. 2, pp. 251–74.

[8] Reich, S. 1998. *What Is Globalization?: Four Possible Answers* 261. Helen Kellogg Institute for International Studies.

[9] Lerche III, C.O. 1998. "The Conflicts of Globalization." *International Journal of Peace Studies* 3, no. 1, pp. 47–66.

[10] Holm, H.H., and G. Sorensen. 1995. *Whose World Order?: Uneven Globalization and the End of the Cold War.* Westview Pr.

[11] Jones, R.B. 2013. *Globalisation and Interdependence in the International Political Economy: Rhetoric and Reality.* Bloomsbury Publishing.

[12] Carnoy, M., M. Castells, S. Cohen, and F.H. Cardoso. 1993. *The New Global Economy in the Informational Age: Reflections on Our Changing World.* Penn State Press.

[13] Castells, M. 1997. *The Rise of the Network Society.* Cambridge, MA: Blackwell.

[14] Harvey, D. 1999. "Time-Space Compression and the Postmodern Condition." *Modernity: Critical Concepts* 4, pp. 98–118.

[15] Giddens, A. 1990. "The Consequences of Modernity Cambridge." *Polity* 53, no. 83, pp. 245–260.

[16] Giddens, A. 1991. *The Consequences of Modernity.* Oxford: Blackwell.

[17] Giddens, A. 2000. *Runaway World: How Globalization is Reshaping Our Lives.* New York, NY: Routledge.

[18] Gilpin, R. 2000. *The Challenge of Global Capitalism.* Princeton, NJ: Princeton University Press.

[19] Jarvis, D.S. 2007. "Risk, Globalisation and the State: A Critical Appraisal of Ulrich Beck and the World Risk Society Thesis." *Global Society* 21, no. 1, pp. 23–46.

[20] Grevi, G., D. Keohane, B. Lee, and P. Lewis. 2013. *Empowering Europe's Future: Governance, Power, and Options for the EU in a Changing World.* The European Union.

[21] Grevi, G., D. Keohane, B. Lee, and P. Lewis. 2013. *Empowering Europe's Future: Governance, Power, and Options for the EU in a Changing World.* The European Union.

[22] Miroudot, S., R. Lanz, and A. Ragoussis. 2009. Trade in Intermediate Goods and Services.

[23] Baldwin, R.E., and P. Martin. 1999. *Two Waves of Globalisation: Superficial Similarities, Fundamental Differences (No. w6904).* National Bureau of Economic Research.

[24] Maddison, A. 2008. *Historical Statistics for the World Economy: 1-2006AD.* Conference Board and Groningen Growth and Development Centre, Total Economy Database.

[25] Fukuyama, F. June 2013. "The Middle Class Revolution." *Wall Street Journal.*

[26] Bivens, J. 2007. "Globalization, American Wages, and Inequality." The Past, Present, and Future, Economic Policy Institute. Working Paper, 279.

[27] Benvenisti, E., and G. Nolte. 2004. *The Welfare State, Globalization, and International Law.* Springer Science & Business Media.

[28] Gunter, B.G., and R. Hoeven. 2004. "The Social Dimension of Globalization: A Review of the Literature." *International Labour Review* 143, no. 1–2, pp. 7–43.

[29] Stiglitz, J.E. 2003. *The Roaring Nineties: A New History of the World's Most Prosperous Decade.* New York, NY: W.W. Norton & Company.

[30] Geishecker, I., and H. Gorg. 2004. *International Outsourcing and Wages: Winners and Losers.* Manuscript, DIW Berlin.

[31] Stiglitz, J.E. 2005. "More Instruments and Broader Goals: Moving Toward the Post-Washington Consensus." In *Wider Perspectives on Global Development,* pp. 16–48. UK: Palgrave Macmillan.

[32] Beck, U. 1992. *Risk Society: Towards a New Modernity,* 17. Sage.

[33] Scheve, K., and M.J. Slaughter. 2004. "Economic Insecurity and the Globalization of Production." *American Journal of Political Science* 48, no. 4, pp. 662–674.

[34] Khan, S., and A. Najam. 2009. "The Future of Globalization and Its Humanitarian Impacts." *Humanitarian Horizons Project, FIC.* https://wikis .uit.tufts.edu/confluence/display/FIC/The+Future+of+Globalization+and+ its+Humanitarian+Impacts

[35] Fuller, G. 1995. "The Next Ideology." *Foreign Policy* 98, Spring 1995.

[36] Pettersson, T., and P. Wallensteen. 2015. "Armed Conflicts, 1946–2014." *Journal of Peace Research* 52, no. 4, pp. 536–550.

[37] Clausewitz, C.V. 1984. "On War." Edited and Translated by Howard, Michael, and Paret, Peer.

[38] Scholte, J.A. 1996. "The Geography of Collective Identities in a Globalizing World." *Review of International Political Economy* 3, no. 4, pp. 565–607.

[39] Scholte, J.A. 2000. *What is 'Global' About Globalization?* Macmillan.

[40] Oke, N. 2009. "Globalizing Time and Space: Temporal and Spatial Considerations in Discourses of Globalization." *International Political Sociology* 3, no. 3, pp. 310–326.

[41] Havey, D. 1990. *The Condition of Postmodernity.* Oxford: Blackwell Publishing.

[42] O'Riain, S. 2006. "Time-Space Intensification: Karl Polanyi, The Double Movement, and Global Informational Capitalism." *Theory and Society* 35, no. 5, pp. 507–528.

[43] Reich, R. 1991. The *Work of Nations.* New York, NY: Vintage.

CHAPTER 3

Culture in the Contemporary World

Convergence, Divergence, and Cultural Mélange

Convergence

In an interconnected world, consumer goods, labor, capital, people, technology, and more importantly ideas travel across borders much faster and easier than ever. The large multinational corporations capitalize on their substantial power to overcome institutional and legal barriers of nation-states. Across the planet, consumers tend to watch the same television programs, listen to the pop music, consume common global brand products and services, and wear the same or similar clothes [1, 2]. The computerized networks facilitate the fast or free movement of information across national boundaries and surmount the limits of geography, language, and ethnicity [3]. These changes gradually push all the world's nations to embrace the value systems of the established Western capitalistic economies. Local communities are affected by powerful cultures, lose their identities, and ultimately become part of a global culture [1, 4]. According to this perspective, globalization leads to cultural convergence as it forces all cultures toward homogeneity without leaving any room for diversities. For Ritzer [5], cultural convergence is about the Americanization of local cultures [1, 4]. The Americanization is the dominant version of Western culture that is fueled by the huge socioeconomic and technological achievements of the United States in the past century. America is undeniably the dominant culture in telecommunication technology. Some 85 percent of web pages originate from the United States, and American businesses control 75 percent of the world's packaged software market [1, 6]. Furthermore, the American culture is central to the global media, entertainment, and music. The homogenization paradigm implies that the global flow of cultural elements takes place in a one-way manner from the Western industrialized countries, mainly from the United States, to the rest of world. For some people in developing countries, the cultural homogenization is a disturbing and even destructive force. It is an assault of global capitalism on their local cultures, religions, traditions, and identities [1, 7–9].

Divergence

The second perspective on the contemporary world's culture is divergence or heterogeneity. The divergence perspective holds that cultures are in a constant conflict with each other. In a globalized world, people become much more aware of their unique values and take pride in their cultural identities. Globalization makes people aware of their diverse national cultures [1, 10]. The question of "who am I?" gains importance and shapes the sociocultural relations across the world [11]. Since local cultures are the source of identity and pride, people defend them against the perturbing forces of globalization. The intelligentsia in many developing countries complains that globalization does not involve an equitable exchange among the world's nations rather it is a form of cultural imperialism where products, services, and more importantly cultural values from the United States and other Western countries are imposed on the rest of world [12, 13]. They view the changing patterns in consumption, language usage, dress code, human image ideals, education, and sexual behavior as potential threats of globalization to their local cultures and identities. A radical and rapid change of local identities may cause grave psychological and social shocks. For that reason, some local cultures resist the disturbing forces of globalization and tend to protect or even emphasize their traditional values. Based on these arguments, it is possible to suggest that, in addition to cultural convergence, globalization may involve some degrees of cultural divergence.

Cultural Hybridization (Mélange)

The cultural convergence and divergence views, respectively, ignore the local reception of Western culture and the adaptation of its elements to the local cultures. In fact, the interaction between global and local cultures creates a constant battle between convergence and divergence forces, which ultimately leads to cultural hybridization or cultural mélange [12, 14, 15]. The main idea of cultural hybridization is that some elements of the global culture are adapted to the receiving local cultures and gradually become like the indigenous parts. The new cultures integrate both global and local cultures but are neither the former nor the latter [4]. Therefore, globalization becomes a mixture of convergence and divergence forces leading to a complex cultural mélange [12, 16]. The process of cultural hybridization destabilizes the old-fashioned definitions of ethnicity, localness, and traditional ways of life [1, 17]. Since culture has different layers such as basic assumptions, values, and artifacts, the superficial elements of a culture are more likely to be mixed together, but the deeply rooted values and beliefs are hard to change. Therefore, globalization could bring about the processes of convergence and divergence at the same time representing overlapping socio-techno-cultural landscapes [1, 18]. Cultural hybridization could be beneficial to the humanity, as the richest cultural traditions have often emerged at the meeting points of noticeably different cultures, such as Athens, the Indus Valley, and Mexico [1, 19].

Diversity, Multiculturalism, and the Lack of Social Cohesion

A variety of factors including the advances in telecommunication and transport especially globalization have created opportunities for migration from developing countries to industrialized nations over the course of past four decades. Consequently, many of the Western countries are progressively experiencing higher levels of socio-ethnic, cultural, linguistic, and religious diversity. For example, it is estimated that 8 to 10 percent of the population in France is from the North African descent. The black Africans constitute more than 3.5 percent of the French population. Germany, which has received more than one million migrants only in 2016, hosts over three million people of Turkish descent. The large cities of the Western Europe and North America, notably London, Paris, Frankfurt, Brussels, Toronto, New York, Los Angeles, and Chicago, consist of extremely diverse ethnicities. According to Canada's *National Post* newspaper, 51 percent of residents in Toronto were born outside Canada [20]. Based on the 2010 U.S. Census, the populations of people from Indian descent in America grew almost 70 percent between 2000 and 2010 and reached four million in 2015 [21]. Due to significant cultural differences between the home and the host countries, a large number of migrants are not fully integrated into their new communities. Some new-comers remain unemployed and marginalized living in segregated ghet-tos. The marginalized immigrants feel at home neither in their culture of origin nor in the culture to which they have immigrated. On the one hand, they have lost their original culture and, on the other hand, they are not connected to the new culture that they found too different from theirs. Some immigrants experience higher levels of discrimination and feel that their new culture does not accept them because of their distinct race, skin color, ethnicity, religion, or lower socioeconomic status. The greater the cultural distance between the migrants' culture and the host culture, the more likely that marginalization happens. Marginalization may have different forms. For instance, in some cases, the immigrants do not show any commitment to the new culture and stick to their cultures of origin. Occasionally, they lose their culture of origin and do not adopt a new culture. As a result, they may become "cultured," "deterritorial-ized," or "unrooted" [22, 23].

The lack of integration and the resulting social incoherence may cause tensions between the ethnoreligious minorities and the host countries (see Figure 3.1). Some serious riots erupted in Paris in 2005 and in London in 2011 involving the burning of cars, vandalizing public buildings, and damaging private properties [24–26]. Similarly, in the United States, there has been a continuous tension between the African Americans and the law enforcement and, on many occasions, violence, riots, and vandal-ism have broken out.

In 2014, after the fatal shooting of Michael Brown by a white police officer, riots erupted in Ferguson, Missouri, for many weeks caus-ing vandalism, looting, rioting, arson, and gunshots [27]. Similarly, in 2020, following the killing of George Floyd by a police officer, major riots erupted in Minnesota and across the United States for several weeks. Different countries have taken different measures to manage cultural and ethnic diversities. A few countries like Canada allow multiculturalism and

Figure 3.1 Diversity could become a source of social conflict: French police confronting a woman on a beach as part of a controversial ban on the burkini in 2016

Source: https://theguardian.com/world/2016/aug/24.

embrace the coexistence of multiple languages and ethnicities. Some do not recognize the cultural diversity within their borders and others turn a blind eye on diversity or try to deny its existence [28–30]. Even, some countries may take drastic measures to assimilate the minorities into the mainstream society [28, 31]. For instance, France emphasizes the cultural and linguistic homogeneity of the society as the cornerstone of the republican ideal where liberty, equality, and fraternity can best be achieved. After all, it seems that these mandatory measures have not been effective in mitigating the pernicious effects of marginalization in France [28].

The Clash of Cultures/Civilizations

The waves of globalization and by extension Westernization have been perturbing all the world's cultures particularly the traditional ones. Globalization is accompanied by the prevalence of modern values such as rationality, secularity, individualism, freedom of speech, and self-expression that are in evident conflict with the traditional values like religiosity, collectivism, and submissiveness to authority [32, 33]. As such, globalization and westernization may lead to cultural anxiety and cultural clash. The forms and scales of the reactions to globalization vary across the world from nuanced and limited resentment to revolution and social tur-moil. In much of the Western world including the United States, Europe, Australia, Canada, and Japan where modern values are already dominant, cultural reactions to globalization have been limited or nonexistent. The intelligentsia in some European countries such as France sporadically expresses their concerns about the disruptive effects of globalization on art, music, and literature, but as a whole, their public does not consider globalization an existential threat [34]. By contrast, the developing and particularly Islamic countries have shown ambivalent and contradictory attitudes toward globalization, westernization, and the associated cultural consequences. On the one hand, these societies are embracing the global capitalism, are consuming its products, and are benefiting from the subse-quent technological innovations. On the other hand, they see the advent of a new era as an existential threat to their traditional values and life-styles. Truly, many Muslim countries cannot withstand the rapid socio-economic and cultural changes of globalization and remain desperate in a struggle between tradition and Western secular modernity.

In addition to the constant tension between traditional and global/modern values, the world is prone to significant cultural conflicts at the civilizational fault lines. Samuel Huntington suggested that, after the epochs of colonialism and the Cold War, the world entered a new stage, in which the cultural and civilizational clashes are more likely to happen because the most important divisions among populations become cul-tural rather than ideological, political, or economic [35]. According to Huntington's famous thesis, the world can be divided into eight major civilizations/cultures as the lasting constitutions of human societies (see Figure 3.2). These eight major civilizations/cultures are demarcated by a combination of religious, linguistic, historical, and geographical factors.

1. Sinic: the common culture of China and Chinese communities in Southeast Asia including Vietnam and Korea
2. Japanese: Japanese culture as uniquely different from the rest of Asia
3. Hindu: identified as the core Indian civilization
4. Islamic: originating on the Arabian Peninsula and spreading across North Africa, Iberian Peninsula, and Central Asia. The Islamic culture includes Arab, Persian, Turkic, and Malay subdivisions

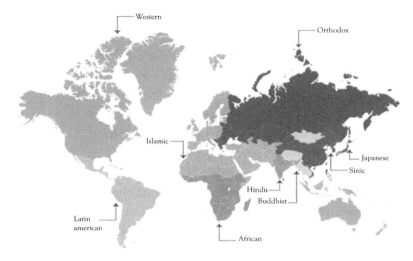

Figure 3.2 According to Samuel Huntington, the present time is marked by increasing level of conflict among the world's civilizations, particularly between the Islamic and Western civilizations

5. Orthodox: the culture centered in Russia that is separate from Western Christianity

6. Western: the civilization/culture centered in Europe and North America

7. Latin American: The Catholic culture of Central and South American countries with a history of authoritarian rule

8. Africa: multiple African cultures that are increasingly gaining assertiveness

Huntington identified the Buddhist areas of Bhutan, Cambodia, Laos, Mongolia, Myanmar, Sri Lanka, and Thailand as separate areas from other civilizations, but maintained that these areas do not constitute a major civilization.

According to Huntington's thesis, new patterns of conflict will occur along the boundaries of different world cultures. He particularly anticipated a coalition of Islamic and Chinese cultures to work against the West as their common enemy. According to Huntington, there is historical ground for a conflict between Islamic and Christian cultures that has been aggravated in the recent times.

Both Islamic and Christian religions pursue an expansionist agenda and may see each other as the potential rivals. The West attempts to universalize its cultural values and institutions that are deeply rooted in the Christianity, and Enlightenment may collide with the Islamic traditional values. The increased communication and contact between Islam and the West has inflated the perceived differences between the two civilizations. Furthermore, without the common threat of communism, the West and Islam increasingly perceive each other as enemies. The recent revival of Islam has given Muslims a reassertion of the relevance of Islam compared to other religions. In the past decades, the Muslim population growth has created large numbers of jobless and disgruntled youth that could become suitable recruits to Islamic causes. This may only amplify the magnitude of cultural collision between the West and Islam [35].

Temporal Acceleration

One of the main features of the modern age is temporal acceleration. Simply put, the world is turning faster than ever. German philosopher Luebbe suggests that Western societies experience the "contraction of the present" because of the accelerating rates of cultural and social innovation [36]. Acceleration is almost about everything in our life, from politics and economics, to work, love, and even leisure [37]. According to Rosa, we may identify three types of acceleration: (1) the acceleration of technological change, (2) the acceleration of social change, and (3) the acceleration of the pace of life [36]. The acceleration of technological change is the most obvious type and can be defined as the speeding up of intentional processes of transport, communication, and production. It is widely accepted that we are communicating, traveling, and processing data much faster than the previous generations. In the past 15 years, the different features of microcomputers such as processing speed, price, memory capacity, and even the number and size of pixels in digital cameras have been upgraded exponentially. According to Butters' Law, the amount of data that we can transmit using optical fiber is doubling every nine months [38]. Depending on the criteria used, computer performance has increased since manual computing by a factor between 1.7 and 76 trillion [39]. The acceleration of social change is classified as

speeding up of society itself, including attitudes and values, fashions and lifestyles, social relations and obligations, groups, classes, milieus, and languages. The acceleration of the pace of life involves the individuals' experience of time, so they consider time as scarce, feel hurried, and experience time pressure and stress [36].

Temporal acceleration is a complex phenomenon that is caused by a combination of economic, cultural, and structural factors. Within a capitalist economy, time is perceived as a highly valuable and crucial factor of production that can be translated into economic profit or loss. An acceleration of production is more efficient, more competitive, and naturally more profitable. Therefore, the processes of production, as well as distribution, and consumption constantly accelerate to create more competitive products and services. The dominant cultural ideals of modernity are associated with social change. That is why the modern Western cultures have a natural tendency to destroy the tradition and embrace novelty. The modern cultures love change for the sake of change. They define the good life as a fulfilled life that is rich in experiences and developed capacities. A fulfilled life can be attained only by doing more, by seeing more, by enjoying more, by tasting more, by being more, and by living more. Living more is possible mainly by accelerating the pace of life, having more options, and overcoming the scarcity of time. In addition to the economic and the cultural factors, the high levels of complexity of modern societies generate a higher number of options and relations whose processes require temporal acceleration. The typical family structure in a traditional society was very stable over time with generational turnover leaving the basic structure unchanged. In classical modernity, this structure was built to last for just a generation: it was organized around a couple and tended to disperse with the death of the couple. In late modernity, the family structure often lasts less than an individual life span as an increasing number of marriages are dissolved and the divorced couples remarry and build new families. Likewise, the life cycle of employment in traditional societies tended to last over many generations as the children inherited the father's profession. In classical modernity, the life cycle of employment got shorter and lasted for a life span as the children were supposed to choose their own occupations. In the postmodern societies, the life cycle of employment has become even shorter as the typical workers can change their employment multiple times during their professional lives. The effects of temporal acceleration can be seen on the product life cycle curves in electronics as they are becoming progressively steeper and shorter in the past two decades. Indeed, the average life span of a computer has shrunk from four or five years to two years in the past decade. The short and steep product life cycle curves are indicative of the effects of temporal acceleration on production, purchase, and consumption of many products, particularly electronic devices. First, temporal acceleration pushes the producers to create more innovative and performing devices because there is only a narrow opportunity to earn profits on a new product before the competition catches up. Then, temporal acceleration pushes the consumers to rush and buy the latest devices to fulfill their lives by buying and doing faster. That is why a large proportion of sales in electronic devices happen soon after the introduction of the product. Finally, temporal acceleration destroys stability by making the electronic devices obsolete shortly after their introduction.

Short-Termism and Myopic Management

According to Sennett, short-termism is one of the main characteristics of the contemporary culture [40]. The need for prompt responses caused by powerful communication technologies means that the future progressively shortens and ultimately melts into an extended present [41]. In other words, the limits of the future move increasingly closer to the present. Long-term strategic planning is replaced by quick and temporary fixes. High-speed, short-termism, and the imperative for an immediate response characterize our contemporary culture [42]. We are living in a world where the old work ethic based on the deferred gratification, self-discipline, and long-term planning is giving way to myopia, simultaneity, and casino capitalism. Economic organizations are focusing solely on quarterly and short-term profits and are moving away from what once constituted the foundation of capitalism. We are witnessing a growing inclination toward short-term relationships in work and organization, including employment discontinuities and unstable cooperative relationships [43]. As a result, there is a shift from the Fordist mode of capitalist production to faster, more flexible, and globally coordinated economic paradigms and techniques such as just-in-time production, outsourcing, and financial globalization.

Short-termism is a pervasive cultural phenomenon whose manifestations can be found in a wide range of areas from investment, capital markets, organizational planning, strategic management, marketing, product life cycle, innovation, technology, trade, and political decision making, to more personal matters such as conjugal relations. Thanks to powerful computers and programmed algorithms, high-frequency traders whose time horizons are normally limited to fractions of a second conduct the majority of trades in financial markets. It has been suggested that the financial crisis of 2007 through 2009 was caused, at least partly, by short-termism because the market participants including mortgage originators, credit default-swap sellers, rating agencies, and investors focused only on short-term profits and neglected the markets' fundamentals. The financial markets were misled by short-term gains but, when the fundamentals emerged, house prices declined, subprime mortgages defaulted, short-term credit markets froze up, and ultimately the bubble collapsed [44]. Short-termism is an important cause of the insecurity of financial institutions [45]. Sennett argues that, by encouraging the opportunistic quest of interests, a short-term perspective may ruin trust-based mechanisms and social relationships [46]. Short-term results, often expressed as quarterly statements, could deceive managers and shareholders by hiding the essential realities of organizations. Short-termism may push managers to inflate the quarterly results and cause some early gains in the form of higher current income and stock price, but it ultimately leads to underperformance and failure. Furthermore, short-termism may encourage managers to commit unethical and even illegal behavior to reach their short-term milestones [47].

Transformation of Cultural Values

The contemporary world is experiencing significant changes in cultural values. The unprecedented economic growth in the Western countries, after the Second World War and more recently in the emerging countries, is generating systematic changes in cultural values. According to modernization theory, cultural values are shaped mainly by socioeconomic conditions and a dearth or an abundance of resources [32]. As societies attain economic development and higher standards of living, they move from traditional to modern cultural values. Traditional societies emphasize the importance of parent and child ties in traditional families, deference to authority, and absolute moral standards. Furthermore, traditional societies are more likely to reject divorce, abortion, euthanasia, and suicide [32, 33]. On the other hand, modern cultures have the opposite preferences on all of these matters and are marked by secular, bureaucratic, and rational values. Interestingly, those nations with a high percentage of their workforce employed in agriculture tend to emphasize traditional values, while those with a high percentage employed in industry and service are likely to embrace modern cultural values [32, 33].

In the past four decades, due to the economic development and rising standards of living, an increasing share of the population in the Western Europe and North America has grown up taking survival for granted. As a result, the cultural values in these societies have shifted from materialism and traditional values to the postindustrial values, emphasizing subjective well-being, self-expression, and quality of life. For example, a growing number of people in the Western societies are showing support for abortion, homosexuality, and same-sex marriage as they are becoming more tolerant than the previous generations used to be. The American religiousness is changing rapidly as, in one decade, the proportion of religiously unaffiliated Americans has more than doubled from 8 percent in 2003 to 22 percent in 2013 [48]. Similarly, the strong supporters of the same-sex marriage legalization have grown from 9 percent in 2003 to over 35 percent in 2013 [48]. It seems that, with some delay and imperfection, the populations of the emerging countries are following the path of cultural modernization. In China, individualist cultural values are gaining importance among the urban population, whereas collectivist cultural values are in decline [49]. The differences between the cultural values of people in rich and poor societies follow a consistent pattern. Therefore, as developing countries are getting richer, they are likely to embrace the modern cultural values such as individualism, secularity and rationality, tolerance of divorce, abortion, and homosexuality (see Figure 3.3). In other words, economic development brings predictable and consistent changes in cultural values and pushes societies to move from traditional, religious, and survival values

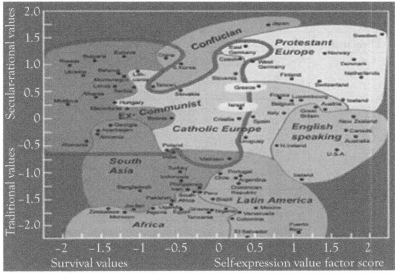

Figure 3.3 According to modernization theory, as societies attain economic development, they move from traditional to modern cultural values

toward secular, rational, and self-expression values [50, 51]. It is important to bear in mind that while economic conditions account for a considerable amount of variation in cultural values, other societal, historical, and geopolitical factors are of considerable importance.

The Culture of McDonaldization

The contemporary culture is marked by what George Ritzer labeled "McDonaldization." According to Ritzer, McDonaldization is the process by which the principles of fast-food restaurants are coming to dominate multiple sectors of American society as well as of the rest of the world [5]. McDonaldization could be considered as a continuation of the Weberian bureaucracy. Ritzer argues that the success of McDonaldization can be explained through four dimensions (see Table 3.1). The first dimension is efficiency. The restaurant offers an efficient way to go from hungry to full. Workers at McDonald's also operate efficiently by following predesigned steps of a process. The second dimension is calculability that focuses on the quantitative aspects of McDonald's products. Examples include portion size, cost, and the amount of time it takes for the customer to get the

Table 3.1 The four dimensions of McDonaldization according to George Ritzer

Dimension	Explanation	Examples
1. Efficiency	The optimal method for accomplishing a task	The fastest way to get from being hungry to being full Minimization of time
2. Calculability	The quantification of objectives	Quantity is translated into quality A large amount of product delivered to the customer in a short amount of time is the same as a high-quality product
3. Predictability	The standardization and uniformity of products and services	Always the same product, the same service, and the same task
4. Control	Influencing the customers and employees via automation	Limited menu, limited choice, and limited time for customers Limited and repetitive tasks for employees

product. This is important because people in the United States now view quantity as being as important as quality. People also calculate how much time it will take for them to get to a McDonald's restaurant rather than eating at home. Predictability is the third dimension. When people go to McDonald's, they can be sure that the product is going to be the same as the previous one. The fourth dimension of McDonaldization is control. This is exerted over the customers with the use of lines, limited menus, and uncomfortable seats. These methods of control cause people to eat quickly and leave.

Although the fast-food industry did not create the desire for efficiency in society, it helped efficiency turn into a universal reality. The streamlined process of McDonaldization has spread to other restaurants within the fast-food industry. The frozen food industry sprang up as a result of the demand to speed up and simplify home cooking. Some other areas of society that have been affected by McDonaldization include shopping, higher education, health care, and entertainment. The department stores, shopping malls, and even gas stations have all become streamlined stores allowing consumers to buy products quickly and efficiently. In the education system, universities give tests that can be graded by a machine, leaving the professors more time dedicated to research and publication.

Now even more efficient modes of entertainment are available as Netflix and Amazon.com allow consumers to have movies delivered directly to their homes. People can also now listen to audio books instead of taking the time to read them.

A McDonaldized society like the United States emphasizes quantity over quality. The emphasis on quantity in the fast-food restaurants leads to the lower levels of quality, but customers are not the only people suffering from the restaurants striving for quantity instead of quality. The most efficient way to produce mass quantities of food is to have the food preparation process broken down into several individual parts. Like Henry Ford's assembly line, each worker is conducting one small task repetitively leading to their alienation and feeling no sense of personal meaning or pride in their work. In a McDonaldized society, everything must be quantifiable. For example, in the current educational system in the United States "the focus seems to be on how many students ('products') can be herded through the system and what grades they earn rather than the quality of 'what' and 'how' they learn" [5]. The entire educational system has become quantified in the sense that the students are now evaluated by their grade point average (GPA) and how their GPA ranks against that of their fellow classmates. Similarly, colleges, hospitals, businesses, libraries, municipalities, and other organizations have become quantified by how they rank against their counterparts. Other products and services like books, magazines, movies, and television shows are constantly reviewed, rated, and ranked. When customers walk into a McDonald's anywhere in the world, they will get the same experience regardless of location. The employees will be wearing the same uniforms and addressing the customer with the same basic responses. The same repetitive tasks not only increase efficiency but also enable companies to produce the same products consistently each time, thus making the employee's duties predictable. Predictability has spread to other sectors and industries including entertainment, retail, transport and aviation, automotive, medicine, and education. The textbooks, curricula, and college degree programs are becoming increasingly standardized and predictable across the world. It does not matter whether you do your MBA in the United States, in Romania, or in Singapore.

In a McDonaldized culture, the nonhuman technology controls both employees and customers. For instance, customers face a variety of structural constraints and follow the norms when they enter a fast-food restaurant. The effects of nonhuman technology can be seen in universities, hospitals, and supermarkets. Fast-food restaurants today have little preparation. Everything is precooked, wrapped, cut, and seasoned. The nonhuman technology increases the control over the employees, making sure that they are doing the right orders. In hospitals, the main doctor is not the solution anymore as he used to be. A person's doctor is just the start of a long pathway that has been previously prepared. In the aviation industry, the pilots are not piloting the plane as they used to do. Instead, the computers guide the plane between takeoff and touchdown. Due to the growing effects of nonhuman technology, the human artisanship and creativity are losing their importance and are becoming worthless. In addition to its dehumanizing effects on the society, McDonaldization may paradoxically involve some inefficiencies and irrationalities. A McDonaldized society can become inefficient when there is an excess of regulations and processes. For instance, in a McDonaldized society, customer service is becoming standardized and void of any real friendliness, thus it is becoming ineffective. By giving the priority to quantity over quality, the McDonaldization process may imply negative effects on customers and employees. A McDonaldized school offers quick and cheap programs but fails to deliver a high-quality education.

References

[1] Hassi, A., and G. Storti. 2012. "Globalisation and Culture: The Three H Scenarios." In *Globalization Approaches to Diversity*, ed. H. Cuadra-Montiel, pp. 3–20. Rijeka, Croatia: InTech Press.

[2] Prasad, A., and P. Prasad. 2006. "Global Transitions: The Emerging New World Order and its Implications for Business and Management." *Business Renaissance Quarterly* 1, no. 3, pp. 91–113.

[3] Castells, M. 1996. *The Network Society*, Vol. 469. Oxford: Blackwell.

[4] Ritzer, G., and Z. Atalay, eds. 2010. *Readings in Globalization: Key Concepts and Major Debates*. John Wiley & Sons.

[5] Ritzer, G. 2008. *The McDonaldization of Society*, 5. Pine Forge Press.

[6] Jaja, J.M. 2011. "Globalization or Americanization: Implications for Sub-Saharan Africa." In K.G. Deng, Globalization-Today, Tomorrow, ed. 113–124. Sciyo, Rijeka, Croatia.

[7] Beck, U. 2000. *What Is Globalization?* Cornwall, UK: MPG Books, Bodmin Ltd.

[8] Berger, P. 2002. "The Cultural Dynamics of Globalization." In *Many Globalizations: Cultural Diversity in the Contemporary World*, eds. P. Berger and S.P. Huntington, pp. 1–16. New York, NY: Oxford University Press.

[9] Pieterse, J.N. 1995. "Globalisation as Hybridisation." In *Global Modernities*, eds. M. Featherstone, S. Lash, and R. Robertson, pp. 45–68. London: Sage.

[10] Tomlinson, J. 2003. "Globalization and Cultural Identity." In *The Global Transformations Reader*, eds. D. Held and A. McGrew, 2nd ed., 269–778. Cambridge, UK: Polity Press.

[11] Deng, N. 2005. "On the National Literature's Tactics in the Globalization's Language Environment." *Journal of Human Institute of Humanities, Science, and Technology* 1, pp. 39–41.

[12] Burton, R.E. 2009. "Globalisation and Cultural Identity in Caribbean Society: The Jamaican Case." *Caribbean Journal of Philosophy* 1, no. 1, pp. 1–18.

[13] MacKay, H. 2004. "The Globalisation of Culture?" In *A Globalizing World? Culture, Economics Politics*, ed. D. Held, pp. 48–84. New York, NY: Routledge.

[14] Pieterse, J.N. 2006. "Globalization Goes in Circles: Hybridities East-West." Retrieved from http://social-theory.eu/texts/pieterse_globalization_goes_in_circles.pdf (accessed May 28, 2008).

[15] Cvetkovich, A., and D. Kellner. 1997. "Introduction: Thinking Global and Local." *Articulating the Global and the Local*, pp. 1–30.

[16] Robertson, R. 2001. "Globalization Theory 2000+: Major Problematics." In *Handbook of Social Theory*, eds. G. Ritzer and B. Smart, pp. 458–471. London, UK: Sage Publications.

[17] Pieterse, J.N. 1996. "Globalisation and Culture: Three Paradigms." *Economic and Political Weekly* 31, no. 23, pp. 1389–1393.

[18] Appadurai, A. 1990. "Disjuncture and Difference in the Global Cultural Economy." *Public Culture* 2, no. 2, pp. 1–24.

[19] Hamelink, C. 1983. *Cultural Autonomy in Global Communications*. New York, NY: Longman.

[20] A snapshot of Toronto: 51% of residents were born outside Canada, Vital Signs Report finds. http://news.nationalpost.com/toronto/a-snapshot-of-toronto-51-of-residents-were-born-outside-canada-vital-signs-report-finds.

[21] ACS Demographic and Housing Estimates—2009–2013. American Community Survey 5-Year Estimates. *United States Census Bureau*. Retrieved May 8, 2015.

[22] Giddens, A. 2000. *Runaway World: How Globalization Is Reshaping Our Lives*. New York, NY: Routledge.

[23] Tomlinson, J. 1999. *Globalization and Culture.* Chicago: University of Chicago Press.

[24] Cesari, J. November 2005. "Ethnicity, Islam, and Les Banlieues: Confusing the Issues." *Social Science Research Council* 30.

[25] Canet, R., L. Pech, M. Stewart. November 2008. "France's Burning Issue: Understanding the Urban Riots of November 2005." SSRN 1303514 Freely accessible.

[26] London disturbances—Sunday August 07, 2011. https://theguardian.com/uk/blog/2011/aug/07/tottenham-riots-police-duggan-live.

[27] "School Segregation, the Continuing Tragedy of Ferguson." *ProPublica.* Retrieved November 25, 2015.

[28] Tomlinson, J. 2003. "Globalization and Cultural Identity." *The Global Transformations Reader* 2, pp. 269–277.

[29] Conversi, D. 2002. *Walker Connor and the Study of Nationalism.* London: Routledge.

[30] Grant, N. 1997. "Democracy and Cultural Pluralism: Towards the 21st Century." In *Cultural Democracy and Ethnic Pluralism: Multicultural and Multilingual Policies in Education,* eds. R. Watts and J.J. Smolicz, 25–50. Frankfurt am Main and Berlin: Peter Lang.

[31] Skutnabb-Kangas, T., and R. Phillipson. 1998. "Language in Human Rights." *Gazette: The International Journal for Communication Studies* 60, no. 1, pp. 27–46.

[32] Inglehart, R. 1997. *Modernization and Postmodernization: Cultural, Economic, and Political Change in 43 Societies.* Princeton University Press.

[33] Inglehart, R., and C. Welzel. 2005. *Modernization, Cultural Change, and Democracy: The Human Development Sequence.* Cambridge University Press.

[34] Lieber, R.J., and R.E. Weisberg. 2002. "Globalization, Culture, and Identities in Crisis." *International Journal of Politics, Culture, and Society* 16, no. 2, pp. 273–296.

[35] Huntington, S.P. 1997. *The Clash of Civilizations and the Remaking of World Order.* Penguin Books India.

[36] Rosa, H. 2003. "Social Acceleration: Ethical and Political Consequences of a Desynchronized High-Speed Society." *Constellations* 10, no. 1, pp. 3–33.

[37] James, G. 1999. *Faster: The Acceleration of Just About Everything.* New York: Pantheon.

[38] Robinson, G. 2000. "Speeding Net Traffic with Tiny Mirrors." *EE Times.* Retrieved August 22, 2011.

[39] Nordhaus, W.D. 2007. "Two Centuries of Productivity Growth in Computing." *The Journal of Economic History* 67, no. 1, pp. 128–159.

[40] Sennett, R. 2011. *The Corrosion of Character: The Personal Consequences of Work in the New Capitalism.* WW Norton & Company.

[41] Petrick, K. 2016. "Strategic Planning in the 'Empire of Speed.'" *Globalizations* 13, no. 3, pp. 345–359.

[42] Hassan, R. 2003. *The Chronoscopic Society: Globalization, Time, and Knowledge in the Network Economy* 17. Peter Lang Pub Incorporated.

[43] Brose, H.G. 2004. "An Introduction Towards a Culture of Non-Simultaneity?" *Time & Society* 13, no. 1, pp. 5–26.

[44] Dallas, L. 2012. "Short-termism, The Financial Crisis, and Corporate Governance." *J. Corp. L.* 37, p. 265.

[45] Revisiting Short-termism, supra note 12, at 42. See also Emeka Duruigbo, Tackling Shareholder Short-termism and Managerial Myopia 16, 46 (April 04, 2011) (unpublished manuscript), available at http://ssrn.com/abstract=1802840

[46] Sennett, R. 2007. *The Culture of the New Capitalism.* Yale University Press.

[47] Patelli, L. 2012. *Short-termism and Behavioral Ethics.* School of Accountancy Daniels College of Business University of Denver.

[48] Jones, R.P., D. Cox, and J. Navarro-Rivera. 2014. *A Shifting Landscape: A Decade of Change in American Attitudes About Same-Sex Marriage and LGBT Issues.* Public Religion Research Institute.

[49] Zeng, R., and PM. Greenfield. 2015. "Cultural Evolution Over the Last 40 Years in China: Using the Google Ngram Viewer to Study Implications of Social and Political Change for Cultural Values." *International Journal of Psychology* 50, no. 1, pp. 47–55.

[50] Inglehart, R., and W.E. Baker. 2000. "Modernization, Cultural Change, and the Persistence of Traditional Values." *American Sociological Review*, pp. 19–51.

[51] Welzel, C., R. Inglehart, and H.D. Kligemann. 2003. "The Theory of Human Development: A Cross-Cultural Analysis." *European Journal of Political Research* 42, no. 3, pp. 341–379.

CHAPTER 4

The Changing Landscape of Global Affairs

A Multipolar World Order

Since the end of the Cold War, we have witnessed the formation of a new multipolar world ruled by several centers of political and economic decision making [1]. The collapse of the Soviet Union and communist regimes in the 1990s marks the end of global bipolarity that had started shortly after the Second World War. While during the Cold War the two undisputable superpowers namely the United States and the Soviet Union dominated the world arena, in the past two decades, a multipolar system has been developing where numerous nations including the European countries, Russia, China, India, Japan, and Brazil are progressively gaining importance [2]. The dynamism of the new order is shaped by the presence of numerous nonstate actors including multinational corporations (MNCs), investment banks, private investors, financial markets, tech giants, and supranational and regional organizations. Because of competition among various actors on the world stage, the global governance has become more diverse and more complex [3]. In tandem with the changes in the geopolitical system, the world economy has entered a multipolar phase [4]. Globalization has resulted in the ascendance of many emerging economies that are not categorized as socially advanced and completely industrialized [5]. In terms of economic growth, many developing countries have been growing much faster than developed nations of the West in the past two decades. For instance, some emerging countries including India and China grew at or above 6 percent per year between 2005 and 2010, while the developed countries grew at 2 percent or less [4]. While the global economy is not necessarily a zero-sum game, the rise of emerging countries could be the cause of the decline in the developed economies of the West (see Figure 4.1). The effects of economic growth in emerging economies are easily noticeable. For instance, gross national income (GNI) per capita increased more than sevenfold in China between 1990 and 2008. In 1990, almost 60 percent of Chinese population lived on under $1.25 per day, but in 2005, that portion was only 16 percent [4]. Similarly, other developing countries such as Brazil, India, and South Africa have experienced significant improvements in their standards of living in the past few years. The share of global exports originated in developing and emerging countries has risen from 28 percent in 1990 to 42 percent in 2007. Likewise, the share of inward flow of global foreign direct investment (FDI) to emerging countries has increased from 18 percent in 1990 to 33 percent in 2006 [5]. The FDI flows from developing economies have rapidly increased from $12 billion in 1990 to nearly $328 billion in 2010, which is equivalent to 24.8 percent of the world FDI [6]. In the past two decades, Japan and the United States' shares of the world's FDI have fallen, while those of developing countries have risen significantly [7, 8]. Currently, the developing countries account for more than half of the global GDP, are champions of economic growth, and consume more than half of the world's energy resources. The number of emerging markets' multinationals in the Fortune Global 500 list of the world's biggest companies is going up steadily as they are expanding and acquiring new businesses across the globe at a frantic pace [9, 10, 11].

The emerging countries enjoy fairly well-developed physical and financial infrastructure but have less well-developed processes and systems of governance, regulation, and education than the world's most

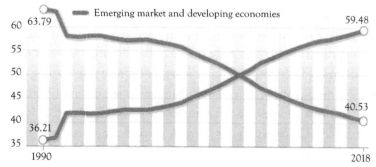

Figure 4.1 The rise of emerging countries involves a relative decline of advanced economies

Source: International Monetary Fund, World Economic Database, 2016.

advanced countries [12]. As of 2020, the MSCI Emerging Markets Index included the following 21 countries: Brazil, Chile, China, Colombia, Czech Republic, Egypt, Hungary, India, Indonesia, Korea, Malaysia, Mexico, Morocco, Peru, Philippines, Poland, Russia, South Africa, Taiwan, Thailand, and Turkey (http://msci.com). According to Goldman Sachs' projections, the four largest emerging economies namely Brazil, Russia, India, and China will overtake the economies of the group of seven largest industrialized countries (the United States, Japan, Germany, France, the United Kingdom, Italy, and Canada) by 2040 [13]. Consistent with the same projections, Brazil, Russia, India, and China along with the next 11 economies (Bangladesh, Egypt, Indonesia, Iran, South Korea, Mexico, Nigeria, Pakistan, Philippines, Turkey, and Vietnam) will be larger than the Group 7 soon after 2030.

Developing and emerging countries are capitalizing on their increased economic power to gain more influence on the global stage. In the past two decades, the Bretton Woods institutions have come under growing pressure to allow more voting power to emerging-market countries such as Brazil, India, and China [14]. The Group-20 (G-20) has replaced the Group-8 (G-8) in 2008 to include the emerging countries' influence. Similar organizational changes have occurred at the IMF [5]. Likewise, the North Atlantic Treaty Organization (NATO) membership has been expanded to include emerging countries and a reform of the United Nations Security Council seems likely [5]. In short, emerging countries are gaining influence in many aspects of global management, including environment protection, energy, health, education, pollution, climate change, migration, and security. The rise of emerging nations implies that the Western countries are facing fierce competition from numerous new players that are gradually enhancing their capabilities. For the first time since the industrial revolution, a small group of Western nations does not dominate the world economy [15]. Indeed, Europe has experienced relative political and economic decline to the benefit of Asian countries in the past 20 years. The rise of emerging countries has been described as a seismic change in the world economy, perhaps "the biggest shift since the Industrial Revolution of the 18th century" [13]. In the same vein, Zakaria suggests that we are witnessing the third great power shift in modern history [1]. The first shift was the rise of the Western world, around the 15th century that made the modern world and brought about considerable revolutions in science, technology, commerce, and capitalism and ultimately the dominance of the Western world. The second shift happened in the final years of the 19th century and led to the rise of the United States as the undisputed global superpower. While in the past 20 years, America's superpower status in every realm has been largely unchallenged, there are visible indications of the rise of emerging countries, what Zakaria called "the rise of the rest." Evidently, at the military and political levels, the United States is still the unquestionable superpower, but along every other dimension including industrial, financial, social, and cultural, the distribution of power is shifting rapidly to other players mainly to emerging countries [1].

What Decline? Do Not Bet Against America!

"The rise of the rest" implies the assumption that a power shift is happening and, as a result, the United States of America is facing a drastic economic decline. This may allow others to take advantage of America's feebleness to challenge its role as the global superpower. Ordinary Americans and even many commentators and pundits have subscribed to this idea and have seen a looming American decline for a long time [16]. The so-called declinists remain cynical and view globalization and the subsequent rise of the emerging countries with a sense of apocalypse and doom. They await grave consequences for the American foreign policy and the world stability as a whole [17]. In addition to the geopolitical and economic indicators, the declinists point to many sociopolitical problems such as an inadequate education system, a weakening middle class, and a paralyzed political system in the United States to defend their pessimistic predictions about America [18]. Interestingly, the prediction of an American decline is hardly new. Since the 1960s, the commentators have been constantly forecasting dire things for the United States, every time claiming that the decline could be imminent [19, 20].

First, it seems that the commonly accepted views about China and other emerging countries rising to challenge the United States and other major Western states are based on an exaggeration of events. The facts are quite simple. The United States is and will remain the world's largest economy for a near future. The indications of American economic supremacy are abundant. Despite the rise of emerging economies, the United States has lost little of its preeminent share of world GDP over the past three decades [4]. With less than 5 percent of the world's population, America accounts for almost a quarter of the world's GDP, which the World Bank estimates to be $74.1 trillion in total. China, with almost 20 percent of the world's population, is far behind the United States and accounts only for 14.84 percent of the world's economy [4]. California alone has a larger economy than Brazil and Russia. Texas' economy is nearly as big as Russia's and somewhat smaller than India's. The U.S. economy is larger than the next four largest economies altogether namely China, Japan, Germany, and the United Kingdom. Based on the standard of living, we find similar results. While standards of living are rising and poverty is declining for millions of people in emerging countries, the United States continues to be ahead by a long way. The standard of living in the United States is on average four times higher than that in Brazil, six times higher than that in China, and as much as 15 times higher than that in India. Furthermore, the United States has some incomparable advantages in size, geography, climate, energy, and natural resources that will make it an exceptional superpower. Perhaps, one of the most important advantages of the United States over all other nations resides in its control over the global financial system particularly by imposing dollar as the reserve currency. As former French President Charles de Gaulle rightly mentioned, using the dollar as the world reserve currency gives America an "exorbitant advantage" unlike any other. Through a dollar-based international monetary system, the United States is virtually taxing every other state, so it is able to reap more than it pays out in the provision of public goods [21].

The strength of the United States resides not only in the size of its economy but also in its astonishing competitiveness. The emerging economies such as China, India, and Brazil are large but are not necessarily efficient and competitive in comparison with the United States. According to the World Economic Forum surveys, the United States has been one of the most competitive economies of the world for the past decade, while China, Russia, India, and Brazil have occupied the ranks on the bottom of the list [22]. Closely associated with competitiveness is the capacity of an economy to innovate. Innovation is perhaps the most outstanding strength of America. The United States accounted for 40 percent of total world research and development in 2008. Two-thirds of most cited researchers in science and technology are originated in the United States [22]. The United States remains the most innovative country in the world with more patents than all other countries combined. The declinists claim that the United States is sliding down the innovation list, but they cannot deny that, despite the rise of research and development in other countries, the United States still ranks among the fourth most pioneering countries of the world.

On top of all these advantages, the United States is benefiting from strong and highly competitive corporations. In 2020, 22 of the top 50 corporations were American [23]. The emerging countries' multinationals remain mainly uncompetitive and dependent on natural resources and government support. For example, a large number of corporations in China are under state control, operate within the national market, lack managerial expertise, and are deficient in terms of transparency, global branding, and sound strategic planning [24]. Another undeniable advantage of the United States resides in its military supremacy and its capacity to project power across the globe from Asia and Africa to the Middle East and Europe. The military power of other countries is not even comparable with that of the United States. While Chinese military budget has risen consistently since 1989, it is less than one-fifth of the American spending. Indeed, the United States was the world's biggest military spender in 2020 with $778 billion, accounting for 39 percent of the global expenditure [25]. Another remarkable advantage of the United States resides in its capacity to build and lead wide alliance systems across the world.

Finally, in addition to all the economic, military, and political forces, America is enjoying a significant soft power thanks to a pluralist sociopolitical culture and an open system. The American education system continues to attract a large number of talented students from all over the world, even from those countries that are well-known to have a critical view of the U.S. policies including China and Russia. Getting an education in an American college is believed not only to improve only the professional credentials but also to offer the much-needed analytical skills. It is interesting to note that the United States was home to 8 of the top 10 world's universities in 2020 [26, 27]. While the United States continues to act as a magnet for international students, the emerging countries, namely Brazil, Russia, China, and India, are facing tremendous difficulties to raise the standard of their educational systems [28]. One may suggest that one of the main causes of continuity in American/ Western strength is the underlying cultural dynamism that started with the Greek philosophers, perfected during the Enlightenment in Europe, and prospered under the American capitalism.

The European Union: An Economic Giant and a Political Dwarf

With 27 member states, 447 million inhabitants, a GDP of $20 trillion, high standards of living, and a rich cultural heritage, the EU is certainly an important power on the world stage. A long history of colonialism, diplomacy, and international trade make the EU an active member of the global community. Europe was developed over the past five centuries through industrialization and colonization, becoming the leading power in the current system of international relations. Most of the modern international organizations are originated in the Western Europe particularly in countries such as Britain, France, and Germany. As such, the European countries in conjunction with the United States are benefiting from a great advantage in designing, affecting, and enforcing the international rules in the areas of security, cooperation, finance, trade, culture, sport, science, and technology. The European interests influence a large number of key international organizations including the United Nations, the Security Council, the IMF, and the World Bank. For example, France is a permanent member of the Security Council, and another two or three European states could serve as rotating members in any given year [29].

Since 2003, the EU has expressed its readiness to assume major global responsibilities. The EU has globally been recognized as a civil power standing for peace, development, human rights, and multilateralism across the world. The EU has played a benevolent role in troubled zones such as peace process in the Middle East, the Iranian nuclear deal, and the climate change accord. As such, it is possible to contrast the EU's influence with the unilateral approach of the United States to international affairs.

Consequently, in many parts of the world, the EU enjoys a high level of trust that could serve as a foundation for an effective multilateralism [30]. Nevertheless, due to its military limitations, the EU has often made only partial contributions to the stability and security of the international system. When comparing the EU with the United States, China, Russia, and other world powers, we need to keep in mind that the EU is by nature a different entity that relies mainly on its diplomatic approaches and soft power. The EU is an ongoing, avant-garde, and utopian project relying on multilateralism, cooperation, and peace. For that reason, the EU has been often characterized as "economic giant and political dwarf" [30].

Apparently, the EU is suffering from multiple weaknesses and challenges that limit its influence in the global affairs. A very pressing challenge is about the single currency crisis and the associated fiscal problems that have hurt the EU's credibility around the world [29]. The single currency has made the EU model less attractive not only to the member states but also to a large number of the EU citizens. As the European Council on Foreign Relations noted, "the continent seems to be losing its agency: where it was once seen as a critical part of the solution to international problems, it has now become a problem to be dealt with by others" [31]. Furthermore, the EU is suffering from a lack of coherent and independent security and defense strategy. While the member states such as France have their own national defense programs, the EU as a whole is not equipped with an effective apparatus to project hard power across the world or to defend its own security. Furthermore, the EU is still short of implementing a common foreign policy vis-a-vis global and geopolitical upheavals. The war in Iraq in 2003 showed that significant disagreements exist among the EU nation-states such as France, Germany, Italy, and Spain. If the EU can reach a higher level of political and economic integration, it will be able to overcome these challenges and express a united voice with respect to global crises. Otherwise, it is possible to predict that the EU's influence on the world stage will decline as the emerging powers, particularly Russia and Asian countries, will gain economic and political weight. With the rise of emerging countries, there is an expectation for a more equitable distribution of power across the world to the detriment of the European countries that are overpresented in many international organizations from the United Nations and the Security Council to the IMF [29].

The Rise of Nonstate Actors

The Treaty of Westphalia in 1648 created the modern world order based on the principle of state sovereignty. It implied that each nation-state has sovereignty over its territory and domestic affairs, to the exclusion of all external powers, on the principle of noninterference in another country's domestic affairs. After the Cold War and toward the end of the 20th century, the principle of state sovereignty has come under a growing pressure. Globalization, the new telecommunication technologies, and the integration of national economies have increased the involvement and importance of nonstate actors in international relations. The current landscape of global affairs is marked by the emergence of nonstate actors in addition to national governments. Nonstate actors are nonsovereign entities that exercise significant economic, political, or social power and influence at the national and international levels [32]. Nonstate actors may include a wide range of entities such as international organizations, MNCs, scientific experts, civil society groups, networks, partnerships, private military and security companies, and even transnational criminal and drug-trafficking networks [33, 34, 35, 36].

The rise of nonstate actors has contributed to a growing fragmentation of the global governance system [37]. As a consequence, we are gradually witnessing a power transfer from nation-states to nonstate actors. Nation-states and nonstate actors are both collaborating and competing on many global issues. The large corporations benefit from colossal business volumes, advanced technologies, and rare resources that enable them to have greater margins for maneuver and adaptability. The number of MNCs, has risen from an estimated 7,000 in 1972 to some 82,000 in 2008 [38, 39]. Likewise, nongovernmental organizations (NGOs) are private, self-governing, voluntary, nonprofit, and task- or interest-oriented advocacy organizations that are increasing in number and importance [40]. As of 2008, more than 3,000 NGOs were registered as consultative groups with the United Nations Economic and Social Council [38]. Due to their flexibility, some NGOs may outcompete narrow-minded national governments. Indeed, in areas such as business, civil society, and science, nonstate actors already play a more important role than national governments do [38]. The super-rich and dominant individuals are other nonstate actors that rely on their immense wealth or power to exert their influence on the global affairs. They might include prominent industrialists, financiers, media moguls, celebrity activists, and religious leaders. These individuals often wield their influence through lobbyist groups, NGOs, MNCs, charity foundations, and other categories of for- or nonprofit organizations [40]. In the past two decades, the criminal and terrorist organizations have become important players on the global stage. Some nonstate violent groups such as the Lebanese Hezbollah are well positioned to exert a huge influence and even overshadow the national governments [41]. Violent organizations might have close connections to their communities and better support them by offering public goods, especially in war-torn regions.

A Comeback of Nuclear Arsenals

Currently, there are more than 16,000 nuclear weapons in nine countries including the United States (7,200), Russia (7,500), France (300), China (260), the United Kingdom (215), Pakistan (130), India (120), Israel (80), and North Korea (10) [42]. Each of these weapons could lead to loss of thousands of lives, catastrophic levels of destruction, and long-term and lasting radioactive contamination. Due to their massive destructive capacity, the nuclear warheads are supposed to safeguard their owners against potential aggressions. Ironically, the nuclear weapons themselves might become a cause of war, conflict, and aggression [42]. In 1970, the five nuclear states namely the United States, the United Kingdom, France, China, and Russia introduced the Nuclear Nonproliferation Treaty to prevent the spread of nuclear weapons and to promote cooperation in the peaceful uses of nuclear energy [43, 44]. Furthermore, in order to enhance the nuclear stability, the nuclear states agreed upon some limitations on heavy intercontinental nuclear missiles and warheads. Thanks to these measures and the constant negotiations between the United States and the Soviet Union during the Cold War, the international relations experienced some level of stability and humanity avoided the risk of a full-fledged nuclear conflict. Despite the introduction of the Nuclear Nonproliferation Treaty, other countries including India, Pakistan, and Israel continued on their nuclear programs and acquired nuclear weapons between 1970 and 1998. More recently, North Korea performed its first nuclear test in 2006 and joined the club of nuclear states [42].

The United States has an undisputable military superiority at the conventional level over all other rivals; therefore, it is considering the nuclear weapons less important. By contrast, for smaller military powers such as Russia, India, China, and Pakistan, the importance of nuclear arsenals is growing because their security relies mainly on the nuclear deterrence.

China as a major Asian power is reluctant to negotiate any restriction on its nuclear arsenal. In addition to rivalry with India, China is particularly concerned about the U.S. military presence in Asia. In the recent years, the U.S.-Indian rapprochement and the American technical support of Indian nuclear program have become a source of concern for China. That is why China is in the process of modernizing its nuclear arsenal to acquire a more robust nuclear second-strike capability [42]. India and Pakistan that have joined the club of nuclear nations more recently are in political conflict and rely on their nuclear arsenal to promote their geopolitical agenda. India is committed to keep and modernize its nuclear arsenal because it faces a powerful rival as China in the East and an archenemy like Pakistan on the West. Pakistan has one of the fastest-growing nuclear arsenals as it is in a race with its archrival India. Pakistan is capable of producing about 20 nuclear warheads a year. Considering the political instability of the country and the presence of multiple terrorist groups, the nuclear arsenal of Pakistan is a source of serious concern for the entire world. Furthermore, Pakistan reserves the right to first use of nuclear weapons in the case of an Indian conventional attack. Likewise, Israel as a small country is relying on a suspected nuclear arsenal to politically deal with its hostile neighbors and push forward its geopolitical interests. The last member of the nuclear club, North Korea has good reasons to expand its nuclear arsenal to overcome the geopolitical pressure coming from the United States and its Asian allies namely Japan and South Korea. In the case of any conflict or friction, Japan and South Korea would be able to develop nuclear weapons within a short timeframe as they already have advanced civilian nuclear infrastructure.

Russia has the largest nuclear arsenal with an estimated 7,500 warheads and boasts of its nuclear capability as a competitive advantage both politically and militarily. Considering the relative weakness of Russians at the conventional level, nuclear weapons are the source of superpower standing for Russian leaders. While the United States considers little use for nuclear weapons, Russia continues to view nuclear arms as advantageous even in ordinary military conflicts [45]. According to the *Financial Times,* in a bellicose gesture, Russia moved nuclear-capable Iskander missiles into Kaliningrad between Lithuania and Poland in 2016, warning that an impudent behavior by America may involve nuclear dimensions [46]. Similarly, in 2017, a member of Russia's parliament has declared that Russia would use nuclear weapons in any conflict in which the United States or the NATO forces entered eastern Ukraine and Crimea [47].

Based on these indications, we can observe that the significance of nuclear weapons in international relations is rising again. The nuclear capacities are defining the power relationships between the United States/NATO and Russia. In Asia, the relations between India and China, on the one hand, and India and Pakistan, on the other hand, are highly affected by their respective nuclear readiness. North Korea as a rogue state is relying on its nuclear capacity to defend its communist ideology. In the Middle East, Israel is relying on its nuclear arsenal not only to guarantee its security but also to gain a competitive advantage over its neighbors. Iran that has been suffering from many decades of isolation is giving up on part of its advanced nuclear program to gain economic benefits. Both the United States and Russia are modernizing their nuclear forces to enhance the accuracy and the power of their warheads. More recently, even countries such as Japan and South Korea are thinking about acquiring nuclear weapons on their own. Unfortunately, the increasing importance of nuclear power in international relations is not matched by effective efforts to control the nuclear race. The nuclear powers are not showing any serious willingness to manage the dangers of the nuclear weapons. The United States and Russia, the two largest nuclear powers, are explicitly accusing each other of having violated the previous nuclear agreements. Therefore, one may suggest that the reliance on nuclear arsenals is becoming an evident reality weighing on the global affairs.

References

[1] Zakaria, F. 2011. *The Post-American World: Release 2.0 (International Edition)*. New York, NY: W.W Norton and Company.

[2] Schweller, R.L., and X. Pu. 2011. "After Unipolarity: China's Visions of International Order in an Era of US Decline." *International Security* 36, no. 1, pp. 41–72.

[3] Chan, G. 2013. "The Rise of Multipolarity, the Reshaping of Order: China in a Brave New World?+." *International Journal of China Studies* 4, no. 1, p. 1.

[4] Zoellick, R. April 14, 2010. *The End of the Third World?* Address Delivered Before the Woodrow Wilson Center for International Scholars, Washington, DC.

[5] Berliner, J. 2010. "The Rise of the Rest: How New Economic Powers are Reshaping the Globe, The Second in a Series of White Papers on the American Economy in a New Era of Globalization." NDN.com

[6] Dohse, D., R. Hassink, and C. Klaerding. 2012. "Emerging Multinationals, International Knowledge Flows and Economic Geography: A Research Agenda." Kiel Working Paper, No.1776.

[7] Kothari, T., M. Kotabe, and P. Murphy. 2013. "Rules of the Game for Emerging Market Multinational Companies from China and India." *Journal of International Management* 19, no. 3, pp. 276–299.

[8] Ramamurti, R. 2012. "Competing with Emerging Market Multinationals." *Business Horizons* 55, no. 3, pp. 241–249.

[9] Kumaraswamy, A., R. Mudambi, H. Saranga, and A. Tripathy. 2012. "Catch-Up Strategies in the Indian Auto Components Industry: Domestic Firms' Responses to Market Liberalization." *Journal of International Business Studies* 43, no. 4, pp. 368–395.

[10] Lorenzen, M., and R. Mudambi. 2012. "Clusters, Connectivity, and CatchUp: Bollywood and Bangalore in the Global Economy." *Journal of Economic Geography* 13, no. 3, pp. 501–534.

[11] Moghaddam, K., D. Sethi, T. Weber, and J. Wu. 2014. "The Smirk of Emerging Market Firms: A Modification of the Dunning's Typology of Internationalization Motivations." *Journal of International Management* 20, pp. 359–374.

[12] Banalieva, E.R., L. Tihanyi, T.M. Devinney, and T. Pedersen. 2015. "Introduction to Part II: Emerging Economies and Multinational Enterprises." In *Emerging Economies and Multinational Enterprises (Advances in International Management)* 28, pp. 43–69. Emerald Group Publishing Limited.

[13] Van Agtmael, A. 2007. "The Emerging Markets Century: How a New Breed of World-Class Companies is Overtaking the World." Available at SimonandSchuster.com

[14] Birdsall, N., and F. Fukuyama. 2011. "The Post-Washington Consensus-Development After the Crisis." *Foreign Affairs* 90, p. 45.

[15] Yeganeh, K.H. 2016. "An Examination of the Conditions, Characteristics, and Strategies Pertaining to the Rise of Emerging Markets Multinationals." *European Business Review* 28, no. 5, pp. 600–626.

[16] Layne, C. 2012. "This Time It's Real: The End of Unipolarity and the Pax Americana." *International Studies Quarterly* 56, no. 1, pp. 203–213.

[17] Quinn, A. 2011. "The Art of Declining Politely: Obama's Prudent Presidency and the Waning of American Power." *International Affairs* 87, no. 4, pp. 803–824.

[18] Luce, E. 2012. *Time to Start linking: America in the Age of Descent.* New York, NY: Atlantic Monthly Press.

[19] Calleo, D.P. 2009. *Follies of Power: America's Unipolar Fantasy.* Cambridge University Press.

[20] Wade, R. 2013. "The Art of Power Maintenance: How Western States Keep the Lead in Global Organizations." *Challenge* 56, no. 1, pp. 5–39.

[21] Norrlof, C. 2010. *America's Global Advantage: US Hegemony and International Cooperation.* Cambridge University Press.

[22] Galama, T., and J. Hosek. 2008. *US Competitiveness in Science and Technology.* Santa Monica, CA: Rand Corporation.

[23] The Forbes Magazine List: www.forbes.com/just-companies/#473da3f62bf0

[24] Shambaugh, D. April–June 2012. "Are China's Multinational Corporations Really Multinational?" In *East Asia Forum Quarterly* 4, no. 2, pp. 7–14.

[25] da Silva, D. L., N. Tian, and A. Marksteiner. 2021. "Trends in world military expenditure, 2020." *SIPRI.*

[26] QS World University Rankings—2012, available at https://topuniversities.com/university-rankings/world-university-rankings/2012

[27] www.forbes.com/sites/nickmorrison/2020/09/02/oxford-keeps-top-spot-but-china-is-the-real-winner-as-us-declines/?sh=6a81e8c742a7

[28] Luce, E. 2012. "Time to Start linking: America in the Age of Descent." Grove/Atlantic, Inc.

[29] Smith, K.E. 2013. "Can the European Union be a Pole in a Multipolar World?." *The International Spectator* 48, no. 2, pp. 114–126.

[30] Messner, D. 2007. *The European Union: Protagonist in a Multilateral World Order or Peripheral Power in the "Asia-Pacific" Century?*

[31] European Council on Foreign Relations. 2012. "Introduction." *European Foreign Policy Scorecard 2012,* 9. http://ecfr.eu/content/entry/european_foreign_policy_scorecard_2012

[32] La-Porte, M.T. 2015. *The Legitimacy and Effectiveness of Non-State Actors and the Public Diplomacy Concept.*

[33] Moravcsik, A. 2010. "Europe, the Second Superpower." *Current History* 109, no. 725, p. 91.

[34] Dingwerth, K., and P. Pattberg. 2006. "Global Governance as a Perspective on World Politics." *Global Governance: A Review of Multilateralism and International Organizations* 12, no. 2, pp. 185–203.

[35] Biermann, F., and P.H. Pattberg, eds. 2012. *Global Environmental Governance Reconsidered.* MIT Press.

[36] Karns, M.P., and K.A. Mingst. 2013. "International Organizations and Diplomacy." In *the Oxford Handbook of Modern Diplomacy.* Oxford, UK.

[37] Jang, J., J. McSparren, and Y. Rashchupkina. 2016. Global Governance: Present and Future.

[38] Falkner, R. 2011. "Global Governance: The Rise of Non-State Actors: A Background Report for the SOER 2010 Assessment of Global Megatrends." European Environment Agency.

[39] UNCTAD (United Nations Conference on Trade and Development). 2009. *World Investment Report 2009.* Retrieved February 18, 2010.

[40] Bieler, A., R. Higgott, and G. Underhill, eds. 2004. *Non-State Actors and Authority in the Global System.* Routledge.

[41] Jakobi, A.P. 2010. "Non-State Violence and Political Order: A View on Long Term Consequences of Non-State Security Governance."

[42] Strategic Trends 2016 is also electronically available at www.css.ethz.ch/publications/strategic-trends

[43] Treaty on the Non-Proliferation of Nuclear Weapons (NPT). https://un.org/disarmament/wmd/nuclear/npt/

[44] "North Korea Nuclear Tests: What Did They Achieve?" *BBC News,* September 03, 2017. http://bbc.com/news/world-asia-17823706

[45] Russia's Nuclear Weapons: Everything You Always Wanted To Know (But Were Afraid To Ask). Published on *The National Interest.* http://nationalinterest.org

[46] Russia: Putting the 'Nuclear Gun' Back on the Table. Retrieved from November 15, 2016, https://ft.com/content/03dfeb98-aa88-11e6-9cb3-bb8207902122

[47] Russian Lawmaker: We Would Use Nukes if US or NATO Enters Crimea. http://defenseone.com/threats/2017/05/russian-lawmaker-we-would-use-nukes-if-us-or-nato-enters-crimea/138230/

CHAPTER 5

Challenges to Security and Governance

The Hybrid Warfare

Since the turn of the century, we are witnessing the rise of a new type of conflict known as "hybrid warfare." NATO has used the concept of hybrid warfare as an umbrella term including various adverse circumstances and actions [1]. We may suggest that the hybrid warfare is a response to an emerging group of global threats that go beyond the traditional area of any single government agency [2]. Indeed, the complexity of international environment implies that conflicts and armed encounters cannot be won by military means alone. Therefore, the hybrid war may consist of different modes of fighting such as conventional capabilities, irregular tactics and formations, terrorist acts, indiscriminate violence and coercion, and criminal disorder [3]. The hybrid war is a war without rules and restrictions transcending the limits of the battlefield, the weapon, the military, and the state [4]. The hybrid warfare may involve the use of a very comprehensive and nuanced variety of military activities, resources, programs, and applications. In other words, in a hybrid fighting, the military force is only a small part and war operations include various paramilitary, military and civilian, direct and hidden actions that can be conducted by both state and nonstate actors [3]. In the hybrid war, the social and institutional softness, in conjunction with the military weakness, is targeted. The conflict in Ukraine in the past five years can be categorized as a good example of a hybrid war [1]. Russia's war in Ukraine capitalizes on multiple acts such as conducting covert small military operations, creating criminal disorder, hijacking social media, collecting intelligence, distributing malware, and supporting local militias to deal with the West as a much stronger rival [5]. Similarly, the conflict between Israel and the

Lebanese Hezbollah in 2006 is a typical example of a hybrid warfare as it included both state and nonstate actors, conventional military power, as well as political, social, diplomatic, and informational components and operations [6]. Due to its hybridization, there is no distinctive and politically well-defined line between war and peace [1, 7]. The hybrid wars are generally marked by their long durations as they could last for several decades. Furthermore, the hybrid wars require strong leadership, well-informed decision making, and comprehensive strategies that enable the application of all facets of state power to achieving a suitable resolution to the conflict [2].

The Rise of Asymmetrical Warfare

In a globalized, complex, and interdependent world, asymmetrical warfare is becoming increasingly an important type of rivalry. Asymmetrical warfare can be considered as any type of fighting that uses comparative advantages against an opponent's weaknesses [8]. In an asymmetrical warfare, "have-nots" undertake the warfare against "haves" by applying their specific advantages against the weaknesses of a much stronger adversary [9]. For that reason, asymmetrical warfare is a war that is not defensible with a conventional military force. In the past decades, the chances of full-fledged conventional conflicts among large nation-states have diminished. At the same time, the incidences of asymmetrical conflicts among nation-states or between nation-states and nonstate actors have increased. For instance, in the past 20 years, more American citizens have been killed in asymmetrical warfare than in conventional military battles [10]. What makes the asymmetrical warfare difficult is that it is carried out by the individuals or groups that are not directly connected to a state or nation. Furthermore, the targets of asymmetrical warfare are not limited to military facilities and may include a wide range of political, economic, and cultural interests. The asymmetrical attacks often seek to cause psychological and emotional damage [8]. The asymmetrical attackers may use various techniques and devices such as airplanes, cars, trucks, postal systems, computers, chemicals, viruses, and biological weapons. Because of rapid technological innovations, the asymmetrical attacks are becoming constantly more frequent and more damaging. Considering these various and complex features, winning the asymmetrical warfare is extremely difficult.

Cyberattack and Cyber-Espionage

Cyberattacks may include any intended actions to change, interrupt, or destroy computer systems and the associated information and programs [11]. Some cyberattacks may be categorized as cyber-espionage as they do not interrupt or destroy the computer networks; rather they aim at stealing information for intelligence purposes. Depending on the importance of targeted computer networks, the effects of cyberattacks could vary from interrupting a website to disruption or even destruction of critical information systems. The importance of cybersecurity is continuing to grow exponentially as cyberspace is expanding too many aspects of our lives. Indeed, the complexity of information systems is growing much faster than the technical capability to protect them [12]. The most expected targets of cyberattacks are critical networks that if interrupted would disrupt normal life and would inflict significant financial, technological, or human loss [13]. Cyberattacks may be used to interrupt financial and air traffic control systems, commit financial fraud, steal corporate information and intellectual property, and penetrate into state and military secret services. It is estimated that, in 2008, cyberattacks in the United States have resulted in a loss of intellectual property of more than $1 trillion [11]. Considering their significant implications, some types of cyberattacks may ignite political tensions and escalate to full-fledged international conflicts. Both state and nonstate adversaries who are able to acquire the required competence may perpetrate cyberattacks. The cyberattackers could include anybody who possesses the technical capabilities to exploit the computer systems' vulnerabilities [14]. Cyberattackers constitute diverse groups ranging from petty and organized criminals to state-backed institutions, fundamentalist religious groups, terrorists, and pressure groups. Indeed, some cyberattackers have been as young as 13 years old. For these reasons, it is very easy to launch cyberattacks, and it is extremely difficult to track, identify, and prosecute the perpetrators. Another problem with the cyberattack and cyber-espionage is that the terrorists do not need to travel to enemy's territory, rather they can launch their attacks via the Internet even when they are thousands of miles away. Unlike other types of warfare, it is not clear who should be held accountable for a cyberattack. Even when the cyberattack is attributed to a nation, it is very difficult to decide about a proportionate riposte or punishment. Consequently, cyberattack is the perfect asymmetrical warfare as it allows the weak to attack the strong with little weapons and with very little fear of vengeance [8]. In contrast to a cyberattack that disrupts computer networks, a cyber-espionage often does not affect the normal operation of computers, rather it aims at stealing valuable information from the adversaries' computers and servers. As such, cyber-espionage may produce a high return for a small amount of investment. Indeed, a few competent hackers may crawl into computer networks for extremely valuable business or military secrets [14].

The Global Terrorism

The global terrorism is a new phenomenon that may refer to terrorist operations carried out in multiple nations or locations. As the terminology suggests, the global terrorism is a by-product of globalization and the recent advances in telecommunication and transport. Globalization has distorted our commonly held concepts of space and time and has turned our planet into a global village such that every person is in constant and close touch with the rest of the world [15, 16, 17]. Unlike old terrorism, the global terrorism has capitalized on global forces to create the diffuse, decentralized, and nebulous organizational structures that can simultaneously perform violent operations around the world. In contrast to old terrorist groups that typically were defined in a geographical area, the global terrorism is not confined to a particular geographical location. Al-Qaeda and Islamic State of Iraq and Syria (ISIS) are prime examples of the global terrorist organizations that constitute of decentralized global networks of Islamic extremists united by a fundamentalist ideology [18]. Unlike the nationalist and leftist characters of the 1960s through 1980s, the new global terrorism is inspired by religious and spiritual visions [19]. During the Cold War, not a single terrorist group in the world could be categorized as religiously motivated, but by the mid-1990s, the religiously motivated terrorism constituted one-third of all terrorist groups ranging from Christians in the United States, Jewish extremists in the West Bank, the Buddhist in Asia, and various Muslim terrorist groups across the world [20].

Currently, the majority of religiously motivated terrorist groups are inspired by an extremist version of Islam and by what they see as a command of God [21]. Religion is central to their terrorist operations because it offers many advantages. Religions, in general, and the Islamic faith, in particular, can guide in-group morality and out-group hatred, minimize the fear of death by spreading the belief in an afterlife reward, and effectively recruit the youth [22]. Al-Qaeda, ISIS, and other Jihadist terrorist groups openly believe in pursuing a divine mission through violence. They call upon their followers to wage a sacred war against nonbelievers including the Westerners across the world, in order to establish a radical religious state, an Islamic caliphate governed by Sharia law. It is important to note that the Islamic terrorism does not exempt ordinary Muslims from their violence. Indeed, most of the terror attacks perpetrated by Al-Qaeda, Taliban, and ISIS have targeted Muslims in countries such as Iraq, Afghanistan, Turkey, Yemen, and Syria. As such, the Islamic terrorism is primarily a cultural and ideological war that targets the outside world including Muslims, non-Muslims, Westerners, and all those who do not share their strict worldview. In contrast to the old terrorism, the global terrorism does not necessarily intend to assassinate or remove political leaders, rather it targets ordinary citizens and uses psychological warfare as an effective strategy [23]. The subsequent nervousness in the targeted population leads to political pressure that may correspond to the terrorists' interests [24]. The global terrorism seeks to intensify the public's fear by conducting random attacks at soft targets instead of political or military figures. Therefore, globalization and the associated improvements in telecommunication have helped the global terrorism send and amplify its message of intimidation to the general public through the media coverage.

Some terrorist groups in developing countries blame globalization for their local problems and perceive the globalized economy as a continuation of imperialist practices aimed at exploiting and surrendering their countries or cultures. They believe that globalization as a corrupting western project is undermining their culture and their way of life. In that sense, the global terrorism may be described as a backlash against the globalization phenomenon itself. It seems that there is a direct relationship between globalization and the level of terrorist incidents. For instance, the number of terrorist attacks has increased significantly after the Cold War during the 1990s and 2000s [18]. As the different parts of the world are becoming interconnected and thus interdependent, we may expect further increases in the number of terrorist incidents.

The collapse of the World Trade Center buildings, the destruction of parts of the Pentagon, and the death of more than 3,000 civilians on 9/11 may be viewed as a turning point in the development of global terrorism. The world leaders recognized the destructive power of Jihadi fundamentalist groups and implemented some hefty security measures [24]. What makes the Jihadi terrorism particularly vicious is its reliance on suicide attackers who by sacrificing their lives choose the time and place of their attacks to maximize damage. The global terrorist groups have secret relations with some states and influential individuals who provide them with financial, logistical, and military support. Furthermore, some terrorist organizations are relying on criminal activities such as drug trafficking, counterfeiting, kidnapping, human trafficking, and extortion to raise money for their subsistence [25]. In general, globalization has helped funding and coordination of Islamist fundamentalist and terrorist groups around the world. For instance, Al-Qaeda and ISIS have financial and operational links with other Islamic groups around the world. Boko Haram is based in Nigeria, but coordinated operations from Mali, and received funding and training from a UK-based Al-Muntada Trust Fund [25].

In the past several years, the terrorist organizations such as Al-Qaeda and ISIS have aimed at spreading their ideologies through mosques, Islamic charities, community centers, and the Internet. The Internet websites, blogs, and social media overcome the geographic barriers and serve as forums to meet, recruit, and radicalize new members. Since the homegrown terrorists live and work in the Western countries, they are able to effectively infiltrate their local communities and carry out destructive terrorist operations [24]. The new waves of terrorism pose a serious threat to the liberal democratic values in the Western countries because they have to curb the citizen's freedoms to enhance the public security and thwart potential terror attacks. After the recent terror attacks in France, the United Kingdom, and Germany, many Western countries had to restrict the basic rights like the freedom of movement, freedom of speech, and individual privacy [26].

The collapse of the Soviet Union in 1991 resulted in a decrease in the conflict and friction between communist and capitalistic ideologies, but it resulted in the rise of fundamentalist ideologies in some Islamic countries. Similar to communism, the Islamic fundamentalism seeks to offer a social, cultural, economic, and political alternative to the liberal democracies. The Islamic fundamentalist groups promote their political agenda by taking advantage of the populations' frustrations in the Middle East, North Africa, and South Asia where people are suffering from strained economies, high youth unemployment, and oppressive leaderships [27]. In the recent years, the Islamic fundamentalist groups have benefited from the Western military interventions in the Islamic countries, notably Afghanistan, Iraq, Libya, Pakistan, and Syria to blame the Western liberal democracies for the destabilization of their home countries. It is widely believed that abject poverty and lack of education are the main factors underlying the rise of religious fundamentalism [28]. Therefore, the population growth and stagnant economies in many Islamic countries may aggravate the religious fundamentalism.

The Fragile and Failing States

The state strength is the extent to which a state is capable of providing basic socioeconomic and political services, especially physical security, legitimate institutions, economic management, and social welfare [29].

Strong states effectively control their territories and provide the full range of socioeconomic and political services to their citizens. They protect their land from any kind of violence, guarantee political freedom and civil liberties, and make environments favorable to economic growth [30]. Not all states are strong enough. For instance, some states such as Afghanistan are struggling to keep a control on the use of military force. Others may lack the legitimate power to govern institutions and protect the basic rights and freedoms. Some others like Zimbabwe are virtually incapable of managing economic and fiscal matters of their nations. The weak states may become "failing states" if the conditions deteriorate and if they fall short of delivering goods in the four areas of physical security, legitimate political institutions, economic management, and social welfare. Some weak states may fail when they lose foreign support [31]. The main characteristic of the failed states is the loss of control of their territory or the monopoly on the legitimate use of military power. The loss of legitimate authority and the inability to provide public services are other characteristics of the failed states. Very often, the institutions of the failed states are impaired, their infrastructure is damaged, and their education and health care become unavailable to the public [32].

Foreign Policy and The Brookings Institution have recently developed indexes to measure the state weakness. The *Foreign Policy Index* relies on 12 dimensions to measure the fragility of world states, that is, demographic pressures, refugees and internally displaced persons, group grievance, human flight, uneven development, poverty and economic decline, legitimacy of the state, public services, human rights, security apparatus, factionalized elites, and external intervention. In 2016, 179 states were included in the Fragile States Index, of which 22 were classified as "Alert" and 16 were classified as "High Alert" or "Very High Alert." Among "High Alert" or "Very High Alert" states, we can find Somalia, South Sudan, Central African Republic, Sudan, Yemen, Syria, Chad, Congo, Afghanistan, Haiti, Iraq, Guinea, Nigeria, Pakistan, Burundi, and Zimbabwe (see Table 5.1). Many of these fragile or failed states are war-torn countries such as Somalia, Yemen, Syria, Afghanistan, and Iraq, which have experienced foreign invasion or civil war. State failure is becoming the source of a wide range of problems including regional instability, weapons proliferation, narcotics trafficking, and terrorism [32]. Some of the failed states such as Iraq, Afghanistan, Yemen, Syria, Libya, Somalia, and Sudan have become safe havens for terrorist groups that can use large territories within these countries to generate revenue, recruit supporters, construct training complexes, and store weapons and ammunitions. The failed states pose a significant security threat not only to their neighbors but also to the developed Western countries that are becoming increasingly affected by the influx of migrants and terrorist attacks on their land. The state failure or fragility has some pernicious effects for the fight against corruption, the promotion of human rights, good governance, the rule of law, religious

Table 5.1 The top 30 fragile states in 2017 according to Foreign Policy magazine (http://foreignpolicy.com)

1	South Sudan	11	Haiti	21	Cote d'Ivoire
2	Somalia	12	Guinea	22	Kenya
3	The Central African Republic	13	Nigeria	23	Libya
4	Yemen	14	Zimbabwe	24	Uganda
5	Sudan	15	Ethiopia	25	Myanmar
6	Syria	16	Guinea-Bissau	26	Cameroon
7	The Democratic Republic of the Congo	17	Burundi	27	Liberia
8	Chad	18	Pakistan	28	Mauritania
9	Afghanistan	19	Eritrea	29	The Republic of the Congo
10	Iraq	20	Niger	30	North Korea

tolerance, environmental protection, child labor, gender equality, and more importantly the socioeconomic development [33]. Therefore, the failed states contribute to a long list of threats to the world security: poverty, disease, famine, migration influx, global terrorism, organized crime, weapons proliferation, religious intolerance, and the outbreak of violence, ethnic cleansing, and genocide [32].

Transnational Organized Crime

Transnational organized crime is a huge and lucrative business that has been growing in the past two decades. It is very difficult to measure the size of transnational organized crime, but revenues generated from major criminal activities are estimated to vary between $1.6 and $2.2 trillion per year, which is equivalent to around 7 percent of the world's exports of merchandise [34]. Transnational organized crime has hugely benefited from globalization and advances in telecommunication, transport, and international trade in the past three decades. Furthermore, the collapse of the Soviet Union and the subsequent transition from the centrally planned to the market-based economy in the Eastern Europe provided huge opportunities for transnational organized criminal organizations [35]. Transnational organized crime is a dynamic industry motivated by exorbitant levels of illicit profit that adapts to all markets and societies.

It constantly reinvents itself and overcomes the legal, linguistic, and geographical boundaries.

The global drug trafficking is the most lucrative business for transnational organized criminals with an estimated annual value of $426 to $652 billion in 2014 [34]. Cannabis, cocaine, opiates, and amphetamine-type stimulants are responsible for the largest shares of drug trafficking. While amphetamine-type stimulants and cannabis are produced in various countries, cocaine and heroin are produced mainly in South America and Afghanistan [34]. Cocaine is transported from Colombia to Mexico or Central America by sea and then onward by land to the United States and Canada. The size of cocaine market in the United States was estimated around $38 billion in 2008. The European cocaine market is growing in the recent years and was estimated at $34 billion in 2008 [36]. The global market value of heroin is estimated about $55 billion annually. Most of the world's heroin is produced in Afghanistan and is transported to customers in the Russian Federation and Western Europe.

Human trafficking is becoming one of the most lucrative criminal activities in the recent years. Human trafficking refers to all activities involving involuntary or compelled control or exploitation of human beings. It can include involuntary servitude, sexual exploitation, slavery, debt bondage, and forced labor. The victims of human trafficking are often physically, sexually, and emotionally abused [37]. According to the International Labor Organization, an estimated 21 million men, women, and children around the world are victims of human trafficking generating about $150.2 billion in profits annually [34]. Almost half of the human trafficking takes place in the Asia-Pacific region with an estimated 12 million victims. While human trafficking could happen within one single country, it is mainly a cross-national business. According to a recent study by the United Nations Office on Drugs and Crime, the victims of human trafficking can be found in 137 countries. Almost two-thirds of the human trafficking victims are women and 79 percent of them are exposed to sexual exploitation [36]. Very often, the traffickers and victims are of the same nationality. In order to target their victims, the traffickers use employment agencies in the Eastern Europe and Asia, and social and family connections in Africa. Alongside human trafficking, organ trafficking is considered a very lucrative business for criminal organizations, generating between $840 million and $1.7 billion annually [34]. The most trafficked organs include kidney, liver, heart, lung, and pancreas and are used in more than 12,000 illegal or legal transplants. The donors often may participate willingly or under coercion to sell their organs. For instance, organ traffickers may force migrants and refugees to sell kidneys to pay for passage to Europe [34].

Human smuggling is another form of organized crime that consists of assisting people to enter a country illegally. Refugees in war-torn countries and workers in poor countries of Asia, Africa, and South America may pay huge amounts of money and risk their lives to access opportunities in the more prosperous countries. For that reason, they rely on organized criminals to assist them to reach their destinations clandestinely. Migrants' relatives in the country of origin or in the destination often finance the payment to smugglers. There are two main flows of human smuggling: from Latin America to North America and from Africa to Europe. An estimated three million Latin Americans are smuggled illegally across the southern border of the United States every year, generating almost $7 billion annually [36]. According to a joint report by Europol and INTERPOL, 90 percent of the more than one million migrants entering the EU in 2015 used smuggling networks' services. Based on the same report, migrant smugglers made an estimated $5 to $6 billion by smuggling Africans to Europe in 2015 [38].

The trafficking of small arms and light weapons had an estimated market value of $1.7 to $3.5 billion in 2014, which represents 10 to 20 percent of the legal arms trade [34]. The arms trafficking business is growing due to instability in many parts of Africa, South America, and in war-torn countries such as Iraq, Afghanistan, Syria, Libya, and Pakistan.

The trade in counterfeit products and pirated goods is another lucrative crime with an estimated market value of $923 to $1.13 trillion annually [34]. The counterfeit industry includes a wide range of products from books and watches to clothes, food, and pharmaceuticals. Almost 60 to 75 percent of the counterfeit and pirated goods are originated in China. Some counterfeit products such as pharmaceutical drugs and food involve serious health hazards. Due to its intangible nature, the theft of intellectual and cultural properties is very attractive to criminal organizations. The illicit trade of intellectual and cultural properties is estimated at $1.2

to $1.6 billion [34]. Theft of intellectual property includes software, movies, music, video games, trusted brand names, proprietary designs of high-tech devices, and manufacturing processes [37].

Trafficking in natural resources may involve the smuggling of raw materials including timber, wildlife, iron, oil, diamonds, and rare or precious metals. Illegal logging is the most profitable natural resource crime. The value of illegal logging varies between $52 and $157 billion per year. Almost 10 to 30 percent of the world's timber is produced illegally. Southeast Asia, Central Africa, and South America have the highest level of illegal logging, and China is the primary destination for the majority of illegally sourced timber [34]. According to a study by the United Nations Environment Program and INTERPOL, the illegal extraction and trade of minerals are estimated between $12 and $48 billion annually [34]. Diamond, gold, and silver are the most illegally mined materials in Africa and South America. Furthermore, the illegal extraction of crude oil was estimated to be worth between $5.2 and $11.9 billion in 2015. The illegal oil extraction is quite rampant in countries such as Nigeria, Colombia, Indonesia, Mexico, Syria, Russia, and Iraq [34]. The illegal trade in wildlife is estimated between $5 and $23 billion [34]. Elephants, rhinos, pangolins, different types of birds, fish, mammals, and plants are the targets of organized criminals across the world. Similarly, illegal fishing is estimated to generate $15.5 to $36.4 billion annually [34].

Transnational organized crime includes almost all criminal activities motivated by profit. The concentration of illegal wealth and power in the hands of criminal groups is a major challenge to governance at the national and international levels. Moreover, the criminal activities have pernicious implications for public safety, public health, democratic institutions, and economic stability across the globe. Transnational criminal organizations weaken state authority either directly through confrontation or indirectly through corruption. They undermine government monopoly of the use of violence [39]. By accumulating money and power, transnational criminal organizations can threaten democratic institutions and the rule of law, change the elections outcomes, and corrupt institutions. Evidently, many of criminal activities violate human rights, harm the environment, and involve conflicts and loss of life. In some countries with weak institutions, transnational criminal organizations may penetrate the government and cause state authorities facilitate their criminal activities [39]. Considering the substantial accumulated power and wealth of transnational criminal organizations and the global scope of their operations, national responses alone are not suitable to cope with them. Fighting the transnational criminal organizations often requires multilateral and global solutions.

The Maritime Piracy

Maritime piracy is a transnational organized crime because a ship is considered the sovereign territory of the nation whose flag is borne and because it requires significant amounts of planning and expertise [40]. Maritime piracy may involve two offenses: the first is stealing a maritime vessel or its cargo; the second involves kidnapping the vessel and crew until a ransom is paid [41]. Almost 90 percent of the world trade is done via sea routes. Therefore, it is not surprising that, in a globalized economy, maritime piracy is becoming a highly lucrative and a common form of organized crime. In the recent years, piracy has increased due to the growth in the volume of merchandise moving by sea and the desire of transporters to pass through crowded maritime routes [32]. The slack coastal security due to political instability in some war-torn countries, terrorism, and the rise of armed groups are other contributors to the growth of piracy [42]. Facing the rise of piracy, more than 20 countries have formed naval task forces to protect their vessels and enhance the maritime security [43]. The Gulf of Aden near Somalia, the Suez Canal, the Cape of Good Hope, the Persian Gulf, and the Indian Ocean represent some of the most important maritime routes. For instance, almost 33,000 commercial ships travel the Gulf of Aden each year and around 7 percent of the world's maritime commerce passes through the Suez Canal [32]. The terrorist groups may be connected to maritime piracy. It has been reported that al-Shabaab terrorist group is relying on the Somalian pirates to smuggle weapons and jihadist operatives into Somalia [32]. The terrorist networks may use the financial earnings of piracy to fund their activities around the world. In addition to the threat to the maritime security and commercial transit, piracy may have disastrous implications for the environment due to the discharge of oil and other toxic chemicals into the seawater. Despite enhanced security measures, the piracy attacks continue to grow in the horn of Africa and in the Gulf of Aden mainly due to the fragility of Somalian state and the ensuing humanitarian crises. Somalia is engulfed in a devastating combination of conflict, immense displacement, drought, high food prices, and hyperinflation [32]. Furthermore, according to the United Nations Food and Agricultural Organization, foreign ships have taken advantage of the political chaos in Somalia to illegally exploit more than $450 million of fish stocks off the coast of Somalia, stealing valuable food sources from the Somalian people. Along with illegal fishing, European ships have been dumping toxic and nuclear waste, such as radioactive uranium, hospital waste, and industrial chemicals in the waters around Somalia [42]. Under these circumstances, maritime piracy can be viewed as an attractive economic activity to the Somalian criminals who may collect up to $18 to 30 million a year in ransom. In addition to the Gulf of Aden and the greater Indian Ocean, maritime piracy attacks are seen in Southeast Asia and mainly in the Straits of Malacca, through which transit more than 90,000 ships per year, accounting for 40 percent of the world's trade [42]. Likewise, the waters of Nigeria, Tanzania, Bangladesh, and India have seen many maritime piracy predations in the recent years [32]. The direct cost of maritime piracy is estimated between $1 and 16 billion per year, but the indirect cost and the long-term effects could be even much higher.

References

[1] Bachmann, S.D., and H. Gunneriusson. 2015. "Hybrid Wars: The 21st—Century's New treats to Global Peace and Security." *Scientia Militaria: South African Journal of Military Studies* 43, no. 1, pp. 77–98.

[2] Chuka, N., and J.F. Born. 2014. *Hybrid Warfare: Implications for CAF Force Development* (No. DRDC-RDDC-2014-R43). Defence Research and Development Canada CORA Ottawa, Ontario Canada.

[3] Hoffman, F.G. 2007. *Conflict in the 21st Century: The Rise of Hybrid Wars*, 51. Arlington: Potomac Institute for Policy Studies.

[4] Metz, S. 2014. "Strategic Horizons: In Ukraine, Russia Reveals Its Mastery of Unrestricted Warfare." *World Politics Review.*

[5] Pomerantsev, P., and M. Weiss. 2014. *The Menace of Unreality: How the Kremlin Weaponizes Information, Culture, and Money.* New York, NY: Institute of Modern Russia.

[6] Glenn, R.W. 2009. "Thoughts on 'Hybrid' Conflict." In *Small Wars Journal* 13. smallwarsjournal.com/mag/docs-temp/188-glenn.pdf (accessed January 02, 2017).

[7] Munkler, H. 2015. "Hybrid Wars. The Dissolution of the Binary Order of War and Peace, and Its Consequences." *Ethics and Armed Forces* 2, pp. 20–23.

[8] Hartman, W.J. 2002. *Globalization and Asymmetrical Warfare* (No. AU/ACSC/053/2001-04). Air Command and Staff Coll Maxwell AFB AL.

[9] Thornton, R. 2007. "Asymmetric Warfare: Threat and Response in the 21st Century." *Polity.*

[10] Khalilzad, Z., T. LaTourrette, D.E. Mosher, L.M. Davis, D.R. Howell, and B. Raymond. 1999. *Strategic Appraisal: The Changing Role of Information in Warfare.* Rand Corporation.

[11] National Research Council. 2009. *Technology, Policy, Law, and Ethics Regarding US Acquisition and Use of Cyberattack Capabilities.* National Academies Press.

[12] Billo, C., and W. Chang. 2004. *Cyber Warfare: An Analysis of the Means and Motivations of Selected Nation States.* Dartmouth College, Institute for Security Technology Studies.

[13] Bruce, R., S. Dynes, H. Brechbuhl, B. Brown, E. Goetz, P. Verhoest, E. Luiijf, and S. Helmus. 2005. "International Policy Framework for Protecting Critical Information Infrastructure: A Discussion Paper Outlining Key Policy Issues." *TNO Report.* Tuck School of Business at Dartmouth.

[14] Bajaj, K. 2010. "The Cybersecurity Agenda: Mobilizing for International Action." *EastWest Institute Report,* pp. 81–103.

[15] Harvey, D. 1989. *The Condition of Postmodernity.* Oxford: Basil Blackwell.

[16] Giddens, A. 1990. *The Consequence of Modernity.* Cambridge: Polity Press.

[17] Scholte, J.A. 1997. "The Globalisation of World Politics." In *The Globalisation of World Politics: An Introduction,* eds. S. Smith and J. Baylis, pp. 211–244. Oxford: Oxford University Press.

[18] Harvey, D. 2003. *The New Imperialism.* USA: Oxford University Press.

[19] Cronin, A.K. 2006. "How al-Qaida Ends: The Decline and Demise of Terrorist Groups." *International Security* 31, no. 1, pp. 7–48.

[20] Neumann, P.R., and M.L.R. Smith. 2007. *The Strategy of Terrorism: How It Works, and Why It Fails.* Routledge.

[21] Hoffman, B. 2006. *Inside Terrorism, Revised and Expanded Edition.* New York, NY: Columbia University Press.

[22] Thomson, J.A. 2003. "Killer Apes on American Airlines, or How Religion was the Main Hijacker on September 11." In *Violence or Dialogue: Psychoanalytic Insights on Terror and Terrorism,* eds. S. Varvin and V.D. Volkan. London: International Psychoanalytical Association.

[23] Coker, C. 2014. *Globalisation and Insecurity in the Twenty-first Century: NATO and the Management of Risk.* Routledge.

[24] Ganor, B. 2009. "Trends in Modern International Terrorism." In *To Protect and To Serve,* pp. 11–42. New York, NY: Springer.

[25] Vidino, L. 2006. *Al Qaeda in Europe: The New Battleground of International Jihad.* Prometheus Books.

[26] Reich, W, ed. 1998. *Origins of Terrorism: Psychologies, Ideologies, Geologies, States of Mind.* Woodrow Wilson Center Press.

[27] Biscop, S. 2016. *The European Security Strategy: A Global Agenda for Positive Power.* Routledge.

[28] Saeed, F., M. Rahid, H.Z. Rehman, S. Mobin, and S. Ahmed. 2012. "Tackling Terrorism in Pakistan." *International Journal of Peace and Development Studies* 3, no. 1, pp. 1–5.

[29] Ware, A., and V.A. Ware. 2014. "Development in Fragile States and Situations: Theory and Critique." In *Development in Difficult Sociopolitical Contexts,* pp. 24–47. UK: Palgrave Macmillan.

[30] Rotberg, R.I. 2003. "Failed States, Collapsed States, Weak States: Causes and Indicators." In *State Failure and State Weakness in a Time of Terror,* ed. R.I. Rotberg. Washington, DC: Brookings Institution Press.

[31] Wise, W.M. 2004. "American Perspectives on the Threat Posted by Weak and Failing the Asian States." Paper Presented at the US-China Conference on Areas of Instability and Emerging treats, Beijing, February 23–24.

[32] Schreier, F. 2015. *On Cyber Warfare.* Geneva, Switzerland: Geneva Centre for the Democratic Control of Armed Forces.

[33] Doornbos, M., S. Roque, and S. Woodward. February 08, 2006. "Failing States or Failed States? Role of Development Models: Collected works." *FRIDE.* A European Think Tank for Global Action.; Crocker, C.A. September/October 2003. "Engaging Failed States." *Foreign Affairs* 82, no. 5.

[34] May, C. 2017. "Transnational Crime and the Developing World." Global Financial Integrity. http://creativecommons.org

[35] Paoli, L, ed. 2014. *The Oxford Handbook of Organized Crime.* Oxford Handbooks.

[36] UNODC (UN Office on Drugs and Crime). June 17, 2010. *The Globalization of Crime: A Transnational Organized Crime Threat Assessment.* ISBN: 978-92-1-130295-0, available at http://refworld.org/docid/4cad7f892.html (accessed July 15, 2017).

[37] Reichel, P, and J. Albanese, eds. 2013. *Handbook of Transnational Crime and Justice.* Sage Publications.

[38] Smugglers made at least $5 billion last year in Europe Migrant (May 17, 2016) Crisis. https://nytimes.com/2016/05/18/world/europe/migrants-ref-ugees-smugglers.html?mcubz=1&_r=0

[39] Picarelli, J., and P. Williams. 2000. "Organized Crime and Information Technologies." In The *Information Age Anthology, Part II: National Security Implications of the Information Age,* eds. D. Papp and D.S. Alberts. Washington, DC: NDU Press.

[40] Gaibulloev, K., and T. Sandler. 2016. "Decentralization, Institutions, and Maritime Piracy." *Public Choice* 169, nos. 3–4, pp. 357–374.

[41] Marchione, E., and S.D. Johnson. 2013. "Spatial, Temporal and Spatiotemporal Patterns of Maritime Piracy." *Journal of Research in Crime and Delinquency* 50, no. 4, pp. 504–524.

[42] Chalk, P. Summer 2009. "Sunken Treasures, The Economic Impetus Behind Modern Piracy." *Rand Review.*

[43] US Naval Forces Central Command. "Combined Task Force 150." http://cusnc.navy.mil/command/ctf150.html; US Navy. "Focus on Combined Task Force 151." http://navy.mil/local/CTF-151

CHAPTER 6

The Environmental Degradation

The Many Faces of Environmental Degradation

Environmental degradation is a broad concept that may refer to any undesirable and noxious changes made to the environment by human beings or natural causes. According to the United Nations International Strategy for Disaster Reduction, environmental degradation is "the reduction of the capacity of the environment to meet social and ecological objectives and needs" [1]. While the environmental degradation may be produced by natural causes, human beings and their economic activities, particularly after the Industrial Revolution, are known as the main culprits. The environmental degradation includes a wide range of phenomena such as climate change and global warming, gas emissions, air and water pollution, overpopulation and the subsequent resources overexploitation, deforestation, drought, solid waste pollution, and loss of biodiversity. The environmental degradation directly threats human life and indirectly implies several socioeconomic consequences such as poverty, famine, war and armed conflicts, migration, and instability. The harmful consequences of environmental degradation are substantial particularly in developing countries where the risk of environmentally caused diseases is 15 times higher than that in developed countries.

Greenhouse Gas Emissions

In the past 100 years, human beings have burned huge amounts of fossil fuels and have released large quantities of greenhouse gases into the atmosphere. The greenhouse emissions are those gases that trap heat in the atmosphere and thus cause global warming. The gas emissions include a variety of chemicals such as carbon dioxide, methane, nitrous oxide, and fluorinated gases. According to the United States Environment Protection Agency, the use of fossil fuel is the chief source of carbon dioxide, but deforestation, agricultural activities, and waste management all contribute to greenhouse gas emissions as well. The economic sectors or activities that lead to the generation of greenhouse emissions include electricity and heat production (25 percent), industry (21 percent), agriculture and forestry (24 percent), transportation (14 percent), and buildings construction (6 percent) [2]. Global carbon emissions from fossil fuels have extensively increased in the past 100 years, but the pace of surge has accelerated particularly since the 1970s. In the past three decades, the quantity of greenhouse emissions has increased constantly as other developing countries such as China and India have joined the club of industrialized countries. For instance, the global greenhouse emissions from human activities in 2010 reached 46 billion metric tons representing a 35 percent increase from 1990 [3]. For the same period, carbon dioxide that accounts for three-fourths of total global emissions increased by 42 percent. Overall, the emissions have increased by over 16 times between 1900 and 2008 and by about 1.5 times between 1990 and 2008. The energy production and consumption accounted for 71 percent of the total emissions in 2010. According to OECD's reports, global greenhouse gas emissions are expected to increase by about 37 percent between now and 2030 and by 52 percent between now and 2050 [4]. The same reports suggest that in developing countries, the emissions growth will be significantly higher than that in rich and developed countries. While developed countries will reduce their overall greenhouse gas emission, they will continue to have the highest emissions per capita [5]. The greenhouse emissions are growing much faster in Asia and Africa, but the main geographic sources of greenhouse gas emissions are concentrated in the United States, Asia, and Europe that accounted for 82 percent of total global emissions in 2011 [3]. According to the United States Environment Protection Agency, the top carbon dioxide emitters in 2008 were China, the United States, the EU, India, the Russian Federation, Japan, and Canada (see Figures 6.1 and 6.2).

Air Pollution

Air pollution is one of the most flagrant features of the environmental degradation in many developing countries. Air pollution is a major

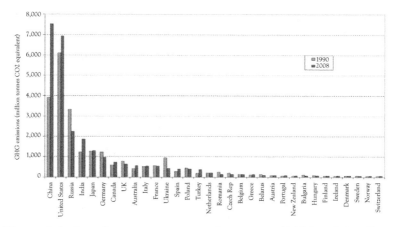

Figure 6.1 Greenhouse gas emissions by country (1990 and 2008)

Source: United Nations Framework Convention on Climate Change.

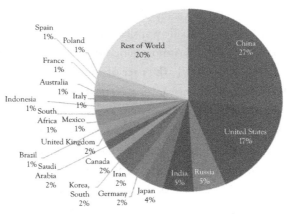

Figure 6.2 Carbon dioxide emissions by country (2011)

Source: United Nations Framework Convention on Climate Change.

environmental risk causing multiple health problems including respiratory infections, heart disease, and lung cancer. According to the World Health Organization (WHO), around 18,000 deaths per day or 6.5 million deaths per year are attributed to the air pollution making it the world's fourth-largest threat to human health [6]. More than 8 out of 10 people live in the urban areas where the air pollutants exceed the WHO's Air Quality Guidelines. Energy production and transport are recognized as the main sources of air pollution [1]. For every gallon of gasoline burned in a vehicle, 25 pounds of carbon dioxide and many other pollutants like carbon monoxides, sulfur dioxide, and nitrogen dioxide are produced [7]. As the number of cars in emerging countries such as China and India are increasing quickly, the air pollution in the urban areas is worsening at an accelerated pace.

Global Warming

Associated with the high levels of greenhouse gas emission is the climate change or global warming. Despite the skeptics' claims, it is scientifically accepted that climate change is a human-made phenomenon. The acceleration of climate warming observed throughout the 20th century is exceptional. Maximum temperatures, numbers of hot days, and the heat index have increased during the second half of the 20th century nearly in all continents [8]. In the past 100 years, the average temperature has climbed about 0.7°C (1.3°F) across the world. The 1980s, the 1990s, and the 2000s have been sequentially warmer at the earth's surface. According to the National Oceanic and Atmospheric Administration, the year 2014 was the hottest since 1880 [9]. The pace of climate warming is accelerating, but the Arctic regions are warming even faster than other parts of the planet [9]. The melting ice has led to sea levels rising at about two millimeters per year [9]. These patterns of global warming will continue in the next few decades, even if all greenhouse gas emissions were terminated now. The average temperature of the earth's surface is expected to increase between 1.4°C and 5.8°C by 2100 [8, 10]. The rising temperatures cause many changes in physical and biological systems across the world: the shrinkage of glaciers, changes in rainfall frequency, shifts in the growing season, early flowering of trees and emergence of insects, and shifts in the distribution ranges of plants and animals in response to changes in climatic conditions [8]. Further increase in the climate temperature could drastically disturb the balance of the world's ecosystems and cause additional irreparable and unpredictable transformations [11]. Some expected climate-induced events include heat waves, flash floods, tropical storms, infectious diseases, droughts, scarcity of renewable resources, sea-level rise, and intensification of natural disasters [12]. Furthermore, the global warming is likely to adversely affect water and fertile soil and thus reduce the agricultural output.

Water Pollution

Water quality can be adversely affected by both human activities and natural factors. Nutrients, sediments, rising temperatures, heavy metals, nonmetallic toxins, pesticides, and biological organisms are among the most notable polluting causes of water resources [13]. Every day, two million tons of dirt and residential, industrial, and agricultural waste materials are released into the world's water resources, lakes, and rivers [14]. It is estimated that around 70 percent of industrial sewage in developing countries is discharged directly into natural waters [15]. The unsafe water supply results in four billion cases of diarrhea each year and causes 2.2 million deaths across the world. A combination of inadequate sewerage and open defecation that are widespread in sub-Saharan Africa and India poses serious threats to water safety [16]. According to the WHO, almost 10 percent of the world's population or 768 million people do not have access to an improved source of water and one-third or 2.5 billion do not have secured access to adequate sanitation [17].

The problem of water pollution is not limited to developing countries. For instance, significant levels of pollution were found in the Japanese water supplies [3]. Due to the high levels of pollution, a significant portion of the world's water resources is not suitable for activities such as fishing and swimming. As the water reserves are becoming increasingly polluted and unusable, the groundwater resources are quickly dwindling due to overexploitation particularly in developing countries. At the same time, global water demand is estimated to surge by 55 percent by 2050 because of increasing demands from manufacturing, agriculture, and domestic use [18]. It is estimated that by 2030, more than 5 billion people or 67 percent of the world population will be deprived of a connection to public sewerage [19].

Land Degradation

Land degradation takes different forms including deforestation, desertification, salinization, erosion, nutrient depletion, carbon loss, and loss of water [20]. Both human-related activities and natural factors may ruin the land, but only humans can cause the accelerated land degradation. Clearance of vegetative cover, soil erosion by wind or water, high-intensity rainfall, invasive species, chemical or bacterial pollution, drought, agricultural practices, urban expansion, and industrial activities are some typical causes of land degradation. For instance, by converting lands and forests into fertile farms for producing certain crops and livestock, farmers change the ecosystems, destroy wildlife, and erase vegetation. Furthermore, the accumulation of toxic substances such as bad minerals, chemical fertilizers, and pesticides could destroy the soil's biological and chemical activities and deteriorate the quality of the soil. Across the world, over 20 percent of cultivated areas, 30 percent of forests, and 10 percent of grasslands have been hurt by land degradation, affecting about 1.5 billion people. Land degradation has touched half of agricultural lands over the last 50 years [21]. It is estimated that 75 percent of the drylands in Latin America and the Caribbean are currently under desertification or other forms of land degradation.

Soil Pollution

Similar to air and water pollution, soil pollution is a major environmental hazard and is defined as the introduction of substances, which harm the quality of the soil. Soil pollutants are various; they range from natural minerals to organic or inorganic chemicals and microorganisms. Likewise, the sources of pollution are almost countless: solid waste, E-waste, nitrogen, heavy metals, radioactive materials, acid or alkali materials, explosives, military weapons, herbicides, pesticides, hydrocarbons, perchlorate, medical waste, nonrecyclable waste, nanoparticles, and so on [22].

Solid waste could contain anything including plastics, cloth, glass, metal and organic matter, sewage, sewage sludge, building debris, and even electronic waste. Plastic bags are mainly nonbiodegradable materials that contribute to soil pollution across the world and pose significant environmental hazards [23]. Industrial operations contribute to soil pollution by creating fly ash, chemical residues, and metallic and nuclear wastes that gradually or suddenly penetrate the soil. Agriculture uses huge amounts of chemicals such as fertilizers and pesticides that constantly pollute the soil. Pesticides are toxic materials that not only harm the soil but also directly hurt humans, animals, and plants [22].

E-Waste

E-waste consists of discarded computers, cell phones, radios, televisions, refrigerators, washing machines, microwaves, and home appliances, which contain plastics, glass, and precious metals. E-waste is a rapidly growing cause of environmental degradation. According to a United Nations University report, the amount of global E-waste reached 41.8 million tons in 2014 [24]. The United States and other developed countries that consume most of the world's electronic products generate most of the world's E-waste. However, the majority of the E-waste is shipped to developing countries. Since the United States has not ratified the Basel Convention, it ships almost 80 percent of its E-waste to developing parts of the world mainly to China, India, Pakistan, and Africa where they dispose of the E-waste using very primitive methods [25]. The trade of E-waste between rich and poor countries is beneficial for both parties: while the rich get rid of the waste, the poor recycle and resell the usable materials. The total value of the global E-waste was estimated around $52 billion in 2014 consisting of 16,500 kilotons of iron, 1,900 kilotons of copper, and 300 tons of gold, and significant amounts of silver, aluminum, palladium, and other useable materials.

In developing countries, vast amounts of E-waste materials are burned or dumped in the agricultural fields, irrigation canals, and along waterways [26]. Burning E-waste results in solid and gaseous toxic chemicals, posing serious threats to the environment (Figure 6.3). The toxic materials may trickle into the ground and contaminate the soil and water, thus affecting the food chain including agricultural crops, fish, and livestock. Among the generated toxic materials, lead, copper, and cadmium are the three heavy metals that persist in the environment for a long time and are likely to be found in plants or in paddy fields [27]. The toxic materials can also go into the atmosphere when primitive E-waste salvaging methods are used.

The adverse effects of E-waste on the natural environment are expected to sharply grow for multiple reasons. As countries get richer, the per capita use of cell phone, computer, and electronics also grows [26]. Over the next few years, the developing countries will make up the bulk of the electronic sales as they draw near to the developed countries [28]. Unlike

Figure 6.3 Most of the world's E-waste is exported to Africa, India, and China

other products, the electronics have shorter life cycles and higher rates of obsolescence that make them rapidly disposable [26]. The tech companies are not only constantly innovating and replacing the old products but also are using some planned obsolescence manufacturing techniques to entice consumers to purchase the latest products and dispose of the old ones. The combination of these factors pushes consumers to replace their electronics unnecessarily, thus generating more E-waste.

Bioaccumulation and Biomagnification

Toxic substances such as arsenic, cadmium, mercury, lead, and selenium that are discharged into freshwater ecosystems easily find their way into the bodies of living organisms such as plankton, benthic invertebrates, plants, birds, fish, and mammals through bioaccumulation [29]. Bioaccumulation is a crucial process allowing animals and plants to absorb and store certain substances that are vital for their survival, including vitamins, trace elements, fats, and amino acids. Because of environmental pollution, many toxic materials could progressively build up to levels that could be harmful to living creatures. A particular case of bioaccumulation is biomagnification (amplification) involving a constant increase of contamination in food webs from prey to predator [30]. Biomagnification can be considered as a secondary poisoning in an ecological system, so the highest levels of contamination are found in animals at the top of the food chain including human beings [31]. The process of bioaccumulation is supported by natural forces because many pollutants have a much higher solubility in organism lipid (fat) than in the ambient water. Many industrial and domestic activities produce wastes with low levels of chemicals that may accumulate in biota over time. Bioaccumulation is the sum of two processes: bioconcentration and biomagnification. Bioconcentration is the direct uptake of a substance by a living organism from the medium (e.g., water) via skin, gills, or lungs, whereas biomagnification results from dietary uptakes. Since contaminants are more soluble in fat than in water, aquatic organisms including phytoplankton and fish that actively filter large amounts of water through their gills are subject to higher amounts of bioaccumulated pollutants. Higher animals such as zooplankton, predatory fish species, lake trout, striped bass, birds, reptiles, and mammals including bear, seal, and ultimately humans biologically magnify the accumulated pollution. The pollutants may cause serious damage to the immune and reproductive systems of living organisms including humans. Some pollutants may be transferred to the offspring instigating various dysfunctions as abnormal sexual development, behavioral dysfunctions, and cancer. Organochlorine pesticides such as DDT (dichlorodiphenyltrichloroethane), chlordane, toxaphene, dioxins, brominated flame retardants, metal compounds, methyl mercury, and tributyltin are among the highly bioaccumulating contaminants [32].

Biosphere Deterioration

Human beings are part of the biosphere. As such, human activities affect and are affected by the biosphere. All socioeconomic activities involve significant changes in the biosphere such as habitat destruction, habitat fragmentation, corridor restrictions, aquatic habitat damage, ecological disequilibrium, reduction of biodiversity, extinction of plant and animal species, deforestation, and creation of invasive species [32]. For instance, activities such as road and home construction involve the consumption of land and the consequent loss of natural habitats of flora and fauna [33]. Habitat fragmentation is often associated with urban or industrial projects that cut through an ecosystem and break it down physically or ecologically. Human activities may block or restrict the established corridors or patterns that animals use in their daily and seasonal movements [33]. Likewise, the aquatic habitats may be damaged because of a wide range of industrial or economic activities. For example, erosion from poorly constructed sites may ruin spawning beds for fish. Alterations of flood cycles, tidal flows, and water levels can distress trophic dynamics by affecting the life cycle of planktons and other aquatic organisms [34]. Ecological disequilibrium happens when the introduction of new plant and animal species in an ecosystem disturbs its dynamic balance to the detriment of native species. In some cases, nonnative species gain a competitive advantage because of a lack of natural controls and subsequently invade the whole ecosystem [34]. Loss of biodiversity is a serious environmental hazard that is caused by human activities particularly agriculture and food production, industrialization, urbanization, road construction, tourism, and aviation.

The Drivers of Environmental Degradation

Human beings are the number one culprit of environmental degradation. Overpopulation, urbanization, energy production and consumption, business activities, agriculture, industrialization, and transport directly or indirectly contribute to the environmental degradation. The world has experienced a steep rise in the global population in the second half of the 20th century from 2.5 billion in 1950 to 6 billion in 2000 and 7.5 billion in 2017 [4]. Despite some slowdown in the world population growth, the number of human beings on the planet will increase in the next decades. The world population is expected to exceed nine billion in 2038 [35]. About 90 percent of the population growth will be concentrated in low- and middle-income countries. The fastest-growing region will be sub-Saharan Africa, and the largest number of people will be added in Asia, particularly in the Indian subcontinent [4]. This huge and fast increase of human populations on the planet implies devastating implications for the environment. Furthermore, the effects of population growth on the environmental degradation are amplified by urbanization. Three decades ago, only 38 percent of the world's population lived in cities, but the share of urbanized population exceeded 50 percent in 2015. The number of the world's urban dwellers is growing fast, and large cities are attracting even more people. By 2050, the share of the urban population is expected to reach 67 percent. Most of the growth in urban population will be concentrated in developing countries and in megacities in Southern and Eastern Asia. This pace of urbanization puts an additional strain on the environment through land degradation, destruction, fragmentation of natural habitats, water pollution, increases in greenhouse gas emissions, and air pollution [4]. Likewise, building and demolition activities in urban centers generate a lot of debris and solid trash, consuming almost one-third to one-half of the world's commodities. The extent of environmental degradation will be particularly significant in developing countries as they are marked by high birth rates and urbanization growth.

Manufacturing is still an important sector of the economic production primarily in emerging countries. Currently, the share of manufacturing is estimated at about 40 percent of the world output. Manufacturing activities rely on the use of different types of resources, consume energy, and generate large amounts of solid or gaseous waste. Due to a manufacturing boom in emerging markets, base and precious metals, biomass, woods, and materials are in high demand. Similarly, global resource extraction has increased vastly in the past decades, from 40 billion ton in 1980 to 58 billion ton in 2005 and is expected to increase to 80 billion ton in 2020 [19].

Agriculture and fishing are other economic sectors that put pressure on the planet's resources and cause the environmental degradation. There is a growing demand for every kind of food because not only human beings are growing in number but also they are eating more. Furthermore, as people in emerging countries attain at the economic prosperity, they tend to consume more protein and meat products. Not surprisingly, the livestock sector is one of the fastest-growing parts of the agricultural economy [36]. The shift from cereal to meat consumption could cause an increase in agricultural production by roughly 50 percent between 2005 and 2030 [19].

Energy and transport sectors are other major contributors to environmental degradation as they generate greenhouse gas and other pollutants. The global primary energy consumption is estimated to increase by 1.8 percent annually [4]. In the recent years, renewable energies such as solar and wind have been promulgated, but the traditional energy resources including fossil fuels and nuclear are still very popular. The total share of fossil fuels in energy consumption is supposed to remain constant at about 85 percent at least until 2030 when it may fall to reach 80 percent in 2050 [19].

The Consequences of Environmental Degradation

First, the environmental degradation has negative effects on human health. Evidently, the phenomena such as air and water pollution, land degradation, and greenhouse gas emissions seriously affect our health and well-being. Water pollution alone is responsible for more than two million deaths across the world annually. Likewise, poor air quality causes more than 6.5 million deaths annually and millions of respiratory diseases such as pneumonia and asthma [6]. The presence of chlorofluorocarbons and hydrochlorofluorocarbons in the atmosphere causes the ozone layer depletion that will emit harmful radiations back to the earth. Chemical and bacterial pollutants enter our food chains and harm produces from fish, meat, and chicken to vegetables, fruits, and beans. The various toxic wastes and harmful chemicals derived from industry, agriculture, and transport cause illnesses and death across the globe. Furthermore, desertification, deforestation, and salinization destroy the natural land cover, deplete the ozone layer, and increase the risk of skin cancer and eye disease.

Poverty is another inevitable consequence of environmental degradation. Across the globe and particularly in developing countries, poverty is related to soil erosion, desertification, water scarcity, and erratic climate changes that cause poor crop yields. Desertification, land degradation, and a shortage of fresh water have negative effects on food production, increase the risks of flooding and droughts, and exacerbate food insecurity particularly in the least developed countries [11]. Additionally, the environmental degradation could result in turmoil and conflict where the resources are already scarce. Due to environmental degradation, the normal business activities could cost the world economy up to 20 percent of global GDP per year [11]. Global warming and the ensuing rising sea levels could destroy the buildings and infrastructures at the coastal zones that are containing about one-fifth of the world's population. Many large cities and important ports are located by the sea or in river deltas, and their populations, infrastructures, industries, ports, oil refineries, and transport systems are at the risk of rising sea levels. Similarly, rising sea levels threaten populations on small islands in the Indian Ocean, the Caribbean, and the Pacific [12]. The densely populated regions in Africa, Asia, and South America are mostly exposed to the risks of climate change because they have limited resources to adapt themselves to the climate change. Even some regions of developed countries in the Western Europe and North America will be affected severely [37].

Rising sea levels and the submergence of large coastal zones may result in territorial disputes over land and maritime borders. Global warming may cause other opportunities and threats in the polar regions and thus trigger competition and conflict among the concerned nations. At the same time, desertification and deforestation could cause clashes over territory leading to political instability and conflict across the planet [11]. Due to water scarcity/pollution or desertification, a large number of affected people have to migrate to other regions or countries. According to the United Nations predictions, there will be millions of environmental migrants by 2020 [11]. The poor and developing parts of Asia, South America, Africa, and the Middle East that have higher birth rates are more vulnerable to environmental degradation and are expected to produce a lot of environmental migrants. By contrast, Europe, North America, and Australia are more likely to receive such environmentally induced migrants.

Facing the horrible effects of environmental degradation, many national and local governments fall short of providing basic services to their citizens. The inability of governments to meet the needs of their populations could generate more frustration and tensions. As the effects of environmental damage become more flagrant, the level of cooperation among nation-states seems necessary. The highly affected nations may blame those responsible for climate change, and as a result, the resentment in the international community could increase. The friction could be especially significant between the developed and developing countries that have diverging economic structures and cultural values [11]. Degradation of the environment under all its forms is responsible for a continuous damage to natural ecosystems and a massive extinction of many living species [38]. The current environmental degradation has resulted in permanent changes in the functioning and status of the earth's ecosystems that ultimately cause a substantial reduction of the biodiversity. In a study conducted by the World Bank, 15 out of 24 ecosystems were degraded [39]. For many living species, the rising temperatures are not tolerable. For instance, an increase of 1°C may be sufficient to extinct 10 percent of land species [39]. Similarly, an increase of 4°C could destroy as much as 30 percent of land species [40]. Therefore, by transforming ecological systems, global warming will severely reduce biodiversity in the next decades.

While environmental degradation affects the entire humanity, those people in poor and developing countries will suffer most, as they are dependent on sectors such as agriculture and fisheries [10]. Furthermore, the capacity of developing countries in adapting to climate change is very limited. Generally, we can say that the least developed countries in the tropical and subtropical areas will be the most vulnerable to the destructive effects of environmental degradation. By contrast, the rich and advanced economies will be able to take measures to mitigate the negative effects of climate change. Africa is for the most part vulnerable to the effects of environmental degradation and may lose between 2 and 7 percent of its GDP due to increased risks of droughts, floods, and pest outbreaks [41]. Currently, North Africa and the Sahel are tackling with growing problems such as drought, water scarcity, soil erosion, and loss of arable land. The Nile Delta in Egypt with millions of habitats is at risk from sea-level rise, soil erosion, and salinization of arable land. In the Horn of Africa, Darfur, and Southern Africa climate change, drought, soil erosion, and food shortages are responsible for increasing levels of ethnic tensions and conflicts [11]. Likewise, the Middle East is experiencing droughts, reduced rainfall, sand storms, air pollution, land degradation, and rising temperatures. Around two-thirds of Arab countries are dependent on sources outside their borders for water [11]. There are tensions over access to water among many Middle Eastern countries such as Jordan, Israel, Palestine, Turkey, Iraq, and Syria. Over time and with the growing trend of environmental degradation, we may expect higher levels of water-related conflict. Substantial drops in fresh water resources in the Middle Eastern countries such as Turkey, Iran, Iraq, Syria, and Saudi Arabia could severely affect their sociopolitical stability [11].

South Asia is a region vulnerable to sea-level rise. Due to a high population density, the lives and belongings of millions of habitats are at risk. It is interesting to note that more than 40 percent of Asia's population or almost two billion people live within 60 km from the coastline [11]. Furthermore, a large portion of Asia's population is still extremely poor and relies on traditional agriculture. Therefore, any kind of damage to agricultural productivity due to water quality, soil erosion, and climate change will have destructive effects on the subsistence of billions of people. It is evident that further strain on natural resources, water, and arable land will result in mass migration, higher levels of conflict, and sociopolitical turmoil. Central Asia is another region vulnerable to the effects of environmental degradation. Most of the Central Asian countries are landlocked and rely on limited water resources for agriculture. The reduction in rainfall, shortage of water resources, and soil erosion are already affecting Kyrgyzstan and Tajikistan. Many coastal parts of Latin American and Caribbean countries are exposed to the sea-level increases. Furthermore, reduction in rainfall and the waning glaciers could affect water availability for human consumption, agriculture, and energy generation in much of Latin America. These changes may imply adverse consequences for food security and local economies.

Global Perils of Water Scarcity

Water covers almost 70 percent of the planet, but only 2.5 percent of all water is suitable for human needs. Currently, some 1.2 billion people or 20 percent of the world's population live in areas marked by water scarcity, and another 1.6 billion people face some degree of water shortage [42]. According to the United Nations reports, as early as 2000, approximately one billion people lacked access to safe drinking water and almost 2.5 billion required acceptable sanitation [43]. It is estimated that, currently, 1.8 billion people or almost 25 percent of the global population uses a source of drinking water contaminated by feces [44]. The rising water demand and lack of access to safe drinking water result in five million deaths each year due to water-related illness. The problem will only worsen as the global growth in water demand is expected to increase by 50 percent over the next two decades. The fast and extraordinary growth in water demand will overtake the ability of many ecosystems and human management to supply clean water [43]. By 2025, 4 billion people will be living in conditions of water stress and another 1.8 billion people will be living in regions with absolute water scarcity [45, 46].

Population growth, climate change, urbanization, agriculture, industrialization, changes in diets and lifestyle, investment and management shortfalls, and inefficient use of existing resources are among the main causes of water scarcity. Water consumption increases at approximately twice the rate of population growth, as more fresh water is required not only for basic drinking needs but also for food production, industry, and improving human health [47]. Globally, 70 percent of water withdrawals are for the agricultural sector, 11 percent for municipal demands, and 19 percent for industrial needs. According to the United Nations Population Division, the world population has more than doubled since the 1950s and is expected to exceed 8 billion in 2024, 9 billion in 2038, and 10 billion in 2056. These levels of population growth will put huge pressure on water resources to meet increased food, energy, and industrial demands. Ironically, food and agriculture are the most water-intensive sectors and account for more than 90 percent of water use [48]. The importance of water resources for food and agriculture is rising, as the world is adding more inhabitants and as developing economies are becoming wealthier and their citizens are shifting from starch-based diets to meat and dairy, which require more water. For instance, producing 1 kg of rice requires about 3,500 L of water, while producing 1 kg of beef needs some 15,000 L [49]. Likewise, water scarcity will be aggravated by energy sector, as all forms of energy require water at the production, conversion, distribution, and consumption stages. Water scarcity has a broad meaning and can refer to physical scarcity or economic scarcity of water. Physical water scarcity implies that there is not enough water to meet demand. Economic water scarcity means an absence of investment and proper management to meet the demand of consumers to use existing water sources [50]. There are many methods to measure water scarcity. For instance, we can compare the size of a population with the amount of available water. According to the United Nations guidelines, water stress for a region happens when the annual water supplies fall below 1,700 cubic meters per person and water scarcity for a region happens when water supplies are less than 1,000 cubic meters per person [45]. Middle East, North Africa, Caucasus, Central Asia, Mongolia, Pakistan, India, Afghanistan, Horn of Africa, and South Sudan are on the top of the list of water-stressed regions (see Figures 6.4 and 6.5). What is more, all these regions suffer from high economic inequality and weak governance. The Asia-Pacific region contains over 50 percent of the world's population, but it detains only 36 percent of the global water resources. All Arab countries are considered water scarce, with less than 500 cubic meters of renewable water resources available per person [48]. Similarly, more than 66 percent of Africa is arid or semiarid, and more than 300 million people in sub-Saharan Africa live on less than 1,000 cubic meters of water resources each. By contrast, North America and Europe enjoy high levels of renewable water resources. For example, Canada and the United States have about 85,310 and 9,888 cubic meters of water resources per person, respectively, whereas Europe has almost 4,741 cubic meters [48]. Apart from its biological and economic importance, water is becoming a hot global and geopolitical issue in some regions. Water insecurity can be aggravated by drought. As water availability decreases, competition for access to this vital but limited resource will increase. Around 60 percent of all freshwater comes from internationally shared river basins that could become sources of cross-national competition [49]. Water scarcity could involve serious socioeconomic risks across the world, including

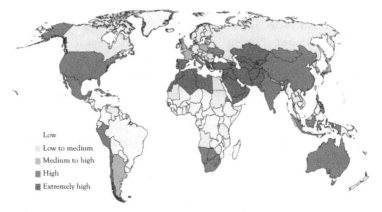

Figure 6.4 Country-level water stress in 2040 under the business-as-usual scenario

Source: [51].

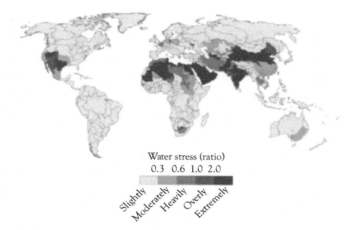

Figure 6.5 *Water stress, shown in the global distribution of water stress index (WSI)*
Source: [46].

famines and food shortages, migratory pressures, regional destabilization, economic downturn, increasing dependence on foreign aid, and diplomatic and national conflict over trans-boundary water resources.

References

[1] Tyagi, S., N. Garg, and R. Paudel. 2014. "Environmental Degradation: Causes and Consequences." *European Researcher* Series A, nos. 8–2, pp. 1491–1498.

[2] Melillo, J.M., T.T. Richmond, and G. Yohe. 2014. *Climate Change Impacts in the United States.* Third National Climate Assessment.

[3] UNEP (United Nations Environment Programme). 2013. *Global Environment Outlook 2000,* 1. Routledge.

[4] Ruta, G. 2010. "Monitoring Environmental Sustainability Trends, Challenges, and the Way Forward." The World Bank Group. https://google.com/url?sa=t&rct=j&q=&esrc=s&source=web&cd=1&ved=0ahUKEwjjgZLBo4nVAhWl7YMKHWc0CrwQFggmMAA&url=http%3A%2F%2Fsiteresources.worldbank.org%2FEXTENVSTRATEGY%2FResources%2F6975692-1289855310673%2F20101209-Monitoring-Environmental-Sustainability.pdf&usg=AFQjCNGbWcJ1qZryp8sdBEI-66kYZYBQeQ&cad=rja (accessed October 06, 2017).

[5] Arto, I., and E. Dietzenbacher. 2014. "Drivers of the Growth in Global Greenhouse Gas Emissions." *Environmental Science & Technology* 48, no. 10, pp. 5388–5394.

[6] World Energy Outlook Special Report. 2016. Energy and Air Pollution. Available at https://iea.org/publications/freepublications/publication/weo-2016-special-report-energy-and-air-pollution.html

[7] Donohoe, M. 2003. "Causes and Health Consequences of Environmental Degradation and Social Injustice." *Social Science & Medicine* 56, no. 3, pp. 573–587.

[8] Kampa, M., and E. Castanas. 2008. "Human Health Effects of Air Pollution." *Environmental Pollution* 151, no. 2, pp. 362–367.

[9] Harris, J.M., and B. Roach. 2007. *The Economics of Global Climate Change.* Global Development and Environment Institute Tufts University.

[10] Solomon, S, ed. 2007. *Climate Change 2007-The Physical Science Basis: Working Group I Contribution to the Fourth Assessment Report of the IPCC* 4. Cambridge University Press.

[11] Holden, E., K. Linnerud, and D. Banister. 2014. "Sustainable Development: Our Common Future Revisited." *Global Environmental Change* 26, pp. 130–139.

[12] Theisen, O.M., N.P. Gleditsch, and H. Buhaug. 2013. "Is Climate Change a Driver of Armed Conflict?." *Climatic Change* 117, no. 3, pp. 613–625.

[13] Carr, G.M., and J.P. Neary. 2008. *Water Quality for Ecosystem and Human Health,* 2nd ed. United Nations Environment Programme Global Environment Monitoring System. Retrieved July 14, 2009 from http://gemswater.org/publications/pdfs/water_quality_human_health.pdf

[14] The World Health Organization, Drinking-water, Fact sheet. Updated July 2017. http:/who.int/mediacentre/factsheets/fs391/en/

[15] Water, U.N., M.PH.A. Mobile, and PT.A. Toilet. 2014. World Water Day.

[16] The World Bank 2010. Environment Strategy 2010: Analytical Background Papers (English). http://documents.worldbank.org/curated/en/355491468333022953/Environment-strategy-2010-analytical-background- papers

[17] WHO/UNICEF. 2013. *Progress on Sanitation and Drinking-Water 2013 Update: Joint Monitoring Programme for Water Supply and Sanitation.*

[18] Marchal, V., R. Dellink, D. Van Vuuren, C. Clapp, J. Chateau, B. Magne, and J. van Vliet. 2011. "OECD Environmental Outlook to 2050." *Organization for Economic Co-operation and Development.*

[19] OECD. 2008. *OECD Environmental Outlook to 2030.* Organisation for Economic Co-Operation and Development, Paris.

[20] Wood, S., K. Sebastian, and S.J. Scherr. 2000. "Soil Resource Condition." In *Pilot Analysis of Global Ecosystems (Page),* pp. 45–54. Washington, DC: IFPRI and World Resources Institute.

[21] Bossio, D., A. Noble, J. Pretty, and F. Penning de Vries. August 2004. "Reversing Land and Water Degradation: Trends and 'Bright Spot' Opportunities." In *SIWI/CA Seminar, Stockholm, Sweden* 21.

[22] Tarasov, D.A., A.N. Medvedev, A.P. Sergeev, A.V. Shichkin, and A.G. Buevich. July 2017. "A Hybrid Method for Assessment of Soil Pollutants Spatial Distribution." In *AIP Conference Proceedings* 1863, no. 1, p. 050015. AIP Publishing.

[23] Xanthos, D., and T.R. Walker. 2017. "International Policies to Reduce Plastic Marine Pollution from Single-Use Plastics (Plastic Bags and Microbeads): A Review." *Marine pollution bulletin* 118, no. 1–2, pp. 17–26.

[24] Balde, C.P. 2015. *The Global E-waste Monitor 2014: Quantities, Flows and Resources.* United Nations University.

[25] Owens, M. 2015. Disposal of E-Waste and Its Impacts on the Ecosystem.

[26] Byster, L., S. Westervelt, R. Gutierrez, S. Davis, A. Hussain, and M. Dutta. 2002. "Exporting Harm: The High-Tech Trashing of Asia." In ed. J. Puckett, 3 vols. Seattle: Basel Action Network.

[27] Luo, C., C. Lui, Y. Wang, X. Liu, F. Li, G. Zhang, and X. Li. 2011. "Heavy Metals Contamination in Soils and Vegetables Near an E-waste Processing Site, South China." *Journal of Hazardous Materials* 186, pp. 481–490.

[28] Van der Meulen, R. March 19, 2015. "Gartner Says Global Devices Shipments to Grow 2.8 Percent in 2015." Retrieved May 01, 2015, from http:// gartner.com/newsroom/id/3010017

[29] Leeves, S.A. 2011. "Bioaccumulation of Arsenic, Cadmium, Mercury, Lead and Selenium in the Benthic and Pelagic Food Chain of Lake Baikal." (Master's thesis, Institute for Biology).

[30] Clayden, M.G., L.M. Arsenault, K.A. Kidd, N.J. O'Driscoll, and M.L. Mallory. 2015. "Mercury Bioaccumulation and Biomagnification in a Small Arctic Polynya Ecosystem." *Science of the Total Environment* 509, pp. 206–215.

[31] Van der Oost, R., J. Beyer, and N.P. Vermeulen. 2003. "Fish Bioaccumulation and Biomarkers in Environmental Risk Assessment: A Review." *Environmental toxicology and pharmacology* 13, no. 2, pp. 57-149.

[32] Galal, T.M., and H.S. Shehata. 2015. "Bioaccumulation and Translocation of Heavy Metals by Plantago Major L. Grown in Contaminated Soils Under the Effect of Traffic Pollution." *Ecological Indicators* 48, pp. 244–251.

[33] Moraes, M.A.F.D., F.C.R. Oliveira, and R.A. Diaz-Chavez. 2015. "Socio-Economic Impacts of Brazilian Sugarcane Industry." *Environmental development* 16, pp. 31–43.

[34] Kabisch, N., S. Qureshi, and D. Haase. 2015. "Human–Environment Interactions in Urban Green Spaces—A Systematic Review of Contemporary Issues and Prospects for Future Research." *Environmental Impact Assessment Review* 50, pp. 25–34.

[35] Bloom, D.E. 2011. "7 Billion and Counting." *Science* 333, no. 6042, pp. 562–569.

[36] FAO (Food and Agriculture Organization). 2009. *The State of Food and Agriculture 2009*. Food and Agriculture Organization of the United Nations, Rome.

[37] Mann, M.E. 2009. "Do Global Warming and Climate Change Represent a Serious Threat to Our Welfare and Environment?." *Social Philosophy and Policy* 26, no. 2, pp. 193–230.

[38] Rockstrom, J., W. Steffen, K. Noone, A. Persson, F.S. Chapin III, E. Lambin, T. Lenton, M. Scheffer, C. Folke, H.J. Schellnhuber, and B. Nykvist. 2009. "Planetary Boundaries: Exploring the Safe Operating Space for Humanity." *Ecology and Society* 14, no. 2.

[39] World Bank. 2010. *World Development Report 2010: Development and Climate Change*. Washington, DC: World Bank.

[40] UNDP (United Nations Development Programme). 2008. "Human Development Report 2007/2008." *Fighting Climate Change: Human Solidarity in a Divided World*. New York, NY: UNDP.

[41] World Bank. 2008. *Climate Change: Adaptation and Mitigation in Development Programs: A Practical Guide*. Washington, DC: World Bank.

[42] UN-Water. 2013. "Water for Life 2005-2015: Water Scarcity." www.un.org/waterforlifedecade/scarcity.shtml (accessed February 20, 2013).

[43] Padowski, J.C., and J.W. Jawitz. 2009. "The Future of Global Water Scarcity: Policy and Management Challenges and Opportunities." *Whitehead J. Dipl. & Int'l Rel.* 10, p. 99.

[44] Metcalfe, C., L. Guppy, and M. Qadir. 2017. *Global Barriers To Improving Water Quality: A Critical Review*. United Nations University Institute for Water, Environment, and Health.

[45] World Water Assessment Programme (WWAP). 2012. *World Water Development Report, Vol. 1: Managing Water Under Uncertainty and Risk*. Paris: UNESCO.

[46] Schlosser, C.A., K. Strzepek, X. Gao, C. Fant, E. Blanc, S. Paltsev, and A. Gueneau. 2014. "The Future of Global Water Stress: An Integrated Assessment." *Earth's Future* 2, no. 8, pp. 341–361.

[47] UN-Water. 2006. *Coping with Water Scarcity-A Strategic Issue and Priority for System-wide Action*. UN-Water Thematic Initiatives.

[48] Water under Uncertainty and Risk. 2012. Paris: UNESCO.

[49] FAO, AQUASTAT. 2013. Available at fao.org/nr/water/aquastat/water_use/index.stm (accessed March 01, 2013).

[50] U.N. Food and Agriculture Organization (FAO). 2012. *Coping with Water Scarcity: An Action Framework for Agriculture and Food Security*. FAO Water Report 38 Rome.

[51] Luo, T., R. Young, and P. Reig. 2015. *Aqueduct Projected Water Stress Country Rankings*. Technical Note.

CHAPTER 7

The Giant Corporations

An Incredible Concentration of Power and Wealth

For a long time throughout the history, the church and the state have been the political and economic centers of decision making [1]. With the advent of modern capitalism in the 18th century, the corporations gradually outshined the church and the state. For a while, the ability of corporations to grow was restrained by the limits of capital accumulation, geographic location, and legal and cultural barriers, but in the second half of the 19th century, the new regulations allowed the momentous growth of corporations. On the one hand, the concept of limited liability made owners of businesses not subject to punishment for their debts. On the other hand, the financial exchanges facilitated the interaction between investors and businesses and thus allowed the rapid accumulation of capital. The steady growth of corporations continued during the 20th century but gained a remarkable momentum in the 1990s. The end of Cold War, the new information technology, and particularly globalization provided unprecedented drivers for a phenomenal concentration of economic power in a number of large corporations. In 1980, the world's largest 1,000 corporations earned $2.64 trillion in revenue, employed 21 million people, and had a total market capitalization of $900 billion. Thirty years later, in 2012, the world's largest 1,000 corporations made an astonishing $34 trillion in revenue, employed 73 million people, and had a total market capitalization of $28 trillion [1]. Currently, the giant corporations are progressively occupying the skylines of big cities and are accumulating huge amounts of wealth (see Table 7.1).

While this method is not an accurate comparison between corporations and nations, it offers a simple impression of the economic influence of large corporations. The world's 10 largest corporations have a combined revenue greater than the government revenue of 180 countries combined,

Table 7.1 The top 100 largest corporations as of 2021

Rank	Company	Location	Sector	Market cap	Rank	Company	Location	Sector	Market cap
1	Apple Inc	The United States	Technology	$2.1T	51	China Merch	China	Financials	$196B
2	Saudi Aramco	Saudi Arabia	Energy	$1.9T	52	Pepsico Inc	The United States	Consumer staples	$195B
3	Microsoft Corp	The United States	Technology	$1.8T	53	Salesforce.com	The United States	Technology	$195B
4	Amazon.com Inc	The United States	Consumer discretionary	$1.6T	54	Merck & Co	The United States	Health care	$195B
5	Alphabet Inc	The United States	Technology	$1.4T	55	Abbvie Inc	The United States	Health care	$191B
6	Facebook Inc	The United States	Technology	$839B	56	Broadcom Inc	The United States	Technology	$189B
7	Tencent	China	Technology	$753B	57	Prosus NV	The Netherlands	Technology	$181B
8	Tesla Inc	The United States	Consumer discretionary	$641B	58	Reliance Inds	India	Energy	$180B
9	Alibaba Grp	China	Consumer discretionary	$615B	59	Thermo Fisher	The United States	Health care	$180B
10	Berkshire Hathaway	The United States	Financials	$588B	60	Eli Lilly & Co	The United States	Health care	$179B

11	TSMC	Taiwan	Technology	$534B	61	Agricultural Bank of China	China	Financials	$178B
12	VISA Inc	The United States	Industrials	$468B	62	Softbank Group	Japan	Telecommunications	$176B
13	JPMorgan Chase	The United States	Financials	$465B	63	Accenture PLC	Ireland	Industrials	$176B
14	Johnson & Johnson	The United States	Health care	$433B	64	Texas Instrument	The United States	Technology	$174B
15	Samsung Electronics	South Korea	Technology	$431B	65	McDonalds Corp	The United States	Consumer discretionary	$167B
16	Kweichow Mouta	China	Consumer staples	$385B	66	Volkswagen AG	Germany	Consumer discretionary	$165B
17	Walmart Inc	The United States	Consumer discretionary	$383B	67	BHP Group Ltd	Australia	Basic materials	$163B
18	Mastercard Inc	The United States	Industrials	$354B	68	Wells Fargo & Co	The United States	Financials	$162B
19	United Health Grp	The United States	Health care	$352B	69	Tata Consultancy	India	Technology	$161B
20	Lvmh Moet Hennessy	France	Consumer discretionary	$337B	70	Danaher Corp	The United States	Health care	$160B
21	Walt Disney Co	The United States	Consumer discretionary	$335B	71	Novo Nordisk	Denmark	Health care	$160B

(Continued)

Table 7.1 (Continued)

Rank	Company	Location	Sector	Market cap
22	Bank of America	The United States	Financials	$334B
23	Procter & Gamble	The United States	Consumer staples	$333B
24	Nvidia Corp	The United States	Technology	$331B
25	Home Depot Inc	The United States	Consumer discretionary	$329B
26	Nestle SA	Switzerland	Consumer staples	$322B
27	IND & COMM BK	China	Financials	$290B
28	Paypal Holdings	The United States	Industrials	$284B
29	Roche Holding	Switzerland	Health care	$283B
30	Intel Corp	The United States	Technology	$261B
31	ASML Holding NV	The Netherlands	Technology	$255B
32	Toyota Motor	Japan	Consumer discretionary	$254B
72	Medtronic PLC	Ireland	Health care	$159B
73	Wuliangye Yibin	China	Consumer staples	$159B
74	Costco Wholesale	The United States	Consumer discretionary	$156B
75	T-Mobile US Inc	The United States	Telecommunications	$156B
76	Citigroup Inc	The United States	Financials	$152B
77	Honeywell Intl	The United States	Industrials	$151B
78	Qualcomm Inc	The United States	Technology	$151B
79	SAP SE	Germany	Technology	$151B
80	Boeing Co	The United States	Industrials	$149B
81	Royal Dutch Shell	The Netherlands	Oil and gas	$148B
82	Nextera Energy	The United States	Utilities	$148B

33	Comcast Corp	The United States	Telecommunications	$248B	83	United Parcel	The United States	Industrials	$148B
34	Verizon Communications	The United States	Telecommunications	$241B	84	Union PAC Corp	The United States	Industrials	$148B
35	ExxonMobil Corp	The United States	Energy	$236B	85	Unilever PLC	The United Kingdom	Consumer staples	$147B
36	Netflix Inc	The United States	Consumer discretionary	$231B	86	AIA	Hong Kong SAR	Financials	$147B
37	Adobe Inc	The United States	Technology	$228B	87	Linde plc	The United Kingdom	Basic materials	$146B
38	Coca-Cola Co	The United States	Consumer staples	$227B	88	Amgen Inc	The United States	Health care	$144B
39	Meituan	China	Technology	$226B	89	Bristol-Myers SQB	The United States	Health care	$141B
40	Ping An	China	Financials	$219B	90	Siemens AG	Germany	Industrials	$140B
41	Cisco Systems	The United States	Telecommunications	$218B	91	Bank of China	China	Financials	$139B
42	AT&T Inc	The United States	Financials	$216B	92	Philip Morris Inc	The United States	Consumer staples	$138B
43	L'Oreal	France	Consumer discretionary	$215B	93	Lowe's Cos Inc	The United States	Consumer discretionary	$136B

(Continued)

Table 7.1 (Continued)

Rank	Company	Location	Sector	Market cap	Rank	Company	Location	Sector	Market cap
44	China Construction Bank	China	Financials	$213B	94	Charter	The United States	Telecommunications	$135B
45	Abbott Labs	The United States	Health care	$212B	95	China Mobile	Hong Kong SAR	Telecommunications	$134B
46	Novartis AG	Switzerland	Health care	$212B	96	Sony Group Corp	Japan	Consumer discretionary	$132B
47	Nike Inc	The United States	Consumer discretionary	$209B	97	AstraZeneca PLC	The United Kingdom	Health care	$131B
48	Oracle Corp	The United States	Technology	$202B	98	Royal Bank of Canada	Canada	Financials	$131B
49	Pfizer Inc	The United States	Health care	$202B	99	Starbucks Corp	The United States	Consumer discretionary	$129B
50	Chevron Corp	The United States	Oil & gas	$202B	100	Anheuser-Busch	Belgium	Consumer staples	$128B

including Ireland, Indonesia, Israel, Colombia, Greece, South Africa, Iraq, and Vietnam [2]. Walmart is ranked the 10th economic entity, and thus, it is considered larger than some major global economies including Australia, South Korea, and India. It is striking to note that the cash that Apple has on hand surpasses the GDPs of almost two-thirds of the world's countries [3]. Apple, Saudi Aramco, Amazon, Microsoft, Alphabet, Alibaba, Facebook, Tencent, Berkshire Hathaway, and Taiwan Semiconductor were ranked the largest global corporation in 2020.

Other financial and nonfinancial measures such as the number of consumers, market share, and growth rate confirm the extraordinary rise of the giant corporations in the past two decades. For example, Google, Amazon, and Facebook experienced rapid and consistent growth in a matter of 10 to 15 years to become giant corporations. Founded in September 1998, Google processes now over 40,000 search queries every second, over 3.5 billion searches per day, and 1.2 trillion searches per year [4]. Similarly, Facebook that was founded in 2004 had more than 2.85 billion monthly active users as of May 2021, a number larger than the population of China and the United States together [5]. Amazon.com that started as an online bookseller in 1995 produced net sales of $386 billion in 2020. The young tech corporations such as Apple, Google, Amazon, and Facebook have become the world's most valuable companies and have reached the astonishing market capitalizations of $2, $1.5, $1.7, and $1 trillion, respectively, as of June 2021.

In the last decade, the global corporations' share of the world's economy has increased drastically, while the competition from small- and medium-sized businesses has fallen by almost the same factor. As a result, a relatively small number of very large corporations have increased their control over global markets, made higher profits, and effectively outcompeted their smaller rivals. Particularly, the tech giants have capitalized on their vast scales to gain market dominance and produce colossal revenues.

A few companies, six or nine, manage the organization of the information economy from an Internet search, advertising, and electronic retailing to clouding and social media. According to the McKinsey Global Institute, 10 percent of the world's public companies generate almost 80 percent of the profits [6]. The simple rule of thumb is that the larger corporations become more competitive because of their economies of scale, political connections, and huge financial and technological resources. For instance, those corporations with more than $1 billion in the annual revenue account for 60 percent of total global revenues [6]. The concentration of wealth in the giant corporations is particularly impressive in the United States where the share of GDP generated by the Fortune 100 biggest American companies surged from about 33 percent of GDP in 1994 to 46 percent in 2013 [6]. Some of these giant corporations such as ExxonMobil, Berkshire Hathaway, Procter & Gamble, Wal-Mart Stores, Pfizer, and Johnson & Johnson have had established themselves many decades ago. Some others like Apple, Alphabet, Microsoft, Amazon.com, and Facebook are tech companies that have joined the club of giant corporations more recently. While most of these giant corporations are originated in the United States, Western Europe, and Japan, some others such as Alibaba, ICBC, and China Mobile belong to the emerging countries.

Doing More With Less: More Revenues and Fewer Employees

Traditionally, the firms' revenues, market capitalizations, and assets were correlated to the number of employees. In other words, those firms that had big revenues also typically had large workforces and substantial assets, as well as large market capitalizations. In the past three decades, with the advent of globalization and new information technologies, the large multinational corporations (MNCs) are doing more with less, meaning that they are generating more revenues with fewer employees and less physical assets [7]. Nowadays, the corporations can be small in assets and employees, but big in revenues and profits (Table 7.2). This feature may be found particularly in high-technology sectors that offer intangible services. Facebook with only 58,000 employees in 2020 generated revenues of $86 billion and had a market capitalization of $750 billion. Netflix with a market capitalization of over $226 billion and revenues of almost $25 billion had only 9,000 employees in 2020. The examples of firms with large revenues and huge market valuations but very small workforce and insignificant tangible assets are not limited to information technology. In the recent years, automation, global production, and outsourcing have enabled the giant corporations to enhance their productivity and generate more revenues with fewer employees and fewer assets. Nike, Apple, Vizio, Exxon Mobil, and AT&T are other examples of those firms that have increased their productivity by cutting their workforce. Exxon Mobil, the world's most successful oil company, has reduced its workforce from 150,000 in the 1960s to less than 75,000, despite having merged with a giant rival [6]. Those firms that have not been able to reduce the number of their personnel tend to hire low-wage workers that ultimately do not cost them very much. It is interesting to note that large corporations employ a grand majority (66 percent) of low-wage workers in America [8]. The American large corporations have mostly recovered from the recession of 2007 to 2008 and are generally in strong financial positions. They are currently generating more revenues as a percentage of the economy, but wages as a percentage of the economy are at an all-time low. Walmart, which is the largest American employer with more than two million employees, has one of the lowest wages in the United States estimated at $12.94 per hour. Other retailers such as Kroger (400,000 employees), Home Depot (371,000 employees), and Target (347,000 employees) are among top employers. Some fast-food chains including McDonald's and YUM Brands have larger employment rolls but rely heavily on part-time and temporary workers. In other words, top employers in the United States are mainly in retail and fast-food industries where employees face low wages, high turnover, minimal benefits, and low career opportunities. Other giant corporations are increasingly relying on a more flexible organizational structure such as labor on-demand model. More recently, Uber and Airbnb have developed business models that are able to generate colossal revenues independent of their workforce. Based on these observations, it is possible to suggest that rising corporate profits come to the detriment of the American workers [9]. The giant corporations visibly favor shareholders' returns over employees' interests and consider the reduction in their workforce as an important step toward profit maximization.

The Winner-Take-All Capitalism

The giant corporations are benefitting from their immense financial, technological, and managerial resources to develop sophisticated competitive

Table 7.2 The top 50 companies ranked by revenue per employee in 2016; S&P 500 companies with highest revenue per employee

Rank	Company	RPE	Sector
1	AmerisourceBergen	$7.9M	Health care
2	Valero Energy Corporation	$7.6M	Energy
3	Phillips 66	$5.7M	Energy
4	Express Scripts Holding Company	$3.9M	Health care
5	Tesoro Corporation	$3.9M	Energy
6	ONEOK	$3.7M	Energy
7	Gilead Sciences	$3.4M	Health care
8	Cardinal Health	$3.3M	Health care
9	Exxon Mobil Corporation	$3.2M	Energy
10	Altria Group	$3.1M	CS
11	EOG Resources	$2.9M	Energy
12	McKesson	$2.8M	Health care
13	Devon Energy Corporation	$2.4M	Energy
14	Chesapeake Energy Corporation	$2.4M	Energy
15	Reynolds American	$2.3M	CS
16	LyondellBasell Industries	$2.2M	Materials
17	Aflac	$2.2M	Financials
18	Chevron Corporation	$2.2M	Energy
19	Marathon Oil	$2.2M	Energy
20	Hess Corporation	$2.1M	Energy
21	Cabot Oil & Gas Corporation	$2.0M	Energy
22	Archer Daniels Midland Company	$2.0M	CS
23	Netflix	$1.9M	CD
24	Apple	$1.9M	IT
25	Conoco Phillips	$1.8M	Energy
26	Anadarko Petroleum Corporation	$1.7M	Energy
27	D.R. Horton	$1.7M	CD
28	Facebook	$1.6M	IT
29	PulteGroup	$1.6M	CD
30	Anthem	$1.6M	Health care
31	Celgene Corporation	$1.6M	Health care
32	Biogen	$1.5M	Health care
33	Noble Energy	$1.5M	Energy

(Continued)

Table 7.2 (Continued)

Rank	Company	RPE	Sector
34	Concho Resources	$1.5M	Energy
35	Newfield Exploration	$1.5M	Energy
36	Lincoln National Corporation	$1.5M	Financials
37	Cimarex Energy	$1.5M	Energy
38	Murphy Oil Corporation	$1.4M	Energy
39	Range Resources Corporation	$1.4M	Energy
40	Apache Corporation	$1.4M	Energy
41	Marathon Petroleum Corporation	$1.4M	Energy
42	XL Group	$1.4M	Financials
43	NRG Energy	$1.4M	Utilities
44	Viacom	$1.3M	CD
45	Williams Companies	$1.3M	Energy
46	CME Group	$1.3M	Financials
47	Centene Corp	$1.3M	Health care
48	Lennar Corporation	$1.3M	CD
49	Aetna	$1.3M	Health care
50	Twenty-First Century Fox	$1.3M	CD

CD, consumer discretionary; CS, consumer staples; IT, information technology.
Source: businessinsider.com.

advantages against smaller rivals. In the technology sector, a few corporations such as Google, Microsoft, Facebook, and Amazon have become so dominant that practically are stifling the competition from the small- and even mid-sized companies [6]. Likewise, in the financial sector, 5 large banks control 45 percent of American banking assets. The 10 biggest banks control almost 50 percent of assets under management worldwide [3]. The wave of consolidation has swept all the U.S. industries from aviation and telecommunication to insurance, pharmaceutical, news, and media. While the phenomenon of consolidation is particularly striking in the United States, European and Asian countries follow almost the same trajectory. Capitalizing on the global logistics and production, large corporations can conveniently scatter their supply chains across the world and take advantage of local endowments. The global presence especially is advantageous to those digital and knowledge-based companies that rely on a lean workforce and intangible assets to generate significant revenues [6]. In order to overcome the tax codes, the giant corporations often get involved in complex financial engineering and keep their revenues or assets in low-tax countries. According to the United Nations Conference on Trade and Development (UNCTAD), the top 100 largest corporations have an average of 20 holding firms each and more than 500 affiliates that are often domiciled in low-tax jurisdictions [6]. Apple, an American giant that is based in California, set up two bogus companies with no employees in Ireland to avoid significant tax bills in the United States in 2015. According to the *Financial Times* [10], about 90 percent of Apple's foreign profits were reported by Irish subsidiaries, which were highly profitable, but paid little tax because they were not tax-resident anywhere. It is estimated that Apple paid 0.005 percent tax on its European profits in 2014 [11]. As the environment of business is becoming more complex and more regulated, the larger corporations have the luxury of mobilizing the armies of their experienced administrators and consultants to benefit from the legal loopholes, lacunas, and ambiguities at the expense of smaller firms. The result is obvious: The large corporations dodge taxes, but the small- and medium-sized firms have to pay a hefty price.

The very large corporations are increasingly connected to cronyism. They are using their power to maximize their profits unethically and even illegally. General Electric, Boeing Co, Northrop Grumman, Comcast Corporation, Verizon Communications, FedEx Corporation, Exxon Mobil, Lockheed Martin, Pfizer, Amazon.com, Facebook, and Google are on the top of the list in lobbying expenditures [12]. According to Oxfam-documented reports, more than 140 corporations from all sectors including finance, extractives, garment, defense, energy, technology, and pharmaceutical are using their influence to establish political connections to shape national and international policies [13]. In the United States, large corporations spend about $2.6 billion a year on lobbying expenditures. Furthermore, the large multinationals often hire former government officials as their senior managers or members of the board of directors to push their strategic agendas. In addition to keeping a good number of their own lobbyists on Capitol Hill, some firms use professional lobbyists to apply a constant pressure on lawmakers. They know that investment in lobbying is paying good dividends as the federal government extends its power over sensitive areas such as health care, technology, telecommunication, and financial markets [6]. The phenomenon of business lobbying is not limited to American corporations. The centers of political decision making in the EU are flooded with a large number of professional lobbyists who are advancing the corporate causes. For instance, Brussels is home to at least 30,000 business lobbyists who try to influence legislation and regulation for more than 500 million European customers [6]. Some of these professional and well-paid corporate lobbyists are former politicians or government officials who are very knowledgeable about the intricacies of the legislature. While the very large corporations receive special treatments from the governments and lawmakers, the small- and mid-sized businesses struggle to abide by complex rules.

The giant corporations are able to effectively transfer and manage their resources across national borders. They benefit from savings in low-cost countries through outsourcing contracts that do not require large capital investments. Indeed, they can, depending on the markets' conditions, quickly modify or cancel their contracts. By relying on the outsourcing contracts, they are able to evade the responsibility for establishing fair labor practices and meeting environmental standards [14]. In other words, the large MNCs are so powerful that they can create a global job competition across the world, granting shares of production only to those nations who offer them the highest concessions and the lowest demands [15]. Tax breaks, human rights abuses, child labor, and lax environmental standards are some examples of concessions that the host nations offer to the giant multinationals. For instance, Malaysia attracted manufacturing operations from some semiconductor multinationals by offering them tax breaks on earnings and preventing the workers from forming unions [14].

In the past two decades, the large corporations have earned huge efficiencies by scattering their value chain activities across the world, forming strategic partnership and alliances, and capitalizing on the economies of scale. It is estimated that the top 1,000 public American companies generate about 40 percent of their revenues from alliances and acquisitions [13]. The large corporations are able to accumulate huge amounts of cash that allow them to acquire smaller firms, develop new products, innovate, and wage price wars. For example, Apple's enormous cash reserves in 2020 were estimated at $200 billion. Thanks to such massive financial resources, the giant corporations can effectively absorb the market down-turn and survive economic and political crises. Acquiring smaller firms is an effective strategy allowing the acquirer to benefit from the existing technologies, processes, and market shares. Facebook acquired Instagram in 2012 and WhatsApp in 2014, respectively, for $1 and $22 billion to capitalize on their existing platforms. In order to benefit from Indian low-cost and abundant talents, General Electric develops a significant portion of new health care products in India [6]. Thanks to their huge financial and managerial resources, the large multinationals can successfully exploit the cross-national differences with regard to research and development, operations, logistics, and innovation. The large corporations have become so powerful that they are almost killing any competition from other firms even the mid-sized businesses. In the past decades, we have witnessed the demise of Nokia, Motorola, and Blackberry as a direct result of com-petitive pressure from Apple Inc. According to McKinsey, the average company's tenure on the S&P 500 list has fallen from 61 years in 1958 to 18 years in 2011, implying that due to competitive pressure, a relatively big number of companies are disappearing [6].

The Decline of Small Business

In the past four decades, the number of small businesses has continued to fall as the power and market shares of large MNCs have surged. For instance, between 1980 and 2012, the number of construction firms fell by 15,000, while the number of small manufacturers dropped by more than 70,000[16]. For the same period, the number of local retailers dropped by 108,000 or 40 percent relative to population[17]. This pat-tern is seen in other sectors including retail and banking. While in the 1980s, local retailers supplied about half of the goods Americans bought in stores; currently, their share has fallen to one quarter [18]. Between 1997 and 2012, the share of total business revenue going to firms with fewer than 100 employees dropped by more than 20 percent [16]. The opposite trend is the unprecedented growth and consolidation of large MNCs almost in all sectors of the American economy. A wide range of products and brands are offered in supermarkets, but most of them are controlled and owned by a few large corporations. One single business makes nearly every brand of sunglasses in the world [19]. Similarly, the production and retail of some food items such as beef, beer, and milk are highly concentrated [18]. The giant MNCs such as Walmart and Amazon.com are dominating most of American retail. Walmart attracts one of every four dollars Americans spend on groceries and more than half of grocery sales in 40 metropolitan areas [18]. The online retail sector is even more concentrated. In 2015, Amazon.com accounted for 51 percent of the growth in online spending and Amazon's share of the U.S. e-commerce market was about 49 percent [20]. In 2010, the Department of Justice officially raised the threshold at which industry is considered too concentrated for assessing mergers and acquisitions [18]. Nevertheless, according to *The Wall Street Journal*, one-third of industries are still assessed as highly concentrated [21]. Further merger and acquisition will involve even higher levels of concentration in various industries from technology and aviation to pharmaceutical and food. It is obvious that as these industries become more concentrated, starting a new entrepreneurial venture or maintaining an existing one continues to become harder. According to an analysis by Brookings Institution, new business creation has declined sharply in the past four decades. What is more disturbing is that the number of business deaths is larger than the number of business births, meaning that the overall number of small or family businesses is declining across all industries and sectors in all 50 states and in more than 360 U.S. metropolitan areas. It is widely accepted that the decline in entrepreneurship is a direct result of a general bias in favor of large businesses in government policies that started in the 1980s after the election of Ronald Reagan as president. The federal government often does not tackle the high concentration and rarely enforces antitrust laws. We may suggest that the most substantial threat to America's entrepreneurs is not technological change or global trade, but an unholy marriage between giant MNCs and government officials. Obviously, big businesses are more efficient from their own investment perspective, but they are unharnessed in exploiting workers, slashing wages, inflating prices, and abusing customers. Above all, big businesses impede small entrepreneurs from scaling up their operations and increasing their market shares. The result is that the business environment in the United States has become less favorable to small business and entrepreneurship. The decline of small businesses may involve significant social losses because they deliver more value in many sectors and can effectively create and distribute jobs, wealth, and economic growth. Small businesses are central to broad prosperity and a strong middle class. Above all, small businesses disperse economic and political power and thus defend democracy and the rule of law.

Eroding the State Sovereignty and Diluting the Nationhood

The very large corporations take advantage of the international system on the one hand and influence nations' policies on the other hand. Nations need the MNCs in order to attract foreign direct investment (FDI), create jobs, and boost economic growth and development. The presence of MNCs can lead to increased tax revenues that allow the governments to pursue their political programs. Large MNCs can dictate to their host countries what they want. They do not need to use corrupt, illegal, or even unethical practices to influence the local governments in order to attain their objectives. If a state, especially an economically ailing one, decides to rescind a large corporation permit, the corporation has the option to transfer its assets and investments to another country and deprive the state of its investments and operations [22]. This will result in harm to the state's economy rather than to the corporation's interests. Large global corporations have many features that put them at advantage vis-a-vis nation-states. For instance, corporations are mobile and are driven by purely economic interests that, due to globalization and advances in technology, are not impeded by territorial and cultural boundaries [23]. Once the large MNCs obtain access to a country, they become active players not only in the domestic economic sector but also in the political, social, and cultural spheres of the host country. Due to their economic influence, the large MNCs can lawfully lobby governments to change policies and legislation with the aim of increasing profits. Furthermore, corporations may engage directly in social activities to set standards for providing public services such as health care and education. The large corporations may put pressure on smaller states, manipulate them, or even plunder their resources in the name of the business, profits maximization, or charity [24].

Because of their influence, the large multinationals have become an increasing threat to states' sovereignty. They have brought about the fragmentation of political authority. They have blurred the boundary between politics, law, and regulation on the one hand and the market and economic activities on the other hand [25]. While the states remain the most important actors, the large corporations are overshadowing their political power in the new international system. Therefore, we may suggest that due to effects of large corporations, the capacity of states is diminishing in providing public goods and services such as guarding the property rights, maintaining a stable currency system, enforcing contracts, and protecting the natural environment [26].

In the 1950s, General Motors President Charles Wilson famously said, "What was good for our country was good for General Motors and vice versa" [3]. Currently, the interests of corporations and their home countries are separate and to some extent conflicting. The large corporations such as Apple, Walmart, Amazon.com, Unilever, and Black-Rock choose locations for their personnel and operations on the basis of their shareholders' interests, not on the basis of national interests. Some of the largest American corporations including Apple, IBM, Microsoft, and General Electric are exporting jobs to other countries and are hoarding billions of dollars in tax-free or low-tax jurisdictions. Accordingly, national interests are not always prioritized, rather they are often neglected. The world is entering an era in which the most powerful law is not that of national sovereignty but that of profit maximization. By prioritizing their shareholders' interests and by extending their operations beyond national jurisdictions, the large corporations are diluting the very concept of nationhood.

Aggravating Economic Inequality

Large MNCs aggravate the rising economic inequality in different ways. As corporations are becoming more profitable, the profits are passed to the top executives and shareholders, whereas ordinary workers do not benefit very much. In other words, the big corporations enrich the rich to the detriment of the poor and thus contribute to economic inequality. Furthermore, corporations often use their connections to secure lax regulations and lower tax rates that benefit the rich at the expense of the rest. While average people pay more than their fair share, the crony capitalists continue to accumulate wealth and power. Because of the increased consolidation in the past two decades, large corporations have improved their income and thus have been able to direct unprecedented financial resources into stock repurchase. As a result, share prices of large corporations have skyrocketed and those executives who are often compensated with stocks have received colossal financial rewards. Particularly, large technology firms rely on stock options as a larger proportion of compensation than other companies do. Consequently, chief executives have seen their incomes rise steeply, but wages for ordinary workers have barely increased. Maximizing returns to shareholders means paying out a larger share of short-term profits to the wealthy people who own stocks. Tech giants steadily have shown some of the largest profit margins and absolute profits, which are often the result of lack of competition [27]. Large technology companies can make a large amount of revenue with relatively few employees. For example, employees at Apple, Facebook, and Google each generated more than $1 million of revenue per capita in 2015. Cutting corporate tax on large corporations often favors the rich and penalizes the poor. Corporate tax cuts are responsible for much of increase in income inequality [28]. What is more, after the 1980s, large MNCs played an important role in reducing unionization across the United States. In 2013, the American union density was only 11 percent. It is widely accepted that unionization plays an important role in creating shared prosperity and lower levels of income inequality.

The excessive concentration of wealth can depress spending, demand, and economic growth. When wealth is more evenly distributed across the population, it provides a large number of people with spending power, which in turn would boost economic growth and wealth creation. There are some indications that extreme levels of inequality could lead to financial crises [29]. Extreme inequality implies that a large number of people rely progressively on debt to pay for their essential needs. As the levels of individual or household debt increase, the financial system becomes unstable. In other words, insufficient income creates unpayable debt that ultimately shakes the financial system. Extreme economic inequality dents social cohesiveness and reduces social mobility. Extreme economic inequality causes various sociocultural problems such as crime, gun violence, mental disorder, obesity, and health problems [30]. Simply put, economic disparities leave more people living in fear and fewer in hope. Empirical studies have shown that inequality has some negative implications for the health and well-being of people at all levels of income brackets [30]. For example, it is reported that the risks of infectious diseases and heart-related problems are higher in the countries marked by extreme levels of economic inequality.

The Rise of Emerging Markets' Multinationals

An important trend in the contemporary world is the rise of emerging markets' multinationals [31, 32]. China Mobile and Lenovo of China, Embraer and Metalurgica Gerdau of Brazil, Samsung and LG of South Korea, Reliance Industries and Tata of India, and Lukoil and Gazprom of Russia are becoming symbols of a new breed of multinational companies originated in emerging countries. They are expanding rapidly and leaving a permanent mark on global markets. The number of emerging markets' multinationals in the Fortune Global 500 list of the world's biggest companies is going up progressively. The emerging markets' multinationals are aggressively trying to catch up with their counterparts in developed economies and are making their presence felt in the global marketplace [32, 33]. According to the United Nations World Investment Report, in 2010 there were approximately 21,500 multinationals based in emerging markets [31]. Among the top Fortune Global 500 multinationals, there were 95 companies from developing countries in 2010, compared to only 19 in 1990. According to McKinsey, by 2025 some 45 percent of the Fortune Global 500 will be based in emerging economies [6]. Currently, the emerging markets' corporations account for over 40 percent of world exports and around a quarter of outward FDI flows [33].

Central to the rise of emerging markets' multinationals was the increased economic liberalization that happened across the world in the past three decades. The economic liberalization in China started with Deng Xiaoping's reforms in 1978. In India, it led to bureaucratic and economic reforms in the early 1990s and, as a result, reduced governmental intervention in the private sector [34]. In Europe, it was marked by the fall of Berlin Wall in 1989 and the subsequent collapse of the Soviet Union in 1991. The end of centrally planned economies in the Eastern Europe in the 1990s and the advent of neoliberal policies in Latin America and North America intensified further economic liberalization and stimulated market forces across the world, thus creating the right conditions for private businesses to enter global markets [35, 36]. At the same time, the relationships among world businesses were deepened by the formation and expansion of regional blocs such as the EU, NAFTA, ASEAN, and MERCOSUR. Because of the increased openness, companies and individuals gained access to overseas talent, technology, capital, and management practices. Large trade surpluses, high savings rates, and more importantly, less restrictive monetary policies strengthened the rising levels of liquidity and improved financing conditions for emerging markets' multinationals. At the same time, privatization created an "ethos of entrepreneurship," introduced the profit motive to business transactions, and encouraged a healthy desire for excellence and global competitiveness in developing economies. Many developing countries such as China, India, Brazil, and Russia suddenly allowed the accumulation of personal wealth and capital gains from business activities. Additionally, they took measures to promote outward FDI. For example, the Chinese government aggressively promoted the outward expansion of its firms in order to increase the competitiveness of its industries [36].

The most visible characteristic of emerging markets' multinationals is the accelerated pace of their expansion [37]. According to the *Financial Times* Global 500 List, the number of multinationals from Brazil, China, India, and Russia quadrupled from 15 to 62 in 2 years between 2006 and 2008. Thanks to organizational flexibility and innovation, emerging markets' multinationals are capable of competing with the well-established multinationals from advanced countries. For that reason, they often get rid of conventional organizational structures and instead implement flexible, global, and decentralized organizational configurations [37].

Many emerging markets' multinationals are directly supported by their central governments, enjoy strong political connections, and as a result have a political advantage over their Western counterparts. These political capabilities coupled with the high growth rates of their respective countries provide them with the required resources to expand into foreign countries [38]. The emerging markets' multinationals often expand globally, upgrade their capabilities in parallel, and usually enter developed and developing markets simultaneously. Emerging markets' multinationals are not big innovators; rather they are often imitators that copy intellectual property from their rivals in advanced economies. More recently, some emerging markets' multinationals are showing a move toward innovation and creativity [39]. The examples of innovators include Mahindra and Mahindra Scorpio of India, Embraer of Brazil, and Sasol of South Africa. It seems that emerging markets multinationals' innovation is based on developing countries' needs, constraints, cultural values, and customs. For instance, much of Haier's success is attributed to developing products adapted to Chinese customers.

The emerging markets' multinationals from Russia, South Africa, and Brazil have taken advantage of their countries' vast natural resources and those from China and India have capitalized on their large home markets and the availability of low-cost skilled and unskilled labor. Many Chinese MNCs were created as state-owned enterprises and are still receiving considerable backing from the central government, including privileged loans, incentives, technology, and favorable tax regimes. Emerging markets' multinationals have excellent capabilities in adapting new technologies and processes to developing countries' contexts. Ironically, the condition of being a latecomer in global markets might represent an advantage for firms engaging in international activities. In comparison with their Western counterparts, emerging markets' multinationals have a superior capacity to understand consumers' needs and preferences in developing countries, and therefore are able to target them more effectively. They are sensitive to variations in consumer habits caused by differences in culture and geography and swiftly adapt to local market requirements. For instance, the Chinese firms added features not found in Western products to respond to the customers' needs in rural China. Thanks to their sociocultural proximity with developing countries, emerging markets' multinationals also have the ability to manage uncertain, volatile, and even harsh business conditions of emerging markets. The examples include dealing with weak infrastructure, poor road conditions, health or security hazards, vague government policies, and erratic financial markets.

References

[1] Serafeim, G. 2013. *The Role of the Corporation in Society: An Alternative View and Opportunities for Future Research.*

[2] Hardoon, D., R. Fuentes-Nieva, and S. Ayele. 2016. *An Economy For the 1%: How Privilege and Power in the Economy Drive Extreme Inequality and How this can be Stopped.*

[3] Khanna, P., and I.B.E. Rodriguez. March/April 2016. "These 25 Companies Are More Powerful Than Many Countries." *Foreign Policy.*

[4] http://internetlivestats.com/google-search-statistics/

[5] https://zephoria.com/top-15-valuable-facebook-statistics/

[6] The Economist. 2016. *The Rise of the Superstars, Special Report*, September 17, 2016.

[7] Davis, J. 2015. "Capital Markets and Job Creation in the 21st Century." *The Brookings Institution.* www.Brookings.edu/~/media/research/files/papers/2015/12/30-21st-century-job-creationdavis/capital_markets.pdf

[8] National Employment Law Project. 2012. *Big Business, Corporate Profits, and the Minimum Wage, Data Brief.*

[9] http://nationalreview.com/article/388780/myth-corporate-profits-matt-palumbo

[10] https://ft.com/content/3e0172a0-6e1b-11e6-9ac1-1055824ca907

[11] Browning, L., and D. Kocieniewski. September 01, 2016. "Pinning Down Apple's Alleged 0.005% Tax Rate Is Nearly Impossible." Bloomberg Technology (website). https://bloomberg.com/news/articles/2016-09-01/pinning-down-apple-s-alleged-0-005-tax-rate-mission-impossible

[12] Wheelwright, G. September 25, 2016. "What are the Big Tech Companies Lobbying for this Election?" *The Guardian Website.* https://theguardian.com/technology/2016/sep/26/tech-news-lobby-election-taxes-tpp-national- security

[13] Allison, C., E. Fleisje, W. Glevey, and W.L. Johannes. 2014. *Trends and Key Drivers of Income Inequality.* Marshall Economic Research Group, University of Cambridge

[14] Roach, B. 2007. *Corporate Power in a Global Economy.* Medford, MA: Global Development and Environment Institute, Tufts University.

[15] Greider, W. 1998. *One World, Ready or Not: The Manic Logic of Global Capitalism.* Simon and Schuster.

[16] U.S. Economic Census. 1997/2012. Available at: www.census.gov/programs-surveys/economic-census.html

[17] Baldwin, W., and J. Scott. 2013. *Market Structure and Technological Change.* Taylor and Francis, New York.

[18] Mitchell, S. 2016. "The View From the Shop—Antitrust and the Decline of America's Independent Businesses." *The Antitrust Bulletin* 61, no. 4, pp. 498–516.

[19] Dayen, D. 2015. "Bring Back Antitrust." *The American Prospect* 26, no. 4, pp. 46–53. Available at: http://prospect.org/article/bring-back-antitrust-0 (accessed December 02, 2019).

[20] Tabuchi, H. 2015. "It's Amazon and Also-Rans in Retailers' Race for Online Sales." N.Y. Times, December 30, 2015, at B1.

[21] Francis, T., and R. Knutson. 2015. "A Wave of Megadeals Tests Antitrust Limits in the US." *Wall Street Journal* 18. Available at: FT.COM:https://ft.com/content/3e0172a0-6e1b-11e6-9ac1-1055824ca907

[22] Baylis, J., P. Owens, and S. Smith. eds. 2017. *The Globalization of World Politics: An Introduction to International Relations.* Oxford University Press.

[23] Detomasi, D. 2015. "The Multinational Corporation as a Political Actor: 'Varieties of Capitalism' Revisited." *Journal of Business Ethics* 128, no. 3, pp. 685–700.

[24] Sassen, S. 2015. *Losing Control?: Sovereignty in the Age of Globalization.* Columbia University Press.

[25] Kobrin, S.J. 2008. "12 Globalization, Transnational Corporations and the Future of Global Governance." *Handbook of Research on Global Corporate Citizenship.*

[26] Cerny, E.G. 1995. "Globalization and the Changing Logic of Collective Action." *International Organization* 49, no. 4, pp. 595–625.

[27] Chen, L. 2015. "The Most Profitable Industries in 2016." Available at: www.forbes.com/sites/liyanchen/   2015/12/21/the-mostprofitable-industries-in-2016/ (accessed January 20, 2017).

[28] Nallareddy, S., E. Rouen, and J.C.S. Serrato. 2018. "Corporate Tax Cuts Increase Income Inequality (No. w24598)." National Bureau of Economic Research. National Employment Law Project 2012, Big Business, Corporate Profits, and the Minimum Wage, Data Brief.

[29] Hacker, J.S., and P. Pierson. 2010. "Winner-Take-All Politics: How Washington, DC Made the Rich Richer–and Turned Its Back on the Middle Class." Simon and Schuster.

[30] Wilkinson, R.G., and K.E. Pickett. 2009. "Income Inequality and Social Dysfunction." *Annual Review of Sociology* 35, no. 1, pp. 493–511.

[31] Berrill, J., and G. Mannella. 2013. "Are Firms from Developed Markets more International than Firms from Emerging Markets?." *Research in International Business and Finance* 27, no. 1, pp. 147–161.

[32] Goldstein, A., and P. Pananond. 2008. "New Multinationals from Singapore and Thailand: The Political Economy of Regional Expansion." In *New Dimensions of Economic Globalization, World Scientific,* eds. R. Rajan, R. Kumar e N. Virgill (a cura di), pp. 209–249.

[33] Lorenzen, M., and R. Mudambi. 2012. "Clusters, Connectivity and Catchup: Bollywood and Bangalore in the Global Economy." *Journal of Economic Geography* 13, no. 3, pp. 501–534.

[34] Stucchi, T., T. Pedersen, and V. Kumar. 2015. "The Effect of Institutional Evolution on Indian firms' Internationalization: Disentangling Inward-and Outward-Oriented Effects." *Long Range Planning* 48, no. 5, pp. 346–359.

[35] Chen, P.L., and D. Tan. 2016, "Foreign Knowledge Acquisition through Inter-Firm Collaboration and Recruitment: Implications for the Domestic Growth of Emerging Market Firms." *International Business Review* 25, no. 1, pp. 221–232.

[36] Gaffney, N., D. Cooper, B. Kedia, and J. Clampit. 2014. "Institutional Transitions, Global Mindset, and EMNE Internationalization." *European Management Journal* 32, no. 3, pp. 383–391.

[37] Guillen, M.F., and E. Garcfa-Canal. 2009. "The American Model of the Multinational Firm and the New Multinationals from Emerging Economies." *Ke Academy of Management Perspectives* 23, no. 2, pp. 23–35.

[38] Cuervo-Cazurra, A., and R. Ramamurti. eds. 2014. *Understanding Multinationals from Emerging Markets*. Cambridge, MA: Cambridge University Press.

[39] Immelt, J.R., V. Govindarajan, and C. Trimble. 2009. "How GE is Disrupting Itself." *Harvard Business Review* 87, no. 10, pp. 56–65.

CHAPTER 8

The Inequality, the Wealth Concentration, and the Super-rich

The Rise of Economic Inequality in America

For most of the 20th century, inequality in the United States was flat or falling [1]. After the Second World War between 1947 and the early 1970s, all income groups, particularly the poor, benefited from the national economic growth and experienced growth in real annual income [2]. During this period, government policies were linking productivity to workers' compensation, full employment was a priority, unions were strong, and fiscal policies were equitable [2]. As a result, for much of the period between the 1950s and 1970s, inequality was either stable or declining. Things changed since the late 1970s when economic inequality started to rise rapidly. During the past four decades, the economic inequality has constantly risen, and currently, it has reached to the levels not seen since the late 1920s [3–6]. The share of American top 1 percent from the national income jumped from 8 percent in 1979 to more than 18 percent in 2007 meaning an increase of 125 percent. If we include income from capital gains in the calculation, the share of the top 1 percent of the national income reaches over 23 percent, implying a much sharper increase in the economic inequality [7]. Between 2000 and 2008 when George W. Bush was in the White House, productivity grew faster than ever, but the real compensation of all Americans except the top 20 percent was either flat or declining [2]. In other words, gains in wages benefited mostly the rich. In fact, over the last 30 years, the growth in the incomes of the bottom 50 percent has been zero, but incomes of the top 1 percent have grown almost 300 percent [8]. The top 1 percent of Americans control one-third of the assets in the United States. According to *Forbes* magazine, 492 billionaires in America own more than $2 trillion in different types of assets [9]. The median family income in the United States has been stagnant for over two decades. While the rich get richer, the poor are getting even poorer. What is more, this growing economic disparity is happening despite greater productivity per worker in all sectors [10]. The rich have distanced not only from the poor but also from the rest of society including the middle-class citizens. It is interesting to note that the United States is the most unequal member of developed countries. The data collected from OECD, a club of mainly rich countries, show that the United States is marked by the third-highest level of inequality. What is even more striking is that the U.S. tax system does little to mitigate the economic inequality [11, 12]. For example, tax rates on top incomes have continued to fall in the recent years. The top rate of income tax was 70 percent in 1980, but it is now 40 percent [13]. The rich not only accumulate wealth but also hand over some colossal assets to their heirs, and thus make the economic inequality even worse. Another trend in economic inequality is the widening gap between the privileged professionals, managers, and business owners and the regular white-collar and blue-collar employees [14] (see Figures 8.1–8.4).

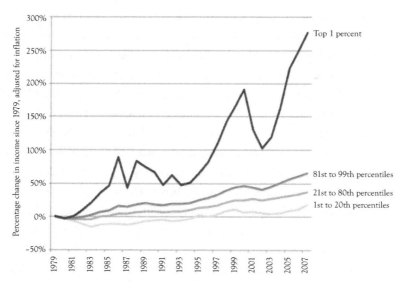

Figure 8.1 A historical overview of the distribution of household income in the United States

Change in share of total income, 1967-2012
relative to 1967, by percentile

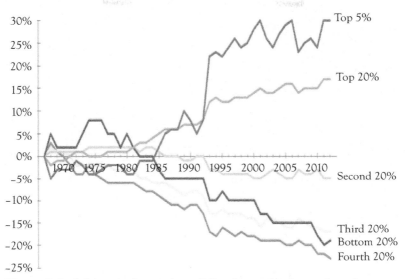

Figure 8.2 A historical overview of the change in share of total income in the United States between 1967 and 2012
Source: CENSUS BUREAU

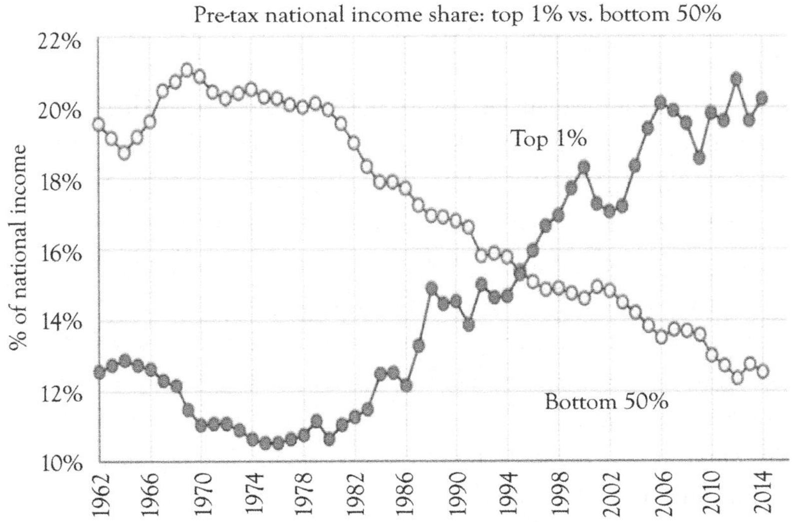

Figure 8.3 Pretax national income shares of the top 1 percent and the bottom 50 percent between 1962 and 2014

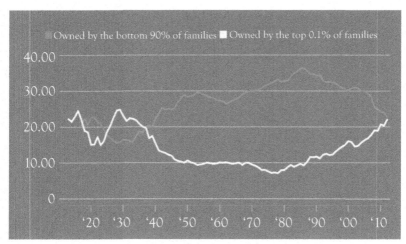

*Figure 8.4 The share of total U.S. wealth owned by the top
0.1 percent and the bottom 90 percent in the past 100 years*

Source: http://gabriel-zucman.eu/files/uswealth/AppendixTables(Aggregates).xlsx

The signs of widening economic inequality and the associated socio-economic segregation can be seen everywhere across the nation from cities and neighborhoods to public schools, colleges, and hospitals. It is estimated that about 50 percent of retirees will run short of their planned financial needs and might have to continue to work after their 60s [3]. The number of bankruptcies, mortgage foreclosures, and car repossessions skyrocketed between 1970 and 2001 [15]. Job loss, medical expenses, and divorce have been reported as the main factors that push the middle-class citizens to file for bankruptcy [11]. Most of the middle-class Americans have insufficient savings or are highly indebted. Compared to the early 1970s, Americans spend 21 percent less on clothing, 22 percent less on food, and 44 percent less on major appliances [3]. Many families are hardly staying afloat with two parents working [16]. They live paycheck to paycheck.

Based on a recent survey conducted by the Federal Reserve Board, almost half of Americans would have trouble finding as little as $400 to pay for an emergency [17]. The United States as the richest country in the world has the highest rates of poverty among the developed nations mainly due to the public and fiscal policies. The poverty rates of American children are on average three or four times greater than those of other developed countries [18]. According to the Federal Reserve surveys, the percentage of household disposable income spent on debt services including mortgage, auto loan, and credit card debt has constantly risen in the past 30 years [3]. The average household owes about $176,000 including $29,000 in auto loans and $17,000 in credit card debt. Furthermore, 44 million Americans are burdened by student loan debt. As of 2016, the total of student loan is estimated over $1.3 trillion implying that the average American graduate has $37,000 in student loan debt. To put things in perspective, it is important to mention that the median household income in the United States has fallen from $67,673 in 1999 to $62,462 in 2014, suggesting that the minimum income needed to be a middle-income household fell from $45,115 in 1999 to $41,641 in 2014 [19]. At the same time, the share of American adults in middle-income households has fallen from 55 percent in 2000 to 51 percent in 2014 [19]. The most conspicuous form of economic inequality is seen along the racial lines. Minorities including African Americans, Hispanics, and women who head families are particularly feeling the financial pressure. The typical white household possesses 12-fold more wealth than the average black household does. More than 61 percent of black and 50 percent of Hispanic households do not possess any type of financial asset, compared with 25 percent of their white households [14].

The Economic Inequality Across the World

The global distribution of wealth both among and within nations is highly skewed. According to the World Bank, those nations with gross GNI per capita of $12,476 or more are categorized as high income, while those with a GNI per capita of $1,025 or less are classified as low-income countries [20]. High-income countries constitute 16 percent of the world's population but produce almost 55 percent of global income [20]. By contrast, low-income countries that account for 72 percent of the world's population generate around 1 percent of global income. Most of the high-income countries are located in North America, the Western Europe, or East Asia. The very poor countries are located mostly in the sub-Saharan Africa and Asia. Due to high economic growth in China in the past three decades, hundreds of millions of Chinese people have been lifted out of poverty [8]. If China is excluded from calculations, it is found that international income inequality has increased significantly between 1980 and 2000 for most of the world's countries. During this period,

Latin America, sub-Saharan Africa, and most parts of the Eastern Europe experienced sharp drops in the level of their GNI per capita. Between 2000 and 2010, the income inequality between the poor and rich countries has been falling mainly because of the fast economic growth across the world and particularly in the low-income nations. Nevertheless, the absolute income gap between the rich and the poor countries has increased from $18,525 in 1980 to close to $32,900 in 2007 [20].

At the individual level, the world is marked by a striking level of economic inequality where 1 percent of humanity controls as much wealth as the bottom 99 percent [21]. According to Credit Suisse, the poorest 50 percent of the world's population collectively have less than a quarter of 1 percent of the global wealth [22]. This outrageous concentration of wealth is part of a long-term trend that is constantly aggravating. In the past four decades, the economic inequality within nations has been growing faster almost everywhere in the world. For instance, between 1988 and 2011, the income of the poorest 10 percent of people increased by less than $3 a year, whereas the income of the richest 1 percent surged 182 times [23]. The growing inequality within nations is not limited to the United States. In the United Kingdom, France, China, and India, economic inequality levels are at all-time high. In China, the top 10 percent of the population earns almost 60 percent of the income. South Africa is becoming one of the most unequal countries, even more, unequal than it used to be at the end of apartheid [24]. Across the world, the incomes of the top 1 percent have increased 60 percent in 20 years and the great financial crisis of 2007 has made the rich even richer [25]. In the years after the Great Recession (2007, 2008), the luxury goods market has shown a strong growth across the globe, indicating the growing purchasing power of the rich (Figures 8.5 and 8.6)

To figure out the level of economic inequality in the world, it is interesting to note that only "eight individuals" own the same amount of wealth as the poorest half of the world [26]. A typical chief executive officer of an FTSE-100 company could earn as much in a year as 10,000 Bangladeshi workers [27]. In Vietnam, the rich could earn more in a day than the poor persons earn in 10 years [28]. What is particularly disturbing about the distribution of wealth is that the children, the youth, and the women often fall in the poorest income quintiles. Due to an abject level of poverty, a large number of women and children are exploited by

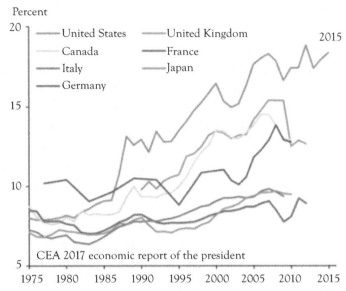

Figure 8.5 Share of income earned by the top 1 percent (1975–2015) in seven advanced economies

Source: World Wealth and Income Database.

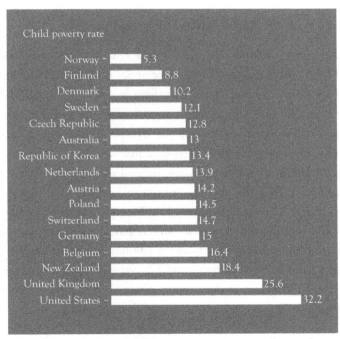

Figure 8.6 A comparison of child poverty rate among advanced economies

Source: www.unicef-irc.org/publications/pdf

multinationals and are forced to work under inhumane working conditions. For instance, the lowest-paid workers in the garment industry in Asia are mostly women and girls [13].

Many empirical analyses confirm that in the past three decades, economic inequality has increased in most of the societies across the world particularly in all transitional and postcommunist societies [29]. The majority of developed countries experienced rising levels of inequality since the 1970s [30]. Currently, economic inequality is higher than during the 1980s, and it is substantially sharper in the developing than in the developed world [30]. Relying on the Gini index, we find that Eastern European and the former Soviet countries have experienced the highest levels of economic inequality between 1990 and 2008. Moreover, across the world, the middle-income countries are marked by the highest levels of economic inequality. Despite some recent improvements, Latin America is categorized as the region with the highest level of income inequality. The patterns of inequality vary across Africa, but sub-Saharan Africa is recognized as extremely unequal [31].

The Causes of Inequality

The deepening economic inequality in the United States and across the world can be attributed to a wide range of political, fiscal, technological, and demographic factors. In the past three decades, technological development has increased the demand for skilled workers to the detriment of less-skilled workers, pushing up the income of more-educated workers and lowering the income of less-educated workers [7, 32]. Advances in telecommunication and transport technologies give a small number of qualified workers the opportunity to expand their local markets and receive higher wages and benefits [33]. Therefore, technology not only lowers the income of uneducated workers but also creates more opportunities for the educated workforce. In addition, globalization has interconnected the world economies and has put the less-educated workers in developed countries in direct competition with their counterparts in low-wage developing countries [7]. Another important factor that could explain the increasing inequality is sectoral shifts. According to this view, the shifts from agriculture to industry and then from industry to service in the past three decades have led to an increase in economic inequality [33]. One explanation is that the service sector usually has a lower union density than industry and manufacturing [33].

The cyclical nature of capitalistic economies and the recurring financial crisis often hit the low and middle classes hardest and bring them the highest levels of indebtedness [34]. On the contrary, the rich not only are immune to periodic financial crises but also can take advantage of economic downturns to acquire assets such as real estate and equities at discount prices. The super-rich have the sufficient capital to spend on the best investment, on the tax or legal advice, and on the estate planning. The wealth held by the super-rich since the financial crisis of 2007 to 2008 has been growing annually by an average of 11 percent [21]. Despite their donations, the super-rich exert a destructive impact on the society simply by pursuing the higher levels of capital accumulation. Both debt and fortune grow exponentially; once a fortune or debt is accumulated, it gains momentum and grows automatically. That is why the gap between the rich and the poor tends to grow over time unless some effective policies are put in place.

The economic inequality, particularly in the United States, is an outcome of government policies regarding minimum wage, income tax code, health care, education, and social programs. According to the Urban Institute-Brookings Institution Tax Policy Center, tax cuts that benefit the most affluent are one of the main culprits of the deepening economic disparities [2]. For instance, during the 1980s due to Ronald Reagan's policies, income taxes became less progressive. A few years later under George W. Bush presidency, some major tax cuts allowed the households with incomes more than $200,000 to receive bigger write-offs for their mortgage interests. The IMF reports show that tax systems in the United States and around the world have become gradually less progressive since the early 1980s, via the lowering of the top rate of income tax, cuts to taxes on capital gains, and reductions in inheritance and wealth taxes [35]. Indeed, many countries are continuing to reduce their taxes on the rich in order to attract more investment. The rich can buy the right to permanent residency in many countries such as the United Kingdom, the United States, Canada, Australia, and Malta with $500,000 to $2 million. In addition to tax cuts, the U.S. governments under Ronald Reagan and George W. Bush have taken measures to reduce the funding for social programs that benefit the poor such as Medicaid, food stamps, affordable health care, and more importantly education [2]. Education yields higher returns in advanced societies and thus plays an important role in creating a more egalitarian society. Nevertheless, the access to higher education has become even more difficult and more expensive in the recent years.

In general, the government policies have focused on fighting inflation and unemployment and finance has played a central role in the American economy. As a result, manufacturing jobs have declined, labor unions have weakened, and the link between workers' productivity and compensation has become less relevant. Workers' unions aim at maintaining consistent wage differentials between skilled and unskilled workers. Therefore, the rapid declines of unionization in the United Kingdom and the United States since the 1980s have contributed to the rising levels of economic inequality [36]. While many high-ranking managers have seen colossal rises in their revenues, wages for frontline workers have hardly increased. The big businesses continue to benefit the rich and deprive the poor of the positives outcomes of economic growth and wealth creation [13]. The frontline workers who are responsible for much of the productivity are not compensated proportionately to their contributions. By contrast, many chief executives receive generous compensation packages equivalent to the wages of thousands of their hardworking employees [21].

In an era of business globalization, low-wage workers across the world see their wages pressed by global supply chains where suppliers compete to provide consumers with the lowest prices. Using the new information technology, the corporations are able to closely monitor their workers, increase pressure on them, and squeeze down the cost of production. All workers particularly blue collars are facing harsher working conditions and less bargaining power as the proportion of the unionized workforce has fallen by nearly 50 percent in the past four decades [37]. Such savings are passed to the top executives and shareholders, while the ordinary workers do not benefit at all. In other words, the big corporations are enriching the rich to the detriment of the poor and thus are contributing to the economic inequality [8]. Furthermore, corporations use their connections to secure lax regulations and lower tax rates that benefit the rich at the expense of the rest. While ordinary people pay more than their fair share, the crony capitalists are accumulating wealth and power.

Though the rich are actively spending a lot of money to influence the political process, the poor often do not participate in elections to exert their most basic right as citizens. The rise of economic inequality has disappointed the poor and underprivileged voters [38]. For example, 9 of 10 individuals in families with incomes over $75,000 vote in presidential elections, while only half of those in families with incomes under $15,000 reported voting [38]. Therefore, American elections are becoming the privileges of the rich to elect those who protect their interests.

The economic inequality could be linked to culture, as some societies attach importance to egalitarianism, whereas others accept and even promote disparity. For example, there are significant cultural differences between the Europeans and Americans with regard to economic inequality. The Europeans tend to be more egalitarian and see the high levels of economic disparity with suspicion. By contrast, Americans fully support private ownership and tend to see economic disparities as the natural consequences of differences in individual talent and effort. These cultural differences may explain why the United States is ranked as the most economically unequal nation among the Western industrialized countries.

The Consequences of Inequality

On the one hand, the rising levels of economic inequality could create incentives for the majority of people to work harder to materialize their financial objectives and ultimately get richer. According to this premise, economic inequality leads to efficiency, creativity, and entrepreneurship. On the other hand, the higher levels of inequality imply that the rich are better positioned to take advantage of economic opportunities than the rest of the population do. As the rich actively aim at increasing their wealth, they use their power to create exclusive entitlements and privileges for themselves and deprive the rest of the society of similar opportunities in the job market, education, and investment. Extreme inequality necessarily reduces the social mobility, so if you are born poor, you will end your life in poverty. A society with highly unequal results is, more or less inevitably, a society with highly unequal opportunity, too [39]. Therefore, we may suggest that while a certain level of inequality motivates economic growth by rewarding hard work and innovation, the extreme levels of inequality could curb the economic growth and cause inefficiencies [40].

The concentration of wealth in the hands of a small number of people depresses spending, demand, and economic growth [41]. When wealth is more evenly distributed across the population, it would provide a large number of people with spending power, which in turn would boost economic growth and wealth creation [42]. There are some indications that the extreme levels of inequality could lead to financial crises [43, 44]. The recent academic research has shown four major paths by which inequality can cause the economic instability and financial crisis: (1) weak demand, (2) rising household debt and asset bubbles, (3) debt-led growth and international imbalances, and (4) financial speculation [43]. Income inequality often causes a sluggishness of demand since lower income groups do not have the sufficient resources to spend and consume. Extreme inequality implies that a large number of people rely progressively on debt to pay for their essential needs. As the levels of individual or household debt increase, the financial system becomes unstable. The debt-led growth in countries such as the United States and the United Kingdom fueled economy artificially and created asset bubbles that were essentially unsustainable. Furthermore, the concentrated wealth at the top generally is more likely to be spent in speculation activities that in turn could involve financial instability.

Wealth is power and, like any form of power, it causes corruption. The bigger the wealth, the bigger is the level of corruption. The rise of economic inequality creates opportunities for the super-rich to abuse of their wealth directly or indirectly. The extreme levels of economic inequality pose a substantial threat to democracy and the rule of law. Even in the democracies such as the United States, the rich spend large amounts of money on shifting the elections outcomes, lobbying politicians, and affecting the political process [24]. Joseph Stiglitz, a prominent American economist and a professor at Columbia University, examined the relationship between the financial industry and the centers of political power in countries such as the United States and the United Kingdom [45]. His analyses reveal that the conservative parties are highly affected by the donations from the financial industry [46]. In the U.S. elections, billionaires provide funding to influence the political decision making and support their favored candidates. Other wealthy individuals openly support some political causes and intervene in the political process. For example, the Koch brothers, two American billionaires, have exerted a significant influence over the Republican Party in the United States and have supported Tea Party movement [21]. Some wealthy individuals directly have run for office in countries such as Georgia, India, Italy, Lebanon, the Philippines, Russia, Ukraine, and the United States [9]. Simply put, the rich can buy votes. The elections represent the dollar values, not the voters' numbers. The impact of the rich on the political process is much more widespread in developing countries due to their weak institutions and rampant corruption. So, it is obvious that inequality has some grave consequences for democracy and the rule of law. A strong middle class is a prerequisite for a stable democracy because, when the majority has insufficient resources to support its demands, the cost of oppression is reduced for the rich [3, 44]. In other words, a more equitable distribution of wealth and property empowers the majority of the population to defend their legitimate rights through democratically established institutions.

The rich afford a better education, an excellence health care, and superior professional services. Thus, they are more likely to occupy higher offices and enrich themselves even more, while the poor flounder to make a living as they go deeper and deeper in financial obligations. The super-rich evade taxes by putting their wealth in tax havens or tax-sheltered accounts. They might also rely on secretive services or legal loopholes to dodge taxes and deprive the government/nation of their fair share. It is estimated that $7.6 trillion of wealth is hidden offshore in tax heavens [47].

Extreme inequality dents social cohesiveness and reduces the social mobility. In the past three decades, the social mobility has sharply fallen in the United States, so one could attain the American dream much easier in Sweden than in the United States [9]. Extreme inequality causes various sociocultural problems such as crime, gun violence, mental disorder, and obesity [48]. Simply put, economic disparities leave more people living in fear and fewer in hope [8]. Empirical studies have shown that inequality has some negative implications for the health and well-being of people at all levels of income and wealth brackets [49]. For example, it is reported that the risks of infectious diseases and heart-related problems are higher in the countries marked by extreme levels of economic inequality. By contrast, the health status of people in the more egalitarian countries tends to be better at all income levels [3, 50]. In addition, extreme inequality has significant damaging effects on the environment. Some studies have shown that the egalitarian countries are more likely to reduce carbon emissions and protect the physical environment [51]. According to a recent report by the World Bank, countries with more equal distribution of wealth enjoy a more sustainable growth [52].

The Plutocrats or the Global Super-rich

Beyond the top 1 percent of the richest people who are mostly multimillionaires, there is a new group of super-rich billionaires or "plutocrats" who are representing only 0.1 percent of the population. According to the 2020 Oxfam report, the world's 2,153 billionaires have more wealth than the 4.6 billion people who make up 60 percent of the planet's population [53]. Wealth continues to accumulate for the super-rich as their returns on investment often surpass economic growth. The distance between the super-rich and the rich (multimillionaires) has been widening fast for the past three decades. Ironically, the deepening divide is no longer between the rich and the poor; rather it is between the rich and the super-rich [54]. The gap between the rich and the poor is obviously very huge, but the one between the super-rich and the rest of the population is even much bigger. For instance, while the average earnings of the top 1 percent are 15 times the income received by 90 percent of the population, the average earnings of the super-rich is 124 times higher [54]. This is a major socioeconomic shift because the super-rich can put pressure not only on the middle-class citizens but also on the multimillionaires and on the rich!

It is estimated that half of the super-rich individuals are from the United States and the rest of the Western Europe or countries such as China, Brazil, Mexico, Japan, and Saudi Arabia [55]. The super-rich often originate in two parts of the world namely Western countries and emerging markets. According to the *Forbes'* 35th annual list, the number of the world's billionaires reached to an unprecedented 2,755 individuals who are worth $13.1 trillion, up from $8 trillion in 2020 [56]. The number of billionaires in Europe is estimated at 468 including 85 in Germany,

47 in the United Kingdom, 43 in France, 35 in Italy, and 26 in Spain with a combined wealth of $1.95 trillion [9]. Most of the super-rich have benefited from a combination of the technological revolution and globalization. The super-rich may consist of the technology elite in Silicon Valley, Wall Street financial sharks, Russian oligarchs, and investment geniuses [54]. The CEOs and CFOs are at the top of the list. Indeed, 40 percent of Americans making over $30 million per year come from the corporate and financial sectors. The recent revolution in telecommunication technology has been a key driver in the rise of the global super-rich who are often self-made, highly educated, and mainly young. The super-rich have the privileges and the abilities to effectively take advantage of the emerging social and economic trends and maximize their fortunes. Mark Zuckerberg, Elon Musk, Steve Jobs, George Soros, Jeff Bezos, and Bill Gates are the prime examples of those who detected the opportunities and responded quickly. For these entrepreneurs, the crises are translated to the best business opportunities. More importantly, the super-rich take advantage of economic and political systems thanks to their proximity to the centers of decision making. In general, the rent-seeking activities do not contribute any values to the economy but serve as shortcuts to wealth accumulation. India, Russia, Brazil, Mexico, South Africa, China, and many other emerging markets are the favorite places of the super-rich rent-seekers. For example, Carlos Slim, one of the richest men in the world with a wealth of more than $50 billion, built his fortune by using his telecommunication companies to influence and exploit the Mexican privatization process [54]. In the United States, the rent-seekers include bankers, hedge-fund managers, CEOs, CFOs, and all those who use their privileged positions to exploit the stock-market imperfections or to commit insider trading.

The super-rich have generally benefited from strong business connections, have studied at prestigious schools, and have accumulated their wealth in their youth. Most of them lead major charitable organizations designed to take advantages of new opportunities, to dodge taxes, to enhance their reputations, and to twist the rules and regulations. The super-rich aim at influencing the world and all aspects of social and even personal life comprising economics, politics, education, culture, art, and nutrition. Emboldened by their vast personal wealth, the super-rich are convinced that their opinions are necessarily beneficial to the society, are engaged in social activities, and seek to promulgate their own worldview. They purchase major news outlets and provide considerable funding for political organizations [9]. The Bill & Melinda Gates Foundation, the Chan Zuckerberg Initiative, and the Soros Open Society Foundations are examples of the super-rich organizations that are intervening in all spheres of our personal and social life. In 2015, Mark Zuckerberg and his wife Priscilla Chan vowed to donate 99 percent of their Facebook shares to "the cause of human advancement" [57]. Pursuing the cause of human advancement is a euphemism that could have many different interpretations. The political and social activism of the super-rich does not receive enough coverage and remains mainly secretive. As the super-rich get more powerful and aim at influencing different aspects of political and economic systems, they represent a significant threat to the democratic rule and the stability of our societies as a whole [54]. The super-rich, whether they are value-creators or rent-seekers, are becoming too powerful to be subject to an effective supervisory structure and legal framework. Simply put, the super-rich are changing the rules instead of abiding by them.

The Popular Myths About Wealth and Poverty

There are certain popular myths about wealth, poverty, and inequality that should be debunked as they continue to mislead the ordinary citizens.

The first myth is about the function of the market. In undergraduate textbooks, students often learn about the rule of supply and demand and make the false assumption that there is a wise and invisible hand behind every market; therefore, the market is always right and self-sufficient. Based on this assumption, some suggest that the role and involvement of government in business should be eliminated or at least minimized. Indeed, no market operates in a vacuum. Every market consists of different participants that affect the prices by their interests. During the past decade, we have witnessed how greed, fear, corruption, cronyism, and abuse of power have led to financial crises and led to government intervention [8]. If unregulated, businesses in the areas such as telecommunication and the Internet, finance and banking, health care, aviation, education, infrastructure, and public safety could severely stifle the small competitors and harm the underprivileged customers. The collapse of the American banking system in 2007 and 2008 pushed the Federal Reserve to hand out colossal amounts of money to the ailing banks and bail them out by the taxpayers' money [58]. If the markets were self-sufficient, then why did the government intervene in the market and bail them out? Some may answer that the American banks were too big to fail and their failure could have triggered a worldwide depression [59]. This argument refutes the principle of market self-sufficiency because it implies that governments should intervene in the market and regulate the banks by preventing them from becoming too big. At any rate, in banking, we need the intervention of government, either by regulating the banks and preventing them from becoming too big or by bailing them out when they are too big to fail.

Another prevalent myth about wealth and poverty is the idea that extreme economic inequality is justified because individual wealth is a sign of success and hard work. Despite abundant evidence, this wrong assumption is strongly supported by most of Americans [60]. Obviously, some degrees of economic disparity are normal as they correlate with individual success and effort, but extreme levels of economic inequality are the results of a dysfunctional economy where individual effort does not lead to success and prosperity. The super-rich gain too much power that can undermine the institutions, the rule of law, and democratic systems. Because of the extreme degrees of economic inequality, a large number of citizens are deprived of their basic needs such as a decent level of education, health care, training, housing, and nutrition. Furthermore, the extreme degrees of economic inequality reduce social mobility and affect the economic productivity negatively. The super-rich often abuse their vast resources to increase their wealth and influence. They continue to enrich themselves without any effort or value creation.

Another popular myth is the notion that businesses exist to maximize their profits at all costs. While the profit maximization is the raison d'etre of any business, it is important to pay attention to all stakeholders, including customers, communities, suppliers, and workers. No business is sustainable unless it has access to reliable workforce, institutions, communities, and customers. When businesses are involved in rent-seeking activities, they may excessively boost the shareholders' gains to the detriment of all other stakeholders. Therefore, the economic inequality rises as the shareholders and managers get richer, whereas the ordinary workers and customers continue to get poorer.

A false assumption about the concentration of wealth and economic inequality is the notion that business and trade are not zero-sum games and everybody can become rich. According to this perspective, we should not criticize the economic inequality; rather, we should avoid envy and instead focus on hard work. The fact of the matter is that everything including wealth is relative and business is essentially a zero-sum game that has some losers and some winners. The accumulation of wealth on the one side necessarily causes poverty on the other side.

Another prevalent assumption is the idea that minorities and women can become as wealthy as others do. In other words, economic inequality is not about race, ethnicity, and gender. As mentioned earlier, the minorities, women, and children are the main victims of economic inequality. In 2007, the median wealth for single women between the ages of 18 and 64 was $15,210 or 49 percent of the median wealth of their single male counterparts. Single women of color and women with children are in a worse financial situation. Despite significant progress in the recent years, there are enormous obstacles to the full participation of minorities and women. In many countries, women continue to receive lower salaries than their male counterparts do. Therefore, the extreme economic inequality is not a matter of effort or talent only; it can be affected by race, ethnicity, gender, birthplace, and zip code.

References

[1] Kalleberg, A.L. 2009. "Precarious Work, Insecure Workers: Employment Relations in Transition." *American Sociological Review* 74, no. 1, pp. 1–22.

[2] Tritch, T. 2006. *The Rise of the Super-rich* 19. New York Times.

[3] Littrell, J., F. Brooks, J. Ivery, and M.L. Ohmer. 2010. "Why You Should Care about the Threatened Middle Class." *J. Soc. & Soc. Welfare* 37, p. 87.

[4] Kawachi, I., and B.P. Kennedy. 2002. *The Health of Nations: Why Inequality is Harmful to Your Health.* New York, NY: The New Press.

[5] Piketty, T., and E. Saez. 2003. "Income Inequality in the United States, 1913–1998." *Quarterly Journal of Economics* CXVII, pp. 1–39.

[6] Reich, R.B. 2007. *Supercapitalism.* New York, NY: Barzoi Books.

[7] Schmitt, J. October 2009. *Inequality as Policy: The United States since 1979.* Center for Economic Policy Research.

[8] Hardoon, D. 2017. *An Economy for the 99%: It's Time to Build a Human Economy that Benefits Everyone, Not Just the Privileged Few.*

[9] West, D.M. 2014. "Wealthification in the United States and Europe." *Intereconomics* 49, no. 5, pp. 295–296.

[10] O'Loughlin, J. 1997. "Economic Globalization and Income Inequality in the United States." *State Devolution in America: Implications for a Diverse Society,* pp. 21–40.

[11] Hacker, J.S. 2007. "The New Economic Insecurity—and What Can be Done about it." *Harvard Law and Policy Review* 1, pp. 111–126.

[12] DeSilver, D. 2013. "Global Inequality: How the U.S. Compares." Pew Research Center. Retrieved December 19, 2013 from http://pewresearch. org/fact-tank/2013/12/19/global-inequality-how-the-u-s-compares/

[13] Rhodes, F., J. Burnley, M. Dolores, J. Kyriacou, R. Wilshaw, D. Ukhova, L. Gibson, and M. Talpur 2016. *Underpaid and Undervalued: How Inequality Defines Womens Work in Asia.* Oxford: Oxfam. http://policy-practice.oxfam. org.uk/publications/underpaid-and-undervalued-how-inequality-defines-womens-work-in-asia-611297

[14] Skocpol, T. 2004. *American Democracy in an Age of Rising Inequality.* The American Political Science Association.

[15] Warren, E., and A.W. Tyagi. 2003. *The Two-Income Trap: Why Middle-Class Parents are Going Broke.* New York, NY: Basic Books.

[16] Smeeding, T.M. February 20, 2004. "Public Policy and Economic Inequality: The United States in Comparative Perspective." Paper prepared for Campbell Institute Seminar, "Inequality and American Democracy." www.max- well.syr.edu/campbell/Events/Smeeding.pdf

[17] Gabler, N. 2016. "The Secret Shame of Middle-Class Americans." *The Atlantic,* pp. 53–63.

[18] Haughton, J., and S.R. Khandker. 2009. *Handbook on Poverty + Inequality.* World Bank Publications.

[19] Morin, R. 2012. *Rising Share of Americans See a Conflict Between Rich and Poor* 11. Pew Research Center.

[20] DeSa, U.N. 2013. "Inequality Matters." *Report on the World Social Situation 2013.* New York, NY: United Nations.

[21] Mayer, J. 2016. "Dark Money: The Hidden History of the Billionaires Behind the Rise of the Radical Right." https://amazon.com/Dark-Money-History-Billionaires-Radical/dp/0385535597/ref=la_B000APC6Q6_1_1/154-3729860-5160132?s=books&ie=UTF8&qid=1480689221&sr=1-1

[22] Credit Suisse. 2016. "Global Wealth Databook." http://publications.credit-suisse.com/tasks/render/file/index.cfm?fileid=AD6F2B43-B17B-345E-E20A1A254A3E24A5

[23] Hardoon, D., S. Ayele, and R. Fuentes-Nieva. 2016. *An Economy for the 1%*. Oxford: Oxfam. http://policy-practice.oxfam.org.uk/publications/an-economy-for-the-1-how-privilege-and-power-in-the-economy-drive- extreme-inequ-592643

[24] Slater, J. 2013. *The Cost of Inequality: How Wealth and Income Extremes Hurt us All*. Oxfam.

[25] Smiley, T. 2012. *Me Rich and the Rest of Us*. Hay House, Inc.

[26] Oxfam Calculations Using the Wealth of the Richest Individuals from Forbes Billionaires Listing and Wealth of the Bottom 50% from Credit Suisse Global Wealth Databook 2016.

[27] Calculations by Ergon Associates Using CEO Pay Data from the High Pay Centre and the Minimum Wage of a Bangladeshi Worker Plus Typical Benefits Packages Offered to Workers.

[28] Nguyen T.L. 2017. *Even It Up: How to Tackle Inequality in Vietnam*. Oxford: Oxfam. http://oxf.am/ZLuU

[29] Cornia, G.A., and T. Addison. 2003. "Income Distribution Changes and Their Impact in the Post-World War II Period." World Institute for Development Economics Research Discussion Paper No. 2003/28.

[30] Lakner, C. 2016. *Global Inequality: The Implications of Thomas Piketty's Capital in the 21st Century*.

[31] Ortiz, I., and M. Cummins. 2011. Global Inequality: Beyond the Bottom Billion—A Rapid Review of Income Distribution in 141 Countries.

[32] Alderson, A.S., and K. Doran. 2010. "How has Income Inequality Grown? The Reshaping of the Income Distribution in LIS Countries." *Inequality and the Status of the Middle Class: Lessons from the Luxembourg Income Study, Luxembourg*.

[33] Allison, C., E. Fleisje, W. Glevey, and W.L. Johannes. 2014. *Trends and Key Drivers of Income Inequality*. Marshall Economic Research Group, University of Cambridge.

[34] Streeck, W. 2014. "The Politics of Public Debt: Neoliberalism, Capitalist Development and the Restructuring of the State." *German Economic Review* 15, no. 1, pp. 143–165.

[35] IMF. 2014. "The IMF Finds that Reductions in the Generosity of Benefits and Less Progressive Taxation have Decreased the Redistributive Impact of Fiscal Policy Since the mid-1990s." *Fiscal Policy and Income Inequality*. https://imf.org/external/np/pp/eng/2014/012314.pdf

[36] Acemoglu, D., P. Aghion, and G.L. Violante. December 2001. "Deunionization, Technical Change, and Inequality." In *Carnegie-Rochester Conference Series on Public Policy* 55, no. 1, pp. 229–264. North-Holland.

[37] Statistical Abstract on the web site of the U.S. Bureau of the Census (www. census.gov/statab/).

[38] Freeman, R.B. 2003. What, Me Vote? (No. w9896). National Bureau of Economic Research.

[39] OECD Publishing. 2015. *In It Together: Why Less Inequality Benefits All.* OECD Publishing.

[40] Berg, A.G., and J.D. Osrty. 2013. "Inequality and Unsustainable Growth: Two Sides of the Same Coin?" *International Organisations Research Journal* 8, no. 4, pp. 77–99.

[41] Ford Company Report. n.d. http://corporate.ford.com/news-center/press-releases- detail/677-5-dollar-a-day

[42] Lowrey, A. 2012. "Income Inequality May Take a Toll on Growth." *New York Times* 16, no. 10.

[43] Martin, A., T. Greenham, and H. Kersley. 2014. *Inequality and Financialization: A Dangerous Mix.* New Economics Foundation.

[44] Acemoglu, D., and J.A. Robinson. 2005. *Economic Origins of Dictatorship and Democracy.* Cambridge University Press.

[45] Hacker, J.S., and P Pierson. 2010. *Winner-Take-All Politics: How Washington Made the Rich Richer—and Turned its Back on the Middle Class.* Simon and Schuster.

[46] Syal, R., J. Treanor, and N. Mathiason. 2011. "City's Influence Over Conservatives Laid Bare by Research into Donations." *Me Guardian.*

[47] Zuchman, G. 2015. *The Hidden Wealth of Nations.* University of Chicago Press. https://doi.org/10.7208/chicago/9780226245560.001.0001

[48] Wilkinson, R.G., and K.E. Pickett. 2009. "Income Inequality and Social Dysfunction." *Annual Review of Sociology* 35, pp. 493–511.

[49] Wilkinson, R.G., and K. Pickett. 2009. *Me Spirit Level: Why an Equal Societies Almost Always Do Better* 6. London: Allen Lane.

[50] Babones, S.J. 2008. "Income Inequality and Population Health: Correlation and Causality." *Social Science & Medicine* 66, no. 7, pp. 1614–1626.

[51] Grunewald, N., S. Klasen, I. Martfnez-Zarzoso, and C. Muris. 2012. *Income Inequality and Carbon Emissions.*

[52] World Bank. 2005. *World Development Report 2006: Equity and Development.* Oxford University Press, Incorporated.

[53] www.oxfam.org/en/press-releases/worlds-billionaires-have-more-wealth-46-billion-people

[54] Freeland, C. 2012. *Plutocrats: The Rise of the New Global Super-rich and the Fall of Everyone Else.* Penguin.

[55] Fuentes-Nieva, R., and N. Galasso. 2014. *Working for the Few: Political Capture and Economic Inequality* 178. Oxfam.

[56] www.forbes.com/sites/kerryadolan/2021/04/06/forbes-35th-annual-worlds-billionaires-list-facts-and-figures-2021/?sh=122d14aa5e58

[57] Mark Zuckerberg is Giving Away His Money, but With a Twist. http://fortune.com/2015/12/02/zuckerberg-charity/

[58] https://economist.com/news/schoolsbrief/21584534-effects-financial-crisis-are-still-being-felt-five-years-article

[59] Ingram, M. December 2015. "Mark Zuckerberg Is Giving Away His Money, But With a Twist." *Fortune.*

[60] Jacobs, D. 2015. "Extreme Wealth Is Not Merited." *Op. cit; The Economist.* Crony-Capitalism Index. http://economist.com/news/international/21599041-countries-where-politically-connected-businessmen-are-most-likely-prosper-planet

CHAPTER 9

The Global Health and Well-Being

Increasing Life Expectancy and Aging Populations

Astonishing increases in life expectancy in tandem with falling fertility rates are changing the world demographic landscape drastically. In the past 50 years, life expectancy at birth has been growing steadily across the world from an average of 46.5 years in 1955 to 65.2 years in 2002. This degree of improvement in life expectancy varies from 9 years in developed countries to 17 years in the high-mortality developing countries including most of Africa and Asia to 26 years in the low-mortality developing countries [1] (Figure 9.1). The improvement in human life expectancy started more than 150 years ago in Europe because of multiple factors including improvement in nutrition, housing, sanitation, hygiene, education, and the new advances in science and technology. Until the mid-19th century, the risk of death was high at a young age and, consequently, only a small proportion of people could reach old age. By contrast, in our modern societies, deaths often happen at older ages. In the recent decades, the health status of adults across the world has improved substantially and, as a result, the risk of death between ages 15 and 60 has dropped from 354 per 1,000 in 1955 to 207 per 1,000 in 2002 [1]. Despite all these achievements, there are significant gaps between life expectancy at birth in the developed nations and the least developed countries of sub-Saharan Africa. For instance, in early 2000, life expectancy at birth could vary from 78 years for women in developed countries to less than 46 years for men in sub-Saharan Africa [1]. In developed countries almost 80 percent of adult deaths happen after 60 years of age; however, this ratio is 42 percent in the case of developing countries [1].

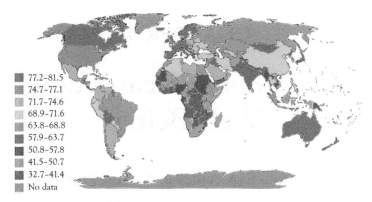

Figure 9.1 Average life expectancy across the globe (years)

Source: Adapted from Global Education Project (2004). Human Conditions: World Life Expectancy Map. Retrieved from http://theglobaleducationproject.org/earth/human-conditions.php

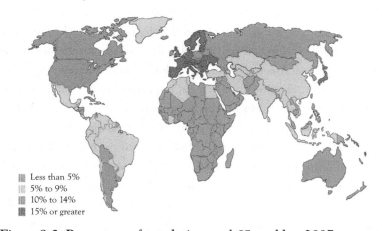

Figure 9.2 Percentage of population aged 65 or older, 2007

Source: Adapted from Population Reference Bureau (2007). 2007 World Population Data Sheet. Retrieved from http://prb.org/pdf07/07WPDS_Eng.pdf.

An interesting trend is that while the developed countries will have the oldest population structure, the fastest aging populations and the massive majority of older people will reside in less developed countries in the next four decades (Figure 9.2). Between 2010 and 2050, the number of older people in developing countries could increase more than 250 percent, compared with a 71 percent increase in developed countries [2]. In 2010, an estimated 524 million people were aged 65 or older representing 8 percent of the world's population. By 2050, the number of people aged 65 or older will triple to reach 1.5 billion or almost 16 percent of the world's population [3]. Since most of the longevity improvement is happening in the developing countries of Asia and Africa, most of the growth in the aging population is expected to be seen in such countries. In East Asia, life expectancy at birth improved from less than 45 years in 1950 to more than 74 years now. Consequently, China and India as the world's two most populous countries will experience the highest increases in the number of senior people. In China alone, the number of people aged 65 and more will surge from 110 million in 2015 to 330 million in 2050. Likewise, India's senior population will grow from 60 million in 2015 to more than 227 million in 2050 [2]. In addition to sharp increases in the number of people over 65 years old, there will be a global surge in the number of the "oldest-old" or those aged over 80 [4]. The number of the oldest-old is expected to rise from 90 million today to more than 400 million in 2050, representing 4 percent of the global population by 2050 [5]. By 2050, China could have more than 100 million people over the age of 80. The rapid aging of the U.S. population is so amazing that by 2050, the number of Americans aged 65 and more will reach 90 million or more than twice the number in 2010 [6].

The increasing levels of life expectancy and the swelling aging populations require that both developed and developing countries take adequate measures to maintain or improve the effectiveness of their health and social care systems [4]. The health-related consequences of these changes are various and may include increased rates of noncommunicable illnesses such as cancer, dementia, diabetes, and cardiovascular diseases, a potential shortage of health care workers/resources, and increasing numbers of people needing long-term care.

The Increased Incidence of Noncommunicable Diseases

As the world's societies undergo economic development, they see significant declines in the rates of mortality and fertility and improvements in life expectancy. Consequently, an epidemiologic shift happens in the pattern of disease and death. In the early 20th century, the major sources of death were related to infectious diseases that often targeted infants and children. Today, noncommunicable diseases that touch adults and older people represent a major threat to the public health. Nevertheless, high mortality rates from infectious diseases are still prevalent in less developed countries because of the abject poverty, lack of sanitation, and malnutrition. As these countries undergo socioeconomic development, they are expected to see lower rates of mortality associated with infectious and parasitic diseases. Therefore, a considerable trend in the contemporary world is the increased incidence of noncommunicable diseases in both developed and developing countries [2]. The main categories of noncommunicable diseases are related to older age groups and include cardiovascular diseases, cancers, chronic respiratory diseases and asthma, diabetes, and mental disorders. It is estimated that over the next 10 to 15 years, people in every world region will suffer more death and disability from such noncommunicable diseases than from infectious and parasitic diseases.

According to the World Health Organization, a variety of factors such as rapid and unplanned urbanization, globalization of unhealthy lifestyles, population aging, unhealthy diets, tobacco and alcohol addiction, and a lack of physical activity can cause the noncommunicable diseases. Furthermore, environmental degradation; exposure to air and water pollution; genetically modified organisms and new food processing techniques; dependence on smartphones; overconsumption of sugar, fat, and salt; and many other manifestations of our modern hectic lifestyles increase the risks of noncommunicable diseases [7]. Obesity is an important risk factor for many noncommunicable diseases and conditions, including stroke, heart disease, cancer, and arthritis [8]. According to the National Health and Nutrition Examination Survey, the prevalence of obesity among older adults is estimated at 34.6 percent in the United States [9].

In 2008, noncommunicable diseases accounted for 86 percent of diseases in high-income countries, 65 percent in middle-income countries, and 37 percent in low-income countries. By 2030, the shares of noncommunicable diseases in middle- and low-income countries will increase, respectively, to 75 and 50 percent. By contrast, infectious and parasitic diseases will account for 10 and 30 percent in middle- and low-income countries, respectively [2]. According to the World Health Organization, noncommunicable diseases are responsible for the death of 40 million people each year representing 70 percent of all deaths. Cardiovascular diseases with 17.7 million deaths per year account for most deaths caused by noncommunicable diseases, followed by cancers (8.8 million), respiratory diseases (3.9 million), and diabetes (1.6 million).

Noncommunicable diseases imply some serious social and economic consequences. At the individual level, noncommunicable diseases lead the patients and their families to poverty, pain, and bankruptcy. It is estimated that about 100 million patients in the world fall into poverty every year due to the costs associated with their treatment [9]. Many businesses and organizations are affected adversely as their workforce lose productivity or are eliminated. The World Economic Forum (2008) estimated that the emerging economies such as Brazil, China, India, South Africa, and Russia might have lost more than 20 million productive life years due to cardiovascular diseases in 2000 [10]. Obviously, the impact of all types of noncommunicable diseases in future will be much more significant as the number of the patients continue to grow drastically. The economic losses of noncommunicable diseases could reach $47 trillion in the next two decades hindering the economic growth and prosperity across the world.

Mental disorders such as dementia and Alzheimer's are other prevalent noncommunicable diseases that are affecting the lives of a large number of people and are often associated with old age. Dementia could have various causes and symptoms, but this disease is often associated with a loss of memory, reasoning, and other cognitive capacities [2]. Dementia, especially in its early stages, is difficult to diagnose and very frequently it remains undiagnosed and underreported even in developed countries. For that reason, the data about the prevalence of dementia across the world are not standard and reliable. Based on the Organization for Economic Cooperation and Development (OECD) reports in 2000, dementia affected about 10 million people in OECD member countries representing 7 percent of people aged 65 or older. Alzheimer's disease is the most common form of dementia and accounted for between two-fifths and four-fifths of all dementia cases. Currently, the number of people affected by dementia is estimated between 27 and 36 million across the world [2]. The prevalence of dementia is very low at a younger age, but it increases sharply after age 65. Based on the OECD studies, only 3 percent of people between ages 65 and 69 were affected by dementia, while the proportion for those between 85 and 89 reached 30 percent. Similar studies in

France and Germany showed that more than half of women aged 90 or older had some forms of dementia [2]. The studies by the Alzheimer's Disease International suggest that by 2050, there will be around 115 million people worldwide living with Alzheimer's or dementia [2]. As the world's population is getting older, the number of affected people is expected to put mounting pressure on health care providers, families, and governments across the world. According to the World Alzheimer Report, the total worldwide cost of dementia was estimated more than $600 billion in 2010 [2]. The cost associated with dementia is expected to rise exponentially, especially in low- and middle-income countries that have insufficient resources for mental health allocating less than 2 percent of their health budget to the treatment and prevention of this disease [7]. Most of the people affected by dementia eventually lose their independence and need constant help with their daily activities causing a heavy economic and social burden on their families and communities [2]. As families become smaller and people have fewer children, there will be fewer family members to look after elderly people affected by dementia.

The Risks of Pandemics

Throughout the history, the world has experienced devastating epidemics of communicable diseases such as smallpox, cholera, typhoid, and measles causing the death of millions of people. For example, an outbreak of influenza killed around 50 million people in 1918. Despite all the advances in medicine and public health, many communicable diseases still claim millions of lives. Malaria, tuberculosis, HIV/AIDS, bacterial diarrhea, and cholera are among the deadliest communicable diseases affecting a large number of people and causing a million deaths annually across the world, particularly in low- and middle-income countries.

Poverty may be considered one of the main causes of communicable disease outbreaks. In many developing countries, sanitary and hygiene standards are extremely low, and a large number of people do not have access to clean water. According to a report by the World Health Organization and UNICEF, a third of the world's population do not have access to adequate toilets [11]. Half the population of India or around 564 million people do not have proper sanitation and defecate in the open, excreting close to 65,000 tons of feces into the environment each day. The open defecation practice is responsible for 188,000 deaths of children under five in India each year [12]. The malnutrition due to poverty is believed to contribute to the spread of communicable diseases through deteriorating the immune system. Furthermore, low levels of education and literacy are directly connected to the personal hygiene. In short, people in undeveloped and low-income countries are more likely to be affected by all sorts of communicable diseases.

It is estimated that between 1.4 and 4.3 million people across the world are affected by cholera of whom 143,000 die every year. The Ebola outbreak in West Africa claimed more than 11,000 lives in 2014. Likewise, 36 million people worldwide are living with HIV/AIDS mainly in sub-Saharan Africa [6]. What is more, we are witnessing the emergence of new communicable diseases every year. For example, more than 300 new communicable diseases have appeared between 1940 and 2004. It seems that genetic mutations and human-caused changes in the environment are responsible for the arrival of new viruses and bacteria. Among the recently emerged communicable outbreaks, SARS in 2003, the bird flu in 2006 through 2010, H1N1 influenza in 2009, Ebola in 2014, MERS in 2015, and Covid-19 in 2020 have caused much harm and fear across the world and have received a good deal of coverage in the media.

The pandemics have always posed a serious threat to human beings, but for multiple reasons, the magnitude of their threat is becoming even more substantial in the recent decades. Industrialization, a massive urbanization across the world, a high density of livestock including pigs, poultry, and dairy cows, and the degradation of our natural environment have prepared a high-risk setting for the generation and transmission of communicable diseases. Furthermore, population growth, poverty, a lack of access to adequate sanitation, and lower health standards in many poor countries have provided an opportunity for a rapid transmission of pathogens. Above all, globalization and the increasing interconnectedness of the world's populations through travel, trade, and transport have facilitated the prompt spread of the new diseases across the planet. In the past decades, the volume of international travel has increased substantially and, as a result, people and products are moving faster across borders. The high volume of international travel can play an important role in spreading the communicable diseases across the world. Therefore, the risks and impacts of epidemics are continuously growing over time. Based on a mathematical modeling, a serious communicable epidemic could spread to all major world cities within 60 days and kill more than 33 million people [6]. It is evident that a virulent outbreak, in addition to its direct mortality, will have serious socioeconomic implications. The recent experiences with Covid-19 show, in order to fight or contain an epidemic, the governments customarily take measures to restrict regular activities and events, close schools and markets, and curb travels. In addition to the official measures, the panic of the disease may lead populations to limit or cancel their ordinary business activities and avoid public places. The fear of disease may have significant economic impacts even on the unaffected populations and countries. Unemployment, market collapse, economic recession, social and political turmoil, poverty, and food insecurity are other consequences of an outbreak. A morbid epidemic not only could claim the lives of affected people but also could paralyze the normal activities and functions of different societies, causing more death and damage, and thus creating a downward spiral in all spheres. Under these circumstances, the low-income countries that have insufficient resources will suffer the most.

The Upsurge in the Medication Expenditure

The global spending on medicines is growing around 6 percent per year and is expected to reach nearly $1.5 trillion by 2021. The United States is the largest pharmaceutical market, growing by 6 to 9 percent over the next 5 years. Currently, China is the second largest pharmaceutical market, but the shares of emerging countries are growing faster [13]. As a general trend, developed economies are gradually descending, whereas developing and emerging countries are climbing the rankings of medication spending. This trend has continued for the past decades and is likely to continue over the next two decades. The 10 largest developed markets for medication consist of the United States, Japan, Germany, the United Kingdom, Italy, France, Spain, Canada, South Korea, and Australia. Likewise, China, Brazil, Russia, India, Mexico, and Turkey are the largest developing pharmaceutical markets [13]. The global amount spent on medicines could double over the next 15 years. The drivers of such growth include oncology with $120 to $135 billion and diabetes treatments with $95 to $110 billion. Furthermore, biologic treatments for autoimmune diseases are expected to continue to see increasing usage across the globe and will reach $75 to $90 billion in spending by 2021. The difference between developed and developing markets spending is that the formers spend on original brands, while the developing markets are attracted to nonoriginal products [13].

Medications are already very expensive in the United States, but their prices are likely to surge even higher in the coming years. Based on a study conducted between January 2006 and December 2015, retail prices for 113 chronic-use brand-name drugs increased cumulatively over 10 years by an average of 188.7 percent [14]. The high cost of prescription drugs puts a heavy financial burden on health care systems, insurers, patients, employers, and providers. In 2015, the average senior American taking 4.5 prescription drugs per month had to pay more than $26,000 per year for the cost of therapy [15]. The prescription drug expenditure constitutes nearly 20 percent of the health care costs, showing a growth of 13.1 percent in 2014 [14]. In recent years, specialty drugs are rapidly gaining acceptance and popularity in the United States. Specialty drugs are difficult to administer and often come in injectable formulations. Originally, specialty drugs were used exclusively to treat chronic diseases such as cancer, rheumatoid arthritis, and multiple sclerosis, but in the last few years, their application has expanded to touch additional diseases. Specialty drugs are generally expensive and accounted for 36 percent of the total drug spending in the United States in 2015. Spending for specialty drugs has grown by 23 percent between 2014 and 2015, compared to growth of 7.8 percent for traditional medicines. Along with this trend, specialty pharmacies are expanding rapidly. Specialty pharmacies are intended to manage the necessary handling, storage, and distribution of complex therapy drugs [16].

The Rising Cost of Care and Shortage of Health Care Workers

Over the course of the next decades, higher levels of life expectancy and aging populations are supposed to put mounting pressure on health care networks in many developed and developing countries. As a result, the patients and governments have to spend much more in order to maintain the health care services at a decent level. In near future, the total global spending on health care is expected to increase by an annual average of 5.3 percent [17]. Since most of the societies are rapidly aging and the share of the economically active population is gradually shrinking, the higher expenditure on health care becomes a difficult proposition. For example, the working age population (15–64 years) in the EU will decline by 48 million by 2050 [18]. In addition to aging and the shrinking portion of economically active populations, the overuse of medical services, overprescription of medications, and advances in treatments and health technologies will contribute to the rising cost of health care services across the world. As new treatments and technologies are developed, the drug makers hike the prices and send to their patient's bills heavier than ever. Some pharmaceutical companies have increased the drug prices as much as 5,000 to 6,000 percent in the past three years [19]. In 2015, Turing, an American drug maker, bought Daraprim, a 62-year-old medicine, for a deadly parasitic disease and then increased the price overnight from $13.50 to $750 a pill [20]. Those people who suffer from multiple chronic and long-term diseases will face more difficulty in getting the health care they need as their treatments are generally complex and expensive [21]. Regardless of their health care model, most countries across the world will experience unsustainable spending on their health care services [22]. In developed countries, the increasing share of older people will gradually place pressure on the health care spending. In such countries, acute care and institutional long-term care services are commonly available, but the aging populations increase the use of health care services and the per capita expenditures. By contrast, many developing countries simply do not have acute care and institutional long-term care services and are establishing baseline estimates of the prevalence and incidence of various diseases.

As well, the increasing pressure on the health care networks will result in a global shortage of health care workers. A study by the World Health Organization (WHO) revealed that, in 2013, out of 186 countries, 118 suffered from a significant shortage of 7.2 million skilled health professionals [23]. Based on the same study, there will be a global shortage of almost 13 million health professionals in the next 20 years [23]. While there is an increasing demand for health care services across the world, the health care workers are retiring or leaving for better-paid jobs without being replaced [23]. To overcome the shortages of their health care professionals, many high-income countries rely on foreign workers to meet their rising demands. In England around 35 percent and in Oman, the United Arab Emirates, and Saudi Arabia up to 80 percent of physicians are foreign nationals. Obviously, the migration of health professionals from low- to high-income countries creates an acute shortage in the home countries [4].

In the Western developed countries, there have been major changes to the traditional nuclear family structure. In the past four decades, many Western societies have seen the makeovers such as higher rates of divorce and remarriage, blended and step family relations, unmarried couples, single mothers, and same-sex relations. Because of these changes to the structure of nuclear families, older people will have few siblings and less familial care and support. The burden of these changes is supposed to grow over time. For example, in the United States, the shares of divorced people for 65 and over, 55 to 64, and 45 to 54 are, respectively, 9, 17, and 18 percent [6]. This pattern implies that the level of family support to older people is expected to decline, as they will have increasingly fewer family relatives. The consequences of such changes to the family structure are more severe for women because unmarried women are less likely than unmarried men to accumulate assets and pension wealth for use in older age.

Toward the Globalization of the Health Care Sector

While manufacturing and many service sectors, including insurance, banking, investment, and software, have been globalized, the health care sector has remained largely local. There are indications that this is going to change. The increasing expenditure of the health care sector is pushing businesses, consumers, and policy makers to take advantage of globalization efficiencies, as no country has all the health care endowments. In the past two decades between 1990 and 2010, national health systems considered a variety of global solutions to their local problems, including the exchange of skilled workers, nurses, and physicians. For instance, the United States and the United Kingdom recruited a large number of Filipino, Caribbean, and South African nurses [24]. These exchanges were beneficial to both home and host countries, as the migrant nurses from the Philippines could earn up to nine times in the United Kingdom what they would earn at home [25]. Similarly, a large number of medical professionals and graduates in the United States were employed from low-cost countries such as India, Pakistan, the Philippines, and English-speaking countries. By some estimates, about 25 percent of the American physicians have received their training in foreign medical schools [26]. The globalization of health care is not limited to the United States and the United Kingdom. The health care systems in more than 50 countries, including Australia, Brazil, Sweden, Malaysia, and the UAE, are relying more and more on foreign professionals [27]. Consistent with this trend, global pharmaceutical companies are going global and continue to develop new drugs in multiple countries. As they are dispersing their research and development operations across the globe, more clinical trials are done in low-cost countries such as India. In the quest for more efficiency and lower cost, some American hospitals have turned to companies in Australia, Israel, India, Switzerland, and Lebanon to decode their CT scans overnight. Another aspect of global convergence in health care is related to the communication and implementation of best practices because the barriers among pharmaceuticals, providers, clinicians, biotech, and payers are lowered. As more advanced technologies are allowing a more efficient exchange of information across the globe, both health care providers and receivers are being affected. The global expansion of pharmaceutical companies necessitates some globally harmonized regulations and standards. Furthermore, health executives need information, metrics, and transparency to streamline decision making. This issue is of prime importance in countries with higher tax rates that benefit from universal health care because citizens demand more transparency about public finances and how their taxes are spent. The globalization of health care is in its early stages, but it is expected to significantly grow in the near future. The globalization of the health care sector creates huge opportunities for large corporations, but at the same time, it may involve major threats to consumers and national health care systems, including swollen costs, uneven or low-quality service, and unfair access.

The Digitization of Health Care

Despite remarkable breakthroughs in health sciences, health care services are lagging behind in digitization in comparison with other industries. The introduction of digital technologies is expected to substantially transform the health care sector in the next two decades. However, the digitization of health care may face major regulatory and economic barriers. Consumers' desire to use digital health care services is not always well responded by the industry. For instance, two-thirds of U.S. physicians are still unwilling to allow patients to access their own health records [28]. Nevertheless, the push for digitization is coming mainly from the rising cost of health services due to global aging populations and new treatment procedures. Even maintaining the existing level of service necessitates more efficiencies that are feasible only via digitization.

Digitization may involve two major transformations namely disruption to the location of health care and disruption to the type of health care [29]. The disruption to the location of health care involves moving care out of the hospital and put it closer to home. On the other hand, the disruption to the type of care involves more prevention and management of diseases rather than their diagnostic and treatment. Digital health care will focus more on the prevention and management of diseases. As a result, consumers will be responsible for handling their own health at home. These changes involve fewer visits to physicians at hospitals. Digital technologies will enable patients to monitor and track their vital signs and receive a virtual care consultation without leaving their homes. This degree of autonomy and self-sufficiency will tremendously reduce the cost of health care services. At the same time, digital health-related services are marked by higher accuracy, because they are data-driven and are likely to be more effective. Virtual care extends access in remote areas and may create a new structure for the health care system. As a result, there will be less focus on building new beds and more attention to developing digital services and improved access at lower cost. The digitization will lead to an emphasis on consumer-centric health care, thus enabling citizens to assume more responsibility for managing their health care. In this new model, consumers will play an important role in using digital tools to improve productivity by reducing the need for professionals. Moreover, the use of precision medicine, robotics, and medical printing will improve patients' health care services at a lower cost. Therefore, digitization is expected to create a major shift toward value-based health care where the gap between the digital and physical worlds is bridged. Data captured by wearable devices, mobile health apps (mHealth), and social media can be used to transform treatment. The global digital health market, including wireless health, electronic medical records, and telehealth, was estimated at $60.8 billion in 2013 and is expected to increase to $233.3 billion by 2020. Five fastest-growing segments of the digital health market include telemedicine, mobile health, electronic patient records, wearables, and social media. Among all sectors, telemedicine is the fastest-growing segment with 315 percent year-over-year growth from 2013 to 2014. Digitization may push companies to offer health kiosks and mobile applications where patients can video conference with physicians who can also access their personal medical records. For example, HealthTap, an interactive health company, aims at reinventing the health care services by incorporating both patients and doctors over the Internet via applications for iPhone, iPad, and Android. It has built a large network of more than 100,000 physicians and 10 million active users [29]. Similarly, Teladoc uses the telephone and video conferencing to offer on-demand remote medical care via mobile devices, the Internet, video, and phone [30]. More than half of the U.S. states recognize virtual health care, as they require health insurers to treat virtual care services as equivalent to face-to-face consultations when reimbursing their customers.

Toward a Personalized, Precise, and Robotic Medicine

Traditionally, medical treatments have been developed to work on average persons; however, the outcomes of treatment can substantially vary from one individual to another. A treatment that is beneficial to one patient could be ineffective or even dangerous for other patients. Approximately 30 to 40 percent of the patients take medications for which the negative effects outweigh the benefits. Along with digitization, advances in genomics sequencing, cloud computing, and analytics are leading to the rise of precision medicine, which aims at adapting medical treatments to an individual's genetic profile and lifestyle. In other words, personalized or precision medicine takes into consideration a patient's lifestyle, genes, and environment to improve disease prevention, diagnosis, and management altogether. Currently, we are at the threshold of a new phase of medical transformation where the new technological advances are allowing the development of targeted treatments. Precision medicine may offer digital diagnostic tools or companion devices. Consistent with this trend, the revenues of businesses focusing on genomics sequencing and data analytics such as Illumina have been soaring. The concept of precision medicine is widely employed to fight cancer by genomic-profiling tests [31]. It is estimated that 60 percent of the patients could benefit from genomics sequencing and data analytics in the next decade. More recently, the new advances in robotics have created multiple applications for medical purposes, allowing complex procedures in surgery. Such procedures not only will improve treatment outcomes but also will substantially lower the cost of health care.

Robot-assisted surgery is increasingly gaining popularity in the past decade. Robots enable minimally invasive procedures and thus reduce the chance of infection, pain, and blood loss. Often, robot-assisted surgeries benefit from faster recovery and fewer complications. Robot-assisted surgeries combined with virtual devices may allow surgeons to connect with their patients remotely. Surgeons can control the robotic arms while sitting at a computer console near the operating table. Currently, the global medical robotics market is estimated to be worth $6 billion and is growing fast [32]. In 2014, Da Vinci robots were used in more than 500,000 surgical operations around the world [33]. In addition to surgical operations, advanced robots may be used in a variety of health care services, including diagnostics and medication. For instance, the Chinese Internet giant Baidu.com is offering an application that uses voice recognition to make instant diagnostic suggestions based on a list of symptoms that users enter into their phones. The early diagnostic may guide the users or patients to the most appropriate health care professionals in their communities. 3D printing is another emerging technology that is becoming popular in personalized medicine. 3D printing is experiencing large growth and is expected to reach $12 billion in 2018 (Columbus 2015). 3D technology has been applied in different areas of health care, including hearing aids, facial reconstruction, personal prosthetics, dental crowns, and surgical implants. The advances in 3D printing are leading to new applications in drug production and medical devices manufacturing. 3D printing technology is often used to manufacture customized and smart medical implants. The main advantage of 3D printing is that the implants, prostheses, pills, and biological structures are becoming more personalized as they are tailored to individuals' differences. At the same time, 3D technology enables manufacturing within hospitals or health care facilities, and thus reduces long waits or expensive costs.

Nano-Medicine

Because of their unique properties, nanomaterials are receiving a good deal of attention from the health and life sciences. Many applications from cell imaging to therapeutics for cancer treatment and biomedical procedures can benefit from nanotechnology. Nanomaterials may gain functionalities by interfacing with biological molecules or structures and can be applied in vivo and in vitro biomedical research. Increasingly, nanomaterials are used in diagnostic devices, analytical tools, physical therapy applications, and drug-delivery vehicles [34]. All these developments have led to a new perspective in medicine labeled as nano-medicine. Nanomaterials can provide medications into specific parts of the human body, thus making the medications more effective and less harmful to the other organs of the body. Nanoparticles can be used to enhance MRI and ultrasound results in biomedical applications of in vivo imaging, as they contain metals whose properties are dramatically altered. Nanoparticles are useful in diagnostics and treatment of soft-tissue tumors because they absorb the energy and heat up enough to kill the cancer cells. The specific targeting will enable medical professionals to selectively reduce the overall drug consumption and its side-effects. Furthermore, certain nanoparticles may prolong the life and effects of drugs inside the body.

In surgical operations, nanotechnology can be used to build tiny surgical instruments and robots capable of executing microsurgeries on any part of the body. In other words, nanotechnology can be applied to perform minuscule, targeted, and accurate surgical operations, without damaging a significant part of the body. Nano-robots or minuscule robots can be introduced into the patient's body to perform treatment on a cellular level. The visualization and control of such surgeries will be done via computers and nano-instruments, which are expected to reduce the chances of a mistake and human error significantly. Furthermore, nanotechnology may be used to produce artificially stimulated cells in order to repair damaged tissues and cells. The tissue engineering capacity can replace conventional treatments, transplantation of organs, and artificial implants [34]. Nanorobotic phagocytes or artificial white blood cells using nanotechnology can be injected into the bloodstream to create a synthetic immune system against pathogenic microbes, viruses, and fungi. Nanorobotic phagocytes can fight the deadliest infectious without negative effects on the patient. They are more effective and faster than antibiotic-aided natural phagocytes. Similar techniques can be used to selectively destroy cancerous cells, clear obstructions from the bloodstream, and prevent ischemic damage in the event of a stroke [34].

References

[1] World Health Organization. 2003. *Global Health: Today's Challenges.* World health report.

[2] World Health Organization. 2011. *Global Health and Aging.* Geneva: World Health Organization.

[3] WHO. 2011. "Global Health and Ageing, National Institute on Ageing and National Institute of Health." U.S. Department of Health and Human Services.

[4] Scrutton, J., G. Holley-Moore, and S.M. Bamford. "Creating a Sustainable 21st Century Healthcare System."

[5] Bloom, D., and R. McKinnon. 2010. "Introduction: Social Security and the Challenge of Demographic Change." *Program on the Global Demography of Aging.*

[6] Dobriansky, P.J., R.M. Suzman, and R.J. Hodes. 2007. "Why Population Aging Matters: A Global Perspective." National Institute on Aging, National Institutes of Health, US Department of Health and Human Services, US Department of State.

[7] Jonas, O.B. 2014. "Global Health treats of the 21st Century." *Finance & Development* 51, no. 4.

[8] US Preventive Services Task Force. "Screening and Behavioral Counseling Interventions in Primary Care to Reduce Alcohol Misuse: Recommendation Statement." US Preventive Services Task Force Website. http://uspreventiveservicestaskforce.org/3rduspstf/alcohol/alcomisrs.htm

[9] Task Force on Community Prevention Services. Preventing excessive alcohol consumption. The Guide to Community Preventive Services Website. http://thecommunityguide.org/alcohol/index.html

[10] Schwab, K., and M. Porter. 2008. *The Global Competitiveness Report 2008–2009*. World Economic Forum.

[11] Billions have no access to toilets, says World Health Organisation report. https://theguardian.com/society/2015/jul/01/billions-have-no-access-to-toilets-says-world-health-organisation-report

[12] Eliminate Open Defecation | UNICEF, available at http://unicef.in/ Whatwedo/11/Eliminate-Open-Defecation The Outlook for Global Medicines Through 2021. 2016. "Balancing Cost and Value." http://static. correofarmaceutico.com/docs/2016/12/12/qiihi_outlook_for_global_ medicines_through_2021.pdf

[13] Healthcare, U. 2012. "Personalized Medicine: Trends and Prospects for the New Science of Genetic Testing and Molecular Diagnostics." United Healthcare Center for Health Reform and Modernization: Minnetonka, Minnesota.

[14] Safran, D.G., P. Neuman, C. Schoen, M.S. Kitchman, I.B. Wilson, B. Cooper, and W.H. Rogers. 2005. "Prescription Drug Coverage and Seniors: Findings from a 2003 National Survey: Where Do Things Stand on the Eve of Implementing the New Medicare Part D Benefit?." *Health Affairs* 24, no. Suppl1, pp. W5–152.

[15] Schondelmeyer, S.W., and Purvis, L. 2016. *Trends in Retail Prices of Brand Name Prescription Drugs Widely Used by Older Americans, 2006 to 2015*.

[16] Emerging Trends in the Specialty Drug Industry. 2016. https://elsevier.com/ clinical-solutions/insights/resources/insights-articles/drug-information/ emerging-trends-in-the-specialty-drug-industryWorld Healthcare Outlook, Economist Intelligence Unit. August 14, 2013.

[17] Commission of the European Communities. 2008. "Regions 2020." Demographic Challenges for European Regions [online], Available at http:// ec.europa.eu/regional_policy/sources/docoffic/working/regions2020/pdf/ regions2020_demographic.pdf

[18] Forbes. February 10. 2017. "Why Did That Drug Price Increase 6,000%? It's The Lawhttps." www.//forbes.com/sites/matthewherper/2017/02/10/a-6000-price-hike-should-give-drug-companies-a-disgusting-sense-of-deja-vu/#7484c92771f5

[19] Los Angeles Times. December 21, 2016. "How 4 Drug Companies Rapidly Raised Prices on Life-Saving Drugs." http://latimes.com/business/la-fi-senate-drug-price-study-20161221-story.html

[20] Deloitte. 2015. "2015 Global Healthcare Outlook." Common Goals, Competing Priorities [online], Available at https://deloitte.com/content/

dam/Deloitte/global/Documents/Life-Sciences-Health-Care/gx-lshc-2015-health-care-outlook-global.pdf

[21] ACCA. 2015. "Sustainable Healthcare Systems: An International Study [online]." Available at https://leaders.accaglobal.com/content/dam/acca/global/PDF-technical/public-sector/tech-tp-sustainable-healthcaresystems.pdf

[22] Global Health Workforce Alliance and WHO. 2013. A Universal Truth: No health without a workforce [online], available at http://who.int/workforcealliance/knowledge/resources/GHWA-a_universal_truth_report.pdf

[23] Mustikhan, A. 2002. Shreveport Times, July 10, 2005; "U.S. Ready to Absorb 3,500 New Pinoy Nurses." Manila Standard, July 23, 2005.

[24] Sison, M. 2003. "Philippines: Health System Suffers a Brain Drain." Migration Stories.

[25] Time.com. 2017. http://time.com/4658651/medical-school-foreign-doctors-study

[26] IFC Global Conference. February 16–18, 2005. Investing in Private Healthcare in Emerging Markets Conference: International Finance Corporation (IFC). Washington, DC.

[27] Munro, D. June 08, 2015. "New Poll Shows Two-Thirds of Doctors Reluctant to Share Health Data With Patients." *Forbes.* http://forbes.com/sites/danmunro/2015/06/08/two%E2%80%92thirds-of-doctors-are-reluctant-to-sharehealth-data-with-patients

[28] Christensen, C. 2008. *The Innovator's Prescription: A Disruptive Solution for Health Care.* McGraw-Hill.

[29] Lapowsky, I. July 30, 2014. "HealthTap's Video Chatting Doctors Want to End Your WebMD Meltdowns." *Wired.* http://wired.com/2014/07/healthtap-prime/

[30] Wieczner, J. 2014. "Thanks to Obamacare, Virtual-Reality Doctors are Booming." *Fortune Magazine.* World Economic Forum. 2016. *White Paper Digital Transformation of Industries: In collaboration with Accenture.* http://reports.weforum.org/digital-transformation/wp-content/blogs.dir/94/mp/files/pages/files/digital-enterprise-narrative-final-january-2016.pdf

[31] Foundation Medicine. 2015. Our Vision. http://foundationmedicine.com/

[32] Global Medical Robotics Market Outlook. 2018. *PRNewswire.* http://prnewswire.com/newsreleases/global-medical-robotics-market-outlook-2018-300077013.html

[33] UnitedHealth Center for Health Reform & Modernization. 2012. "Personalized Medicine: Trends and Prospects for the New Science of Genetic Testing and Molecular Diagnostics." Working Paper 7, http://unitedhealthgroup.com/~/media/UHG/PDF/2012/UNH-Working-Paper-7.ashx

[34] Abeer, S. 2012. "Future Medicine: Nanomedicine." *JIMSA* 25, pp. 187–192.

CHAPTER 10

Food and Agriculture

Global Patterns of Hunger and Undernourishment

The current trends portray a mixed and complex picture of global hunger and undernourishment. Despite a rapidly growing global population, the share of undernourished people has decreased across the planet over the course of the past decades. For instance, the world population has increased by 1.9 billion between 1992 and 2016, but the share of undernourished people has dropped from 18.6 to 10.9 percent [1]. The number of undernourished people has decreased almost by 216 million for the same period [1]. Most of the improvement in fighting malnutrition and reducing hunger was achieved before the 1990s, but since the early 2000s, the rate of improvement in undernourishment has slowed, and in some regions, it has reversed. In the past two decades, the main progress in fighting undernourishment has been concentrated in populous regions such as China, Southeast Asia, and South America [2]. Since the 2000s, the absolute number of people wrecked by hunger continues to grow [3]. According to the Food and Agriculture Organization (FAO) of the United Nations, global hunger is on the rise again, affecting 815 million in 2016 or 11 percent of the global population. The FAO of the United Nations estimates that the global number of undernourished people in 2030 would exceed 840 million.

The distribution of hunger varies significantly across the world. In 2010, almost 30 percent of the population in sub-Saharan Africa was undernourished, while the largest number of undernourished people (600 million) lived in Asia [3] (see Figures 10.1 and 10.2). The global distribution of hunger is so skewed that two-thirds of the world's undernourished people live in seven countries, namely Bangladesh, China, the Democratic Republic of Congo, Ethiopia, India, Indonesia, and Pakistan [4]. According to the United Nations, the world's population will grow by

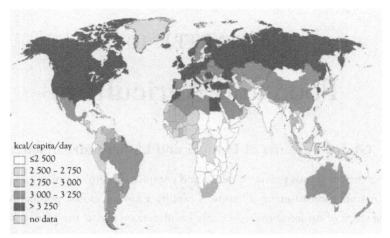

Figure 10.1 World food availability per capita (average 2009–2011)
Source: [5].

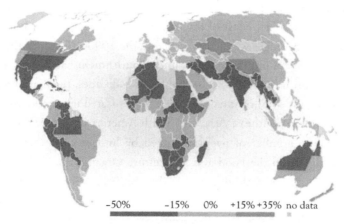

Figure 10.2 Projected changes in agriculture in 2080 due to climate change
Source: [5].

almost two billion people in the next three decades, and most of this growth will happen in sub-Saharan Africa and India. What makes the fight against hunger more difficult is the fact that most of the global population growth happens in extremely poor and undernourished regions. As rural populations grow much faster than employment and productivity in primary agriculture, the undernourishment in rural areas is more prevalent than in urban centers [2]. To reduce the associated undernourishment, governments and policy makers in developing economies should enable the transition of their economies to nonagricultural employment. However, this transition requires some significant instructional and societal reforms. In Asia and Latin America, a large proportion of the rural population is moving to nonagricultural jobs, but in sub-Saharan Africa, the share of rural labor employed in nonagricultural jobs is still negligible [5]. Some countries and regions, including the Caucasus and Central Asia, Eastern Asia, Latin America, and Northern Africa, have shown astonishing progress in reducing undernourishment. By contrast, Southern Asia and sub-Saharan Africa have shown little improvement in the fight against undernourishment and hunger. Therefore, Southern Asia and sub-Saharan Africa account for significantly higher shares of undernourishment in the world. The food security and undernourishment have deteriorated in many parts of sub-Saharan Africa, South Eastern, and Western Asia due to a wide range of factors, including violent conflicts, political turmoil, water scarcity, droughts, climate change, and more recently Covid-19. Recurrent extreme climate conditions and natural disasters increasingly cause economic damage and reduce agricultural productivity.

There is a vicious and reciprocal relationship between violent conflicts and the prevalence of undernourishment or hunger. Indeed, more than 60 percent of food-insecure and undernourished people in the world live in the countries affected by violent conflict. Most of the world's conflicts are concentrated in four regions: the Near East and North Africa, sub-Saharan Africa, Central America, and Eastern Europe. Violent conflicts disturb almost every aspect of agricultural activities and food systems from production, harvesting, processing, and transport to financing and marketing [1]. The causal relationship between undernourishment and conflict seems reciprocal. In other words, undernourishment can be considered as both the cause and consequence of conflict. It is widely recognized that food shortage is among the main causes of conflict. For example, the sociopolitical turmoil in many Arab countries in 2011, known in the media as the Arab Spring, could be attributed to food insecurity and significant surges in the food prices between 2009 and 2010. Likewise, violent conflicts and social turmoil in the Horn of Africa and Eastern Africa have been linked to lingering famine and food shortages.

In addition to acute undernourishment, a large number of people or almost one in three people worldwide are suffering from chronic malnutrition [6]. It is estimated that more than two billion people do not have access to vital micronutrients. The forms of malnutrition are diverse and are expected to involve serious risks. For instance, a growing number of the world population is suffering from the pernicious effects of obesity and diet-related diseases such as diabetes and hypertension. The occurrence of obesity more than doubled between in the last three decades between 1980 and 2014 [1]. More than 600 million adults, almost 13 percent of the world's adult population, are categorized as obese. In Latin America, almost 25 percent of the adult population is currently obese. The share of overweight people is rising in every region and most rapidly in low- and middle-income countries [6]. For example, the number of overweight adults in China is projected to increase 50 percent by 2030.

Growing Demand for Food

The global demand for food is expected to grow in the next three decades, driven by a significant surge in the world population compounded by economic growth and increases in consumption per capita across the globe, and particularly, in developing economies. While the world population growth has slowed since the mid-1980s, it remains at about 1.2 percent per year. Currently, the world population is estimated at 7.7 billion, and according to the United Nations Population Division, it is expected to increase to 9.8 billion by 2050 and 11.2 billion by 2100 [7]. Food consumption follows and often surpasses population growth, especially in the developing economies marked by improvement in the income per capita. The drivers for an improved income per capita include productivity gains, industrialization, better education, government spending on infrastructure, and higher levels of consumption [8]. Food consumption per capita has grown in the past 50 years from an average of 2,280 kcal/person/day in the early 1960s to almost 2,800 kcal/person/day in 2014. The Western industrialized countries reached high levels of food consumption per capita as early as the 1960s, but most of the gains in recent years are attributed to the developing and emerging economies [2].

Each year, the world population increases by more than 100 million of which the majority is in developing economies of Asia and Africa. Africa has the highest growth rate at 2.5 percent, while Europe has the lowest growth rate of 0.04 percent. As a result, most of the global population growth in the next four decades is expected to happen in Africa. Other developing economies, including India, Egypt, and Pakistan, will witness substantial population growth at least until 2050. By contrast, population growth in most developed economies is small or even negative. The significant divergence between the population growth in the rich or developed and the poor or developing economies implies that most of the future demand for food will originate from the latter, not the former. This implies that the demand for all major agricultural commodity groups will continue to grow.

It is hard to predict the future demand for food, but some estimates reveal that the demand for food may increase as much as 70 percent by 2050 [9]. In order to meet the demand in 2050, food production in developing economies should double. For example, the annual cereal production would have to grow by almost one billion tons and meat production by over 200 million tons to a total of 470 million tons in 2050 [9]. Because of the projected economic growth in developing economies, the demand for food products such as livestock and dairy products that are more responsive to higher incomes is expected to grow much faster than that for cereals.

In the past 10 years, production growth is accelerating for some commodities, such as oilseeds, cereals, and milk, while it is slowing down for other, such as eggs and meat [8]. Overall, we can say that the demand for all major agricultural commodities in the developed regions has reached a state of maturity or is growing at a moderate pace, but the demand in the developing regions of the world marked by high population growth is still growing fast. Therefore, the demand for most agricultural products, including milk, beef, and poultry, from developing economies is surpassing the demand from developed economies [8] (see Figures 10.3 and 10.4). The food consumption growth is expected to outpace the population growth for the major commodity groups, mainly due to the increasing income levels. The only exceptions could be meat and dairy products that their consumption levels seem either stable or decreasing. The beef consumption growth rate has dropped below the

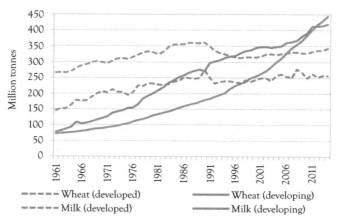

Figure 10.3 Evolution of consumption of wheat and milk in the developed and developing economies

Source: [4].

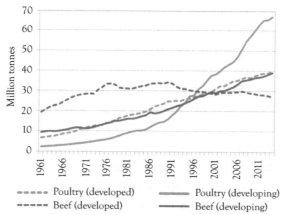

Figure 10.4 Evolution of consumption of poultry and beef in the developed and developing economies

Source: [4].

population growth rate due to a declining consumption in developed economies and rising prices that reduce the products' affordability.

Global Dietary Changes

In recent years, a multitude of factors, including economic development, urbanization, higher income levels, international trade, and cultural adaptation, have contributed to a dietary transformation across the world. Diets have moved away from staples such as cereals, roots, and tubers toward more livestock products, meat, milk, vegetable oils, fruits, and vegetables, in both developing and developed nations [2]. Consumers are adding diverse and more expensive foodstuffs to their diets.

In developed economies, consumers often can afford their preferred foods, and the effects of income increase and economic growth on their diet are generally negligible. By contrast, in developing economies, economic growth and increases in income levels are drastically changing the dietary habits. In these countries, as wages increase, consumers are more likely to pay for packaged, prepared, and processed foods.

In addition to economic development, urbanization may have important effects on consumers' dietary preferences. For the first time in 2007, the world's urban population has surpassed the world's rural population. According to the World Bank reports, the share of the world's urban population has risen from 30 percent in 1950 to more than 54 percent in 2015. Rural residents often consume traditional foods that are high in grains, fruit, and vegetables and low in fat; by contrast, urban residents tend to consume an increased intake of energy, sugar, refined grains, and fats [10]. As urban centers attract large supermarket chains, they make nontraditional foods more accessible to urban populations [11]. Furthermore, urban consumers generally spend less time at home, enjoy higher income levels, have smaller households, and conduct a busy lifestyle. Therefore, urban consumers are more likely to consume processed or fast food. In urban centers, foodstuffs such as bread, noodles, pizza, and pasta are popular, and meat, fruits, and vegetables are preferred [12]. It is widely accepted that urbanization stimulates the global demand for animal proteins, fat, salt, sugar, and refined carbohydrates and discourages the demand for fiber and micronutrient [13]. In addition to urbanization, international business, advertising, and telecommunication are pushing people from developing countries to adopt the North American and European dietary habits [14]. Consequently, the patterns of food consumption are becoming more similar across the world.

At the global level, there has been an increasing pressure on the livestock sector to meet the growing demand for animal protein [6]. Calorie and protein intakes have remained stable in developed economies, while they have been growing sharply in developing economies [8]. Meat consumption in developing economies has grown from 10 kg per person per year in 1964 to 1966 to 26 kg per person per year in 1997 to 1999 and may reach 37 kg per person per year in 2030 [15]. Likewise, the consumption of milk and dairy products in developing economies has risen from 28 kg per person per year in 1964 to 1966 to 45 kg per person per year in 1997 to 1999 and is poised to reach 66 kg per person per year by 2030 [14]. In developing economies, cereals, rice, vegetable oil, sugar, meat, and dairy intake are consumed higher than the last three decades, and the consumption of all animal products, including meat, dairy, fish, and eggs, is growing very fast [8]. There is a strong positive relationship between the level of income and consumption of animal protein [16]. Therefore, as the income levels across the world and particularly in emerging countries increase, there will be more demand for the animal sources of protein, including meat, chicken, fish, milk, and eggs. The increasing interest in meat and animal-derived foods may lead to food shortage. Furthermore, meat production generates more greenhouse gas emissions and causes other environmental damages such as deforestation, farmland degradation, and depletion of water resources [17].

The dietary changes and increasing food consumption per capita, combined with a more sedentary lifestyle, have led to the prevalence of obesity and a number of diet-related and noncommunicable diseases such as type 2 diabetes and heart diseases in developing economies [18–20]. It is increasingly common to see obesity and malnutrition or undernourishment next to each other in developing economies [21]. According to the World Health Organization, in 2014, more than 1.9 billion adults or more than 25 percent of the world's population was overweight. Almost, two-thirds of the overweight people now live in developing countries, particularly in emerging markets and transition economies. Indeed, due to the recent changes in their diets, many developing economies are facing the double burden of malnutrition and obesity at the same time.

Rising Productivity Gaps Between the Developed and Developing Economies

Throughout the 20th century, agricultural productivity has largely increased across the world, and therefore, the food production growth has matched or surpassed the population growth. According to the United Nation FAO, almost 70 percent of the improvement in agricultural productivity is attributable to increasing yields, while the expansion of arable land and increase of the cropping frequency has limited effects on the overall agricultural improved productivity. The noticeable development is that agricultural yields have increased mainly in industrial countries and China. Indeed, developing economies, particularly the sub-Saharan African countries, have shown no or very limited levels of yield improvement [14] (see Figure 10.5). In the past decades, the advent of new technologies has modernized agricultural production in the developed economies of Western Europe, Oceania, and North America. New technologies have delivered the means for motorization and large-scale mechanization, mineral fertilization, treatment of pests, diseases, and conservation and processing of vegetable and animal products in developed economies [14]. As new machines were used in agriculture, smaller farms were consolidated into larger ones, and the share of farmers' population declined substantially [14]. For example, the number of farms in the United States fell from about six million in 1950 to about two million in 2000 [22]. The agricultural sector has continued to become more effective by producing more crops with fewer workers and resources.

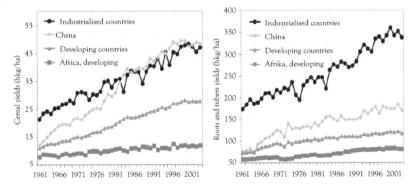

Figure 10.5 Yields of cereals plus roots and tubes in industrialized and developing economies plus in China and Africa, developing from 1961 to 2003

Source: [3].

According to the U.S. Department of Agriculture [19], in 2015, direct on-farm employment accounted only for about 2.6 million jobs or 1.4 percent of the U.S. employment. The agricultural modernization resulted in higher efficiency, thus higher volumes and lower prices of agricultural produces that became competitive in international markets. The transformation of agricultural production in industrialized countries not only liberated a significant share of workers from agricultural production but also provided abundant and cheap food that allowed consumers to spend only a small percentage of their income on food. In 2016, food accounted for almost 12.6 percent of the American households' expenditures [19]. In addition, the consumers in the United States and other developed economies got access to a larger variety of food products from meat, chicken, and fish to fresh fruits and vegetables, independent of season or their geographical location.

The modernization of agricultural production in developing economies has seen significant setbacks. In most developing countries, farms' sizes are usually small, the use of farm planning is not well established, and farming techniques have remained mainly simple and inefficient. Farmers in developing countries generally cannot afford the new agricultural equipment. Because in developing countries, a largely rural population of landless households relies on agricultural production, the arrival of agricultural machines and adoption of new techniques could involve adverse effects on farmers. With the rising competition in international markets, farmers in developing countries have to adopt modern agricultural practices, including the increased use of chemical fertilizers and pesticides. Due to the mounting competitive and international pressures, the farmers in developing countries are forced to concentrate on short-term returns from cash crops [14]. As the farmers emphasize cash crops, local food production declines and the developing countries become more dependent on food imports from industrialized countries [14]. In the early 1960s, developing countries were considered as food exporters and had a general agricultural trade surplus of almost $7 billion per year. However, since the 1980s, the net flow of agricultural commodities between developed and developing countries has reversed direction, and most developing countries have become net importers of agricultural products [2]. The improvement in agricultural productivity and falling real prices of agricultural products are certainly beneficial to world consumers and may increase the economic status of the urban poor in developing countries. However, the abundance of food products due to increased price competition may harm developing countries whose populations traditionally remain dependent on agricultural production to survive [14].

Emerging Techniques in Agriculture and Food Production

The food production is being reshaped by certain emerging technologies in areas such as biology, materials science, seasonal forecasting, and computer science. Agricultural biotechnologies range from low-tech approaches, including artificial insemination, fermentation techniques, and bio-fertilizers, to high-tech approaches and advanced DNA-based methods like genetically modified organisms [23]. The emerging techniques in biological science will deliver crops, pastures, and animals, which could provide higher-value products, including cereals with enhanced health attributes, novel aquaculture breeds and feeds, and designed plants with bio-industrial applications. Modern genetics can improve agricultural productivity, natural resource management, and consumer demand. The emerging genomic techniques can be used to develop more effective farming methods for the dry tropics, shifting crop and animal production systems into new climatic zones, and improved resource-use efficiency across all agricultural systems. The advances in biotechnology may result in the creation of new types of animals and plants that can more effectively supply nutrients. Many new food products may be created directly from genetic manipulation or laboratory processes. Currently, it is possible to produce in vitro meat or the meat cultured directly in a lab. While no cultured meat has been produced for public consumption yet, this product is likely to gain economic justification and consumers' acceptance in the future.

Along with biotechnology, the advances in materials science offer custom design of special ingredients and supplies for agricultural applications, including fertilizer formulations, seed coatings, and germination control. Nanotechnology-based food and health products will be gradually available to consumers worldwide in the coming years [23]. Nanotechnology could not only increase soil fertility but also develop innovative products and applications for agriculture, water treatment, food production, processing, preservation, and packaging [24]. Nanotechnology may be used to control how food looks, tastes, and even how long it lasts. The new information technology could lead to significant improvements in farming automation. In future, the digital farming platforms will allow farmers to use a wide range of robotics, including automated aerial and ground vehicles, drones, and associated intelligent software and data analytics for crops, automated milking, herding and sampling, and animal production systems. Consequently, farmers can boost their productivity, save on the cost of labor, and plan for their operations. The digital technologies such as computational decision and analytics tools, the cloud, sensors, and robots enable farmers to effectively utilize their data and optimize their production [25]. Agriculture will greatly benefit from increases in a better understanding of climate, improvements in observations, modeling techniques, and computer speed that will make seasonal forecasting more accurate. Farmers may rely on satellite imagery and advanced sensors to optimize returns on inputs. Crop imagery may help farmers scan crops as if they are present on the ground. By integrating sensors with satellite imagery, farmers can manage crop, soil, and water more effectively and conveniently. Technologies such as global positioning systems (GPS), geographical information systems, precision soil sampling, proximal and remote spectroscopic sensing, robots, unmanned aerial vehicles, and auto-steered and guided equipment can help farmers substantially increase their productivity [25]. Agricultural robots may be used to automate agricultural processes, such as harvesting, fruit picking, plowing, soil maintenance, weeding, planting, and irrigation. Soil and water sensors can identify moisture and nitrogen levels, so farmers can use this information to determine when to water and fertilize their lands. Some new irrigation technologies can improve crop yields by 30 percent over crops grown without irrigation. Because most developing economies are still relying on traditional irrigation approaches, advanced irrigation technologies may result in significant increases in the agricultural output across the world [17]. The use of protected and greenhouse cultivation is a growing trend in agricultural production that can improve both the quality and quantity of crops. Currently, Spain, the Netherlands, and Israel are the leaders in protected and greenhouse cultivation [24]. Vertical farming could allow farmers to produce food in vertically stacked layers, for instance, in dense areas or within urban environments. All these technological advances will usher farmers into a new digital agriculture very like manufacturing and service sectors. Thus, a nation's agricultural productivity will depend even more on its technological competitiveness and innovation capacity.

Limited Arable Land and Application of Fertilizers

The total world's land area is estimated about 130.7 million km², of which only less than half is arable [26]. The bad news is that almost all of the world's arable land has been already exploited, and significant increases in arable land are practically impossible. A further expansion of arable land may include forests and grasslands or those lands that are too steep, too dry, or too wet. For instance, about 80 percent of deforestation in the past decades has been attributed to developing arable lands [26]. Obviously, deforestation is not a viable solution as it causes many environmental problems, including loss of biodiversity and emission of greenhouse gases. While the expansion of arable land is not feasible, the existing agricultural land areas are gradually becoming less productive due to soil erosion, salinization, waterlogging, urbanization, nutrient depletion, overcultivation, overgrazing, and soil compaction. Soil erosion is the most serious cause of arable land degradation that is associated with agricultural malpractices leaving the soil surface without vegetative cover for an extended period of time and exposing it to the effects of wind and rain [14]. Due to its noxious effects, land degradation should be considered a major threat to food security [27].

In the past few decades, the widespread application of nitrogen-based fertilizers has resulted in securing more agricultural products for the world's growing population, but at the same time, it has caused an accumulation of huge amounts of reactive nitrogen in the soil and natural environment. Increases in reactive nitrogen in the atmosphere are linked to the production of tropospheric ozone and aerosols that affect human health and cause respiratory diseases, cancer, and cardiac diseases. Furthermore, the increased levels of reactive nitrogen may bring about water acidification, biodiversity losses in lakes, habitat degradation in coastal ecosystems, global climate change, and stratospheric ozone depletion [14, 29]. In addition to nitrogen-based fertilizers, agricultural pesticides involve serious toxic effects on the environment. For example, agricultural pesticides may enter surface and groundwater and may be toxic to aquatic organisms, as well as to terrestrial flora and fauna [29]. While the use of pesticides and fertilizers may be harmful to humans and the environment, in many developing regions of the world like Africa, India, and Central America, these chemicals are still underused. Therefore, we can predict that, at the global level, the use of fertilizers such as nitrogen, phosphate, and potash along with their perverse effects will continue to increase in the near future.

Consolidation of Food Production and Distribution Systems

In recent years, the agricultural industry has undergone significant transformations, including the standardization of output, concentration of primary production, and consolidation of farmland [23]. Small landowners have left their farmlands in search of employment and opportunities in large cities. At the same time, food production is changing along with retail channels, and thus, value chains are becoming vertical, marked by the integration of primary production, processing, and distribution. Due to their limitations in financing, market accessibility, transport, and quality, many small- and medium-sized businesses are giving up, and they cannot compete with big players anymore. Food producers are increasingly relying on automation, large-scale processing, and higher levels of capital to boost their output [23]. Because of these trends, the share of fresh food has been declining across the world. For instance, the share of fresh food has remained below 30 percent in upper-middle-income countries and around 10 percent in lower-middle-income countries [23]. In many developed and developing economies, a large number of urbanized consumers are relying on a few supermarket chains to purchase their groceries. The food industry is particularly consolidated in North America where hypermarkets account for more than 93 percent of the food purchase. This pattern is quickly spreading to other parts of the world. The shares of hypermarkets in food distribution in Europe, Latin America, Middle East, and Africa and Asia are estimated, respectively, at 55, 46, 38, and 36 percent [23]. The consolidated and large-scale food producers could help increase the convenience and efficiency of food delivery systems. At the same time, they are likely to introduce processed food products that contain higher levels of sugar, fat, and salt. The share of processed food rose between 2000 and 2014 across the world in low-, middle-, and high-income countries. The significant rise in overweight, obesity, and diet-related noncommunicable diseases across the world confirms the adverse effects of large-scale food producers and distributors on consumers' health.

References

[1] Marx, A. 2015. *The State of Food Insecurity in the World: Meeting the 2015 International Hunger Targets: Taking Stock of Uneven Progress.* Rome: Food and Agriculture Organization of the United Nations.

[2] Wik, M., P Pingali, and S. Brocai. 2008. *Global Agricultural Performance: Past Trends and Future Prospects.*

[3] Giovannucci, D., S.J. Scherr, D. Nierenberg, C. Hebebrand, J. Shapiro, J. Milder, and K. Wheeler. 2012. *Food and Agriculture: The Future of Sustainability.*

[4] FAO. September 14, 2010. http://fao.org/news/story/en/item/45210/icode/

[5] FAO, U. December, 2009. *How to Feed the World in 2050.* In Rome: High-Level Expert Forum.

[6] Vasileska, A., and G. Rechkoska. 2012. "Global and Regional Food Consumption Patterns and Trends." *Procedia-Social and Behavioral Sciences* 44, pp. 363–369.

[7] Desa, U. 2015. "World Population Prospects: The 2015 Revision, Key Findings, and Advance Tables." Working Paper No. ESA/P/WP. 241.

[8] Kearney, J. 2010. "Food Consumption Trends and Drivers." *Philosophical Transactions of the Royal Society of London B: Biological Sciences* 365, no. 1554, pp. 2793–2807.

[9] Alexandratos, N., and J. Bruinsma. 2012. *World Agriculture Towards 2030/2050: The 2012 Revision* 3, 12 vols. FAO, Rome: ESA Working paper.

[10] Hoffman, D.J. 2001. "Obesity in Developing Countries: Causes and Implications." *Food Nutrition and Agriculture* 28, pp. 35–44.

[11] Pingali, P. 2007. "Westernization of Asian Diets and the Transformation of Food Systems: Implications for Research and Policy." *Food Policy* 32, no. 3, pp. 281–298.

[12] Regmi, A., and J. Dyck. 2001. "Effects of Urbanization on Global Food Demand." *Changing the Structure of Global Food Consumption and Trade,* pp. 23–30.

[13] Popkin, B. 2000. "Urbanization and the Nutrition Transition. Policy Brief 7 of 10." *Focus* 3. Achieving Urban Food and Nutrition Security in the Developing World.

[14] Knudsen, M.T., N. Halberg, J.E. Olesen, J. Byrne, V. Iyer, and N. Toly. 2006. "Global Trends in Agriculture and Food Systems." *In Global Development of Organic Agriculture-Challenges and Prospects,* pp. 1–48. CABI Publishing.

[15] FAO, R. 2006. "Prospects for Food, Nutrition, Agriculture, and Major Commodity Groups." *World Agriculture: Towards,* 2030, 2050.

[16] Nishida, C., R. Uauy, S. Kumanyika, and P Shetty. 2004. "The Joint WHO/FAO Expert Consultation on Diet, Nutrition and the Prevention of Chronic Diseases: Process, Product and Policy Implications." *Public Health Nutrition* 7, no. 1a, pp. 245–250.

[17] Food Scarcity-Trends, Challenges, Solutions. http://saiplatform.org/uploads/Modules/Library/Dexia%20AM%20Research%20Food%20Scarcity.pdf

[18] Boutayeb, A., and S. Boutayeb. 2005. "The Burden of Noncommunicable Diseases in Developing Countries." *International Journal for Equity in Health* 4, no. 1, p. 2.

[19] https://ers.usda.gov/data-products/ag-and-food-statistics-charting-the-essentials/ag-and-food-sectors-and-the-economy/

[20] Prentice, A.M. 2005. "The Emerging Epidemic of Obesity in Developing Countries." *International Journal of Epidemiology* 35, no. 1, pp. 93–99.

[21] Doak, C.M., L.S.Adair, C. Monteiro, and B.M. Popkin. 2000. "Overweight and Underweight Coexist within Households in Brazil, China, and Russia." *The Journal of Nutrition* 130, no. 12, pp. 2965–2971.

[22] Pretty, J. 2002. "People, Livelihoods and Collective Action in Biodiversity Management." *Biodiversity, Sustainability, and Human com.*

[23] Global Panel on Agriculture and Food Systems for Nutrition. 2016.

[24] The Future Trends of Food and Challenges. 2017. *Food and Agriculture Organization of the United Nations Rome.*

[25] Van Es, H., and J. Woodard. n.d. *Innovation in Agriculture and Food Systems in the Digital Age.*

[26] Kendall, H.W., and D. Pimentel. 1994. "Constraints on the Expansion of the Global Food Supply." *Ambio,* pp. 198–205.

[27] Breman, H., J.R. Groot, and H. van Keulen. 2001. "Resource Limitations in Sahelian Agriculture." *Global Environmental Change* 11, no. 1, pp. 59–68.

[28] Wolfe, A. H., and J.A. Patz. 2002. "Reactive Nitrogen and Human Health: Acute and Long-Term Implications." *Ambio: A Journal of the Human Environment* 31, no. 2, pp. 120–125.

[29] Environmental Indicators for Agriculture. 2001. "Methods and Results." *Agriculture and Food* 400, 3 Vols. France: OECD Publications Service.

CHAPTER 11

The Sharing Economy

Rise of Sharing Economy

Sharing economy or the collaborative economy is an important global trend that is leading us beyond what we have experienced as consumers, workers, owners, and communities. It is based on our ability to share our possessions, services, and needs. It affects many industries, including hospitality, tourism, transport, and lending. More importantly, sharing economy is driven by multiple technological, social, cultural, and economic forces. As Amazon.com and eBay capitalized on the connectivity of the Internet to create e-commerce business models in the 1990s, some companies such as Uber and Airbnb are currently harnessing the convenience of mobile technologies and wireless connectivity to construct new business patterns. By analogy, we may suggest that as Amazon. com and eBay revolutionized the meaning of retail, logistics, reading, and shopping, the sharing economy businesses are poised to change the meaning of possession, consumption, work, and enterprise. Sharing economy businesses have witnessed a spectacular rise in recent years and are expected to continue their phenomenal growth in the next decade. The sharing economy is growing steadily by incorporating more sectors and its size could grow from roughly $15 billion in 2017 to around $335 billion by 2025 [1]. According to the Pew Research Center survey of 4,787 American adults in 2016, 72 percent have used some kind of shared or on-demand service. Likewise, Owyang et al. reported that 29 percent of the British population had engaged at least once in a sharing transaction and 23 percent had used one or more platforms such as Airbnb, Uber, TaskRabbit, Etsy, and Kickstarter [2]. Based on other estimates, in 2014, 25 percent of the UK population shared online services [3]. According to Goudin, the potential economic gain due to the sharing economy is estimated at around 572 billion euros in annual consumption across the

European Union (EU) [4]. Uber and Airbnb are innovative companies that were founded less than two decades ago, but currently they have operations in a large number of countries across the world. Uber operates in 10,000 cities across 71 countries and has 93 million monthly active riders and 3.5 million active drivers. Uber processed $26.61 billion in gross bookings from its ridesharing business in 2020, and this number is expected to grow in the future. Airbnb is another pioneer of the sharing economy, with an online platform that matches room seekers to homeowners. Founded in 2008, Airbnb currently operates in more than 81,000 cities and 191 countries [5]. Airbnb has more than a million properties listed for rent, making it larger than the world's biggest hotel chains. Airbnb was valued at $90 billion in June 2021. Uber and Airbnb are indicators of a burgeoning trend toward what is termed as sharing or collaborative economy. The business model of Uber and Airbnb can be applied to any other unutilized or underutilized asset or service, including bicycles, apartments, vacation homes, tools, designer clothes, accessories, objects of art, and yachts. With each month that passes, the impacts of sharing economy companies, including Uber and Airbnb, become more prevalent. The sharing economy business models can be applied to share goods, services, ideas, information, and skills through a network of individuals and communities via computers and mobile apps. Despite their apparent differences, all these platforms match the supply and demand in a very accessible and low-cost way. In addition, these platforms create opportunities for buyers and sellers to interact, share feedback, and build mutual trust. Sharing economy releases the potential for peer-to-peer commerce across the globe by relying on the blockchain technology. Perhaps, the most important characteristic of sharing economy enterprises is that they create conditions to reduce the cost of producing each additional unit of good or service until the marginal cost tends toward zero. Interestingly, sharing activities can be for monetary or nonmonetary benefits. As more businesses and consumers join the sharing economy, our societies and markets are undergoing drastic changes and disruptions. According to *Time* magazine, sharing economy is recognized as one of the top 10 trends that are expected to change the world. Some have compared the social and economic implications of sharing economy to those of the industrial revolution [6].

The Essence of Sharing Economy

The concept of sharing economy refers to different terms, including collaborative consumption, collaborative economy, on-demand economy, peer-to-peer economy, zero-marginal-cost economy, and crowd-based capitalism [7]. Sharing economy is based on collaboration and on-demand production or consumption. The sharing economy platforms offer opportunities, so people can share property, resources, time, and skills across online platforms. We may define sharing economy as an economic system built on sharing, swapping, trading, or renting products and services in a way that enables access over ownership, including business-to-consumer, business-to-business, and peer-to-peer transactions [8]. In other words, sharing and exchange of resources take place via information technology without any permanent transfer of ownership [9, 10]. According to Botsman [11], sharing economy is defined as "an economic system of decentralized networks and marketplaces that unlocks the value of underused assets by matching needs and haves, in ways that bypass traditional middlemen." Sharing economy businesses facilitate business-to-consumer or peer-to-peer transactions, can be for-profit or nonprofit organizations, and range from small businesses to multibillion giants such as Uber and Airbnb [1, 6]. The pivotal appeal of the sharing economy is a platform matching buyers and sellers and reducing transactions costs. The platform is generally operated separately from the services exchanged. The whole concept of sharing economy remains fuzzy and ambiguous, as it represents multiple business models that are undergoing constant transformation and innovation. In addition to the large for-profit businesses, there are a large number of small nonprofit entities such as time banks, food swaps, repair collectives, and other grassroot organizations [12, 13]. While the term *sharing* may imply altruistic or positive nonreciprocal social behavior, the services or goods exchanged in a sharing business model are often fee-paying in nature and involve economic benefits [14].

A New Economic Logic

According to Jeremy Rifkin, the sharing economy represents a paradigm shift that he labels the "third industrial revolution" [15]. The sharing economy represents a new economic paradigm because, by reducing and eliminating barriers such as ownership costs and inflexible distribution networks, it could allow greater access to crucial goods and services for people and communities [8]. The sharing economy seems particularly attractive when a large number of workers and consumers are under mounting pressure and are disappointed with the conventional economic model [8]. Under the current socioeconomic circumstances marked by the astonishing levels of inequality, sharing economy is beneficial for both workers and consumers, as they are enabled to act more independently, run their businesses, distribute their products and services, and democratize expensive assets. In this regard, the sharing economy could be viewed as a more humane model than the conventional economy with large-scale corporations and customers [8]. While the conventional economy is dominated by rivalry and opposition, the sharing economy is marked by common development and coordination. The platforms of the sharing economy do not exclude competition, but create economic value by increasing the number of participants on both sides of supply and demand [16]. The sharing economy is gradually transforming some fundamental concepts such as exchange, supply, demand, production, consumption, ownership, and transaction. The new logic of the sharing economy is different, as it is revolutionizing the very concept of production and economic value. It is suggested that the sharing economy hinges primarily on collaboration and altruism, and thus is a game-changing revolution to Western economics [1]. In other words, in the sharing economy, the participants do not pursue the goal of profit maximization; by contrast, self-interest is fulfilled through collaboration. The sharing economy represents a new mode of a market economy where Adam Smith's Economics of egoism is mitigated by altruism. What we have serves others and vice versa. As the number of market participants in the sharing economy increases, more assets are shared and more economic value is added [16]. The most important remark is that the sharing economy is changing the conventional economic model from competition to symbiosis and collaboration. This represents a paradigmatic shift where everyone is involved in production, distribution, and consumption. Furthermore, while the conventional economy focuses on the relationship between the market and government, the sharing economy considers a synergetic relationship between these two entities.

One of the most important features of the sharing economy is its reliance on a combination of new technologies, including data analytics, mobile connectivity, and cloud computing. Because of the recent advancements in telecommunication technology, the sharing economy can create a different type of economic value, which is different from the conventional economy. The created value in the sharing economy is more abstract, more complex, and more multidimensional than that of the conventional economy. Unlike the conventional economy, the sharing economy relies mainly on nonmaterial factors to create value. This is a fundamental change because hard assets such as labor and land and even technology are not the only factors that determine economic growth. In other words, the growth of the sharing economy is derived from the intelligent combination of factors.

In the sharing economy, the creation of wealth depends on all parties who are participating in the supply, distribution, and consumption processes. The sharing economy covers a global marketplace where all producers and consumers across the world are in constant relationships. The created wealth in the sharing economy is social capital illustrated by trust, collaboration, and participation. Furthermore, in the sharing economy, rights and ownerships are separated, and as a result, exclusive products become sharable. In contrast to large and multilevel and large-scale organizations, the sharing economy creates a large number of micro-entrepreneurs who can directly run and manage their own businesses on a daily basis.

The sharing economy is distinguished from the normal economy by offering new modes of consumption, information, wealth, and humanization. The new mode of consumption means that in the sharing economy, utilization is more important than ownership. The new mode of information implies that, in the sharing economy, resources across sectors are reallocated with high efficiency and low costs. The new mode of wealth means that, in the sharing economy, idle things, spiritual resources, cultural resources, and natural resources are shared. The new mode of humanization implies that, in the sharing economy, self-interest is achieved through altruism [16]. Based on these features, it is possible to claim that the sharing economy is a major economic and social force that could eventually revolutionize how we consume, how we work, how we do business, and how we interact with each other.

In conventional economies, the price is the result of a market competition where capital, land, and other physical assets are accumulated to create and accumulate wealth. As a result, a minority of people take control of rare assets and exert their power over the rest of society. The race toward capital accumulation strains human relations, and people exclude each other. By contrast, the sharing economy breaks the structure of conventional economies by attaching value to utilization, rather than possession of assets and by generating wealth from increasing human relations. Trust acts as the building block of sharing economy and brings people together to create economic value. Therefore, the sharing economy makes us aware that we are all part of a social economic and ecological system with common interests and mutual relations, where we can benefit by being benefitted by others. In other words, the sharing economy can be seen as more humane and harmonious than the existing models of the conventional economy [17].

The sharing economy can be seen as an alternative to the dominant models of the 20th century such as the Keynesian and the neoliberal models, as it aims to embed economic dealings once again in social relations [18]. The notion of reciprocity originally is found in noneconomic dealings of premodern societies and in groups such as families, clans, communities. The modern societies eliminated reciprocity by creating solid economic structures and monetary exchanges in commerce and labor. However, it seems that sharing economy again is reviving the notion of reciprocity in our postmodern societies by using advanced technologies to connect people [18].

The Drivers of Sharing Economy

Social Drivers

Currently, the world population is estimated at 7.9 billion and is expected to exceed 8 billion in 2024, 9 billion in 2038, and 10 billion in 2056. As the human population surges, the world resources become rarer. Therefore, a new economic paradigm such as sharing economy that relies on the utilization of assets, rather than their ownership, can be considered as a sustainable and environment-friendly option. In addition to sustainability, the sharing economy creates opportunities for efficient utilization of assets and resources [19].

As the sharing economy promotes utilization, rather than ownership, it becomes very attractive to consumers [20]. As a result, both asset owners and consumers are able to reduce their costs and the number of resources needed. For instance, the average idle time of a car is 23 hours per day. When one car is put into sharing economy, it could reduce the sales of approximately eight cars. According to the former president of General Motors, every car joining the sharing economy may result in a reduction of production by 15 cars [16]. Unlike the conventional economy, in a sharing economy business, consumers have access to a large number of assets and services from a variety of brands, prices, and features. For example, the users of Airbnb have access to a wide range of accommodation options from a small room in a basement to luxurious mansions and middle-age castles.

The rise of the sharing economy is partly because of the transformation of social norms and cultural values. Across the world and particularly in the Western countries, people are getting more comfortable with strangers and trust them, so they can invite strangers into their home for dinner and share their home, vehicle, or vacation with them. Interestingly, as the trust in individuals is increased, the trust in government institutions and large corporations is diminished [11]. One may suggest that the trust that people put in government and large organizations is partially being replaced by the trust they put in their peers.

As the sharing economy creates business opportunities among strangers, it relies primarily on trust among market participants. The consumers must trust that the goods and services delivered via technological platforms will be as described. Indeed, sharing homes, cars, and lives requires a good degree of mutual trust between buyers and sellers. An important aspect of the sharing economy is that, instead of large corporations, governments, church, and other formal organizations, the consumers are putting their trust in strangers [21]. Consumers are free to choose among numerous brands of varying quality, regardless of advertisement, expert recommendations, and celebrity endorsements [20]. A peer evaluation and review system is designed, allowing the consumers to make informed decisions [19].

The sharing economy is a new form of communitarianism as the businesses match different consumers with each other and create opportunities for communication, socialization, and cultural exchange. This sense of community is an important driving force behind the sharing economy models, as the new generations are increasingly living in isolation and seek opportunities for human contact and personal interaction. The sharing economy models can bring people together in ways that conventional businesses do not [17].

The Environmental Awareness

As environmental degradation is becoming a pressing issue, a majority of citizens, particularly the youth, are advocating business practices that are not pernicious to the environment. This new wave of environmental awareness has been a driving force behind the collaborative consumption that emphasizes utilization, rather than full ownership. For instance, the idea of owning a car might become unattractive in the future, as many consumers will focus on getting a ride or renting a car instead of buying it [16]. The sharing economy is a green economy par excellence because it can reduce the substantial amounts of waste created from unused or underused resources.

Sharing and Happiness

By linking happiness to material possession, the conventional economy creates a vicious circle that often leads to human isolation, alienation, and mental disorder. The postindustrial cultural values imply that there is no direct relation between material wealth and happiness. Rather, they claim that happiness should be sought in socialization and collaboration with others. Indeed, some evidence confirms that the growth of the gross domestic product (GDP) in many countries, including the United States, China, and South Korea, has led to increasing levels of unhappiness, mental disorders, and depression [16]. The sharing economy provides opportunities for citizens to interact with each other and experience kindness, which is often absent from the conventional businesses. For instance, one may share their spare room for socializing with people from other cultures [16].

Economic Drivers

In the past three decades, many Western economies have been underperforming, and the inequality has been growing. The sharing economy is a viable alternative, as it can make many products and services more affordable. Furthermore, the sharing economy creates opportunities for market participants to generate additional income by sharing their assets or services. It is ironic that the sharing economy emerged shortly after the great financial recession of 2007 to 2008, claiming to change the world for better by providing a new pattern of consumption and work [13]. As the divide between the upper and middle classes is becoming larger, and the inflationary pressure is rising, the sharing economy can be considered very attractive. The sharing economy creates professional opportunities for many unemployed or underemployed workers. It can lead consumers to focus on utilization, rather than on ownership, and thus reduce unnecessary purchases. A major cause of the rise in sharing economy is its capacity in creating a symbiosis with the conventional economy. For instance, a large number of Uber's drivers work full time or part time in the conventional economy. In other words, the sharing economy can prosper not despite the conventional economy, but thanks to it. In comparison with many other businesses, the sharing economy startups require very little investment and hard assets. For instance, the accommodation giant Airbnb started modestly in a basement, and it still is operating with less than 600 employees.

Technological Drivers

The sharing economy is driven by the recent advancements in information technology that are able to match consumers and service providers. Big data, data analytics, social media, and mobile devices allow more efficiency. In the past decade, the payment systems have improved and allowed secure and prompt financial transactions among users. Thanks to the new technologies, the risks of fraud and error in the financial transactions have been hugely reduced [20].

The recent advances have created Internet Plus that encompasses a variety of high-technology applications in conventional industries. Internet Plus integrates all resources in a platform, activates the elements of sharing economy, offers the business models, and manages new credit systems [16].

Four Industries Revolutionized by the Sharing Economy

The sharing economy businesses offer both private and public resources such as merchandise, service, time, space, and capital surpluses. Some public resources are inherently shared, but the new technological platforms allow a more efficient allocation of such resources among multiple participants and across a larger geographic area [16]. For instance, municipalities, hospitals, libraries, sports facilities, and universities may share their unused or underused resources with remote areas. Currently, the sharing economy is revolutionizing four important sectors or industries: accommodation and hospitality, transportation and mobility, online labor market, and finance and lending.

Transport and Mobility

Transport and mobility are among the sectors that are undergoing significant transformations because of the advent of sharing economy. Two different types of platforms can be identified in the transportation sector. The first type allows the contracting of resources such as cars, motorbikes, and bicycles. Businesses such as ZipCar, EasyCar, Car2go, Autolib, and Velib belong to this first category. The second type allows users to rent vehicles together with labor. BlaBlaCar, Sidecar, Uber, and Lyft are famous examples of this second category. Car2go has more than one million members, is active in more than 29 cities across Europe and North America, and offers transportation on a by-the-minute basis. BlaBlaCar is a car-pooling service with more than 25 million members that allows drivers to share their empty seats with long-distance passengers. Uber is the most valuable business in the sharing economy that matches passengers and drivers [1]. In addition to car-sharing services, bike-share businesses like Bixi, Capital Bikeshare, and Citi Bike also are mushrooming across many metropolitan areas offering residents and tourists viable and convenient transport alternatives. As of 2013, bike-sharing businesses existed in more than 500 cities. Thanks to Internet Plus, users are now able to locate available bikes and open docks via mobile applications. Bike- and car-sharing businesses are expanding rapidly and are creating more convenient and sustainable transportation alternatives in urban centers [17].

These programs are becoming even more popular, as land values rise within metropolitan centers, and private car ownership becomes more expensive and less desirable. Private cars are idle for about 95 percent of the time, and even when they are driven, they are used often with an average of three to four empty seats [22]. The sharing businesses can have cars on the road and out of parking spaces for much of the day. This will result in a substantial reduction of the total number of cars to transport people. Consequently, the demand for parking spots in urban centers could decrease. The consumers can save on the cost of insurance, fuel, and repair [17]. Car- and bike-sharing businesses will change the face of big cities by reducing congestion, noise, and air pollution. For example, parking spaces may be converted into public amenities such as parks, tennis courts, plazas, and farmer markets.

Accommodation and Hospitality

Accommodation and hospitality represent another attractive sector to the sharing economy businesses. Airbnb, HomeAway, HouseTrip, 9Flats, Wimdu, Onefinestay, Roomerama, Sleepout, Love Home Swap, and Holiday Lettings are some well-known platforms through which people can rent out properties or parts of properties. As the cost of housing is rising in many metropolitan areas, shared housing and cohousing are becoming more attractive. In a shared housing, couples or individuals combine their resources to rent and live in a home together. By contrast, in a cohousing, multiple households live in a community or multifamily structure. In the past decade, the millennials have been seeking these affordable options [17]. Banks are recognizing the impact of the sharing economy on lending and are considering appropriate measures. For example, a Credit Union in Canada has developed a product called a mixer mortgage, which allows multiple buyers to share a single mortgage [17]. The sharing economy has witnessed a raid and substantial growth in the short-term rental and accommodation industry. Some businesses such as Airbnb, HomeAway, FlipKey, VRBO, and Roomorama have penetrated the hospitality industry through peer-to-peer rental services. The market of short-term rental is expected to grow significantly in the coming years, as it offers convenience and saving to travelers and additional income to the homeowners. Internet-based search engines, electronic payments, and mechanisms for peer review and ratings to ensure the quality have boosted the market expansion of short-term rentals.

Labor Market

The labor market is supposed to be massively affected by the sharing economy. Currently, there are many kinds of inefficiencies in labor markets. For instance, while many businesses are in a desperate need of qualified workers, almost 30 to 45 percent of the working-age population in countries around the world is unemployed, inactive, or working only part time [23]. The sharing economy platforms can rely on advanced technologies to connect individuals to the right work opportunities and thus increase labor efficiency in many aspects. Many platforms are popping up that specialize in micro-tasking by matching employers and on-demand workers. Some examples in this category include Amazon Mechanical Tusk, Adtriboo, TaskRabbit, Oltretata, Freelancer, Crowdsource, Crowdflower, Clickworker, and Upwork [1]. Upwork is an online platform that connects workers who supply services with buyers who pay for and receive these services across the globe [24]. Using the Upwork platform, workers can contract with any firm directly. Upwork offers a complete management system by recording the time spent on the job, allowing communication between workers and employers, and facilitating electronic monitoring. According to the McKinsey Global Institute, online platforms could add $2.7 trillion, or 2.0 percent, to the global GDP and increase employment by 72 million full-time-equivalent positions by 2025 [23]. The sharing economy creates opportunities for job seekers to find jobs that suit their skills and preferences, offer transparency around the demand for skills, and allow students to make informed choices.

Finance and Lending

The rise of nonbank platforms such as Prosper, LendingClub, Kick-starter, Funding Circle, and Zopa implies that the sharing economy has gained popularity and acceptance in the money lending industry. The sharing economy businesses offer opportunities for financial transactions, which are being conducted between relevant parties without the intermediation of financial institutions [25]. The main advantage of sharing finance is that the lenders and borrowers can interact directly and do not have to pay fees to the banks and financial institutions. Therefore, lenders get fairly high returns, while borrowers benefit from low-cost loans. Like other business models of the sharing economy, the peer-to-peer lending networks represent convenience and efficiency for all market participants as they eliminate some of the difficulty and high costs associated with traditional lending, including advertising, overhead, and infrastructure expenses [6]. Such a collaborative finance is mainly beneficial to low-income borrowers, including students and young couples. While most of the activities are peer-to-peer lending, some platforms such as Kickstarter and IndieGogo match entrepreneurial projects with venture capitalists.

The Consequences of Sharing Economy

The sharing economy offers many opportunities for people to generate a full- or part-time employment and an additional source of income [26]. The flexibility of sharing business models enables people to earn extra income while doing their current occupations or education [27]. For example, many drivers work with Uber because of the flexibility it offers to earn money during their free hours [26]. Workers and suppliers benefit from a good degree of flexibility in choosing when to work or make their assets available, while users and consumers benefit from customized and on-demand services [28]. The sharing economy can moderate some of the consumerist tendencies in the industrialist countries where consumers see no problems with buying more and having more [27]. Furthermore, the sharing economy adopts different economic models, transforms the concept of work, and modernizes the labor market. Therefore, salary systems, social protection, and retirement plans that are historically linked to the conventional economy will have to change. Users of the sharing economy, both consumers and providers are empowered, so they can play an important role in forming the dynamism of markets. Reviews, ratings, and involvement can determine the reputation, prices, and by extension, the value of products and services [28]. As such, the sharing economy businesses have effective self-regulated mechanisms to control the quality of their services. The sharing economy brings about new challenges and disruptions. Most sharing businesses are unregulated and escape the government's scrutiny. As more business activities migrate to the sharing economy, the governments' revenues and taxation could decline, and public services may be disrupted. Sharing economy businesses may squeeze the conventional incumbents by offering lower prices and by tempting their customers.

Environmental Sustainability

The conventional economy is in interminable chase of higher production, consumption, and competition that necessarily put pressure on natural resources and pose various threats to the natural environment. Any efforts to protect the natural environment should focus on reducing consumption. It is impossible to tackle environmental problems such as greenhouse gas emissions, air pollution, global warming, water pollution, land degradation, and E-waste, without reducing the level of global consumption of goods, services, and commodities. The sharing economy focuses on smart utilization of resources, results in lower levels of consumption, and consequently improves environmental sustainability. According to the French Environment and Energy Management Agency, shareable goods account for about one-third of the household waste, implying that the sharing economy can have positive effects on the environment [28]. The most important feature of the sharing economy is its capacity to make the green and responsible consumption a natural component of business activities. Therefore, the goal of environmental protection is not imposed on the economy; rather it becomes part of it and even serves wealth creation. Simply put, in the sharing economy, the environmental protection is achieved through business activity and not despite it.

Workers' Exploitation

While the sharing economy is supposed to rely on the spirit of collaboration and solidarity, a new critical perspective is increasingly gaining acceptance: the sharing economy brings about a new form of workers' exploitation. The proponents of this perspective argue that the sharing economy is destroying standard work arrangements and workers' protections under the pretext of technological innovation and efficiency [13]. They argue that business models such as Uber and Airbnb are damaging the bargaining power of workers because they have little control over the relations of production, benefits, and wages [29]. According to this view, in the sharing economy, the work relations are algorithmically determined, so it is extremely difficult for workers and regulators to understand how businesses operate [30]. As the supply of workers and providers increases, there will be more pressure on workers, and as a result, their work conditions will deteriorate. Furthermore, as most of the sharing economy business models consider workers as independent contractors, they have a good degree of freedom to define the wages, earnings, and work conditions and terminate the contracts. Some empirical studies on the sharing business models confirm that their workers are not generally well compensated, they are responsible for various expenses, and more importantly, they are deprived of benefits and the rights and protections guaranteed to standard employees [31]. Furthermore, the sharing economy workers are exposed to multiple risks, including physical perils and legal risks. What is particularly striking is that, when the sharing economy workers enter the contract out of necessity and as the principal job, the working conditions can be particularly painful and traumatic.

A Utopian View

According to some authors, notably Jeremy Rifkin, the sharing economy ushers us to a utopian society as the most essential goods and services will be produced with near-zero marginal cost [20]. With the advancement of the sharing economy, the free exchange of manufactured products will accelerate over time, the cost of production will decline, and ultimately, the concept of ownership will be eliminated or at least will be weakened. These transformations result in an abundant society where our material needs will be easily, and sometimes, freely satisfied. While this perspective seems naively optimistic, we suggest that the sharing economy may transform the idea of ownership, particularly with regard to some tangible assets such as vehicles and homes.

The Potential for Disruption

An important feature of every innovation, including the sharing economy, is its disruptive effects. According to Christensen, disruptive innovation can be described as "a process by which a product or service takes root initially in simple applications at the bottom of a market and then relentlessly moves up market, eventually displacing established competitors" [32]. A successful disruptive phenomenon does not happen suddenly, rather it grows gradually until it appears more attractive than the existing technologies or options when it becomes part of the mainstream. The sharing economy can bring about disruptions in traditional markets. For example, there are many complaints against unregulated or under-regulated business models such as Uber and Airbnb. People may rent their homes without complying with the existing regulations for hotel accommodation, or they may offer rides without complying with taxi regulations. There is a lack of checks and balances on drivers and vehicles. Workers' compensation is inadequate, and safety does not receive enough attention. Uber has tackled with governments and has experienced partial bans in many cities across the world, including Sydney, Amsterdam, Berlin, Paris, London, New York, San Francisco, and New Delhi.

New Risks

The sharing economy creates new problems and risks for low-income and vulnerable consumers and workers. The risks and problems of sharing businesses are particularly serious, as they often escape the control and scrutiny of the existing regulatory frameworks [33]. For instance, sharing economy businesses gain access to large amounts of users' sensitive information that could be used to their detriment in the future [34]. Furthermore, the sharing economy businesses may pose serious threats to the health and safety of their users, as most of them do not provide sufficient oversight and training because many of the service providers are not their full-time employees. Drivers, passengers, and on-demand workers may be threatened by dangerous, illegal, or unsafe tasks or situations [35]. For example, some Airbnb hosts have had their homes severely damaged and their relations with neighbors deteriorated [13]. Some Uber drivers have been accused of raping passengers or committing sexual assault. As trust is a key component of the sharing economy, lower-income people and visible minorities are at a disadvantage because they are seen as less trustworthy [6].

Benefits for Low-Income and Underserved Groups

The sharing economy models may have positive implications for low-income people and underserved groups by removing barriers of ownership and lowering the barriers to certain goods and services. For example, the lower income groups can benefit from a relatively easy access to cars and vacation homes. It is widely accepted that peer-to-peer platforms offer more inclusive and higher-quality consumption that might be achieved through traditional models [36]. Consumers may rent an entire apartment at the price of a mid-range priced hotel room or order a cab for half the price of a normal taxi fare [12]. Similarly, the sharing businesses can facilitate access to some basic services such as affordable meals, health care, and medical equipment [12]. Similarly, the sharing of business models may have positive effects on communities by strengthening local economies, standards of living, infrastructure, job creation, entre preneurship, and social relations [8]. While the sharing economy has some benefits for low-income consumers, it is not assured whether these benefits can be sustainable in long term.

References

[1] Petropoulos, G. 2017. *An Economic Review of the Collaborative Economy*, no. 2017/5. Bruegel Policy Contribution.

[2] Owyang, J., A. Samuel, and A. Grenville. 2014. "Sharing is the New Buying: Vision Critical & Crowd, Companies." Available at https://visioncritical.com/resources/collaborative-economy-report/

[3] Martin, C.J. 2016. "The Sharing Economy: A Pathway to Sustainability or a Nightmarish form of Neoliberal Capitalism?" *Ecological Economics* 121, pp. 149–159.

[4] Goudin. 2016. *The Cost of Non-Europe in the Sharing Economy.* European Parliamentary Research Service, European Parliament.

[5] https://press.airbnb.com/news/

[6] Economics, D.A. September 20, 2015. *The Sharing Economy and the Competition and Consumer Act.* http://accc.gov.au/publications

[7] Selloni, D. 2017. "New Forms of Economies: Sharing Economy, Collaborative Consumption, Peer-to-Peer Economy." In *CoDesign for Public-Interest Services,* pp. 15–26. Springer, Cham.

[8] "An Inclusive Sharing Economy Unlocking Business Opportunities to Support Low-Income and Underserved Communities." 2016. https://bsr.org/reports/BSR_An_Inclusive_Sharing_Economy.pdf

[9] Taeihagh, A. 2017. "Crowdsourcing, Sharing Economies and Development." *Journal of Developing Societies* 33, no. 2, pp. 191–222. doi:10.1177/0169796X17710072

[10] Dillahunt, T.R., and A.R. Malone. April 2015. "The Promise of the Sharing Economy Among Disadvantaged Communities." In *Proceedings of the 33rd Annual ACM Conference on Human Factors in Computing Systems,* pp. 2285–2294. ACM.

[11] Botsman, R. October 20, 2015. "The Changing Rules of Trust in the Digital Age." *Harvard Business Review.* https://hbr.org/2015/10/the-changing-rules-of-trust-in-the-digital-age

[12] Ehrenfreund, M. 2015. "Where the Poor and Rich Really Spend Their Money." *Washington Post.* https://washingtonpost.com/news/wonk/wp/2015/04/14/where-the-poor-and-rich-spend-really-spend-their-money/

[13] Schor, J.B., and W. Attwood-Charles. 2017. "The 'Sharing' Economy: Labor, Inequality, and Social Connection on for-Profit Platforms." *Sociology Compass* 11, no. 8, p. e12493.

[14] Hamari, J., M. Sjoklint, and A. Ukkonen. 2015. "The Sharing Economy: Why People Participate in Collaborative Consumption." *Journal of the Association for Information Science and Technology.*

[15] Rifkin, J. 2011. *The Third Industrial Revolution: How Lateral Power is Transforming Energy, The Economy, and the World.* Macmillan.

[16] China Council for International Cooperation on Environment and Development. 2016. "Sharing Economy: A New Economic Revolution Led by Lifestyles."

[17] Madden, J. 2015. "Exploring the New Sharing Economy." *NAIOP Research Foundation. White Paper.* Retrieve from https://naiop.org/~Zmedia/Research/Research/Research%20Reports/Exploring% 20the% 20New, 20

[18] Pais, I., and G. Provasi. 2015. "Sharing Economy: A Step Toward the ReEmbeddedness of the Economy?" *Stato eMercato* 35, no. 3, pp. 347–378.

[19] "All Eyes on the Sharing Economy." March 09, 2013. *The Economist.* http://economist.com/news/technology-quarterly/21572914-collaborative-consumption-technology-makes-it-easier-people-rent-items

[20] The Insurance Institute of Canada. 2017. Sharing Economy: Implications for the Insurance Industry in Canada.

[21] Consumer Intelligence Series. 2014. "The Sharing Economy." https://pwc.com/us/en/technology/publications/assets/pwc-consumer-intelligence-series-the-sharing-economy.pdf

[22] Coldewey, D. December 08, 2011. "Exploring Some Implications of Driverless Cars." *TechCrunch.* http://techcrunch.com/2011/12/08/googles-dutta-explores-some-implications-of-driverless-cars/

[23] Manyika, J., S. Lund, K. Robinson, J. Valentino, and R. Dobbs. 2015. "A Labor Market that Works: Connecting Talent with Opportunity in the Digital Age." *McKinsey Global Institute* 20. http://mckinsey.com/~/media/McKinsey/dotcom/Insights/Employment%20and%20growth/Connecting

[24] Horton, J., W.R. Kerr, and C. Stanton. 2017. *Digital Labor Markets and Global Talent Flows,* no. w23398. National Bureau of Economic Research.

[25] Mitręga-Niestrój, K. 2013. "The Sharing Economy and Collaborative Finance-Outline of the Problems." *Studia Ekonomiczne* 173, pp. 13–25.

[26] Hall, J., and A. Krueger. January 15, 2015. "An Analysis of the Labor Market for Uber's Driver-Partners in the United States." Retrieved April 12, 2016, from https://s3.amazonaws.com: https://s3.amazonaws.com/uber-static/comms/PDF/Uber_Driver-Partners_Hall_Kreuger_2015.pdf

[27] van Welsum, D. 2016. "Sharing is Caring? Not Quite." *Some Observations About 'The Sharing Economy.'* World Development Report 2016—Digital Dividends (Background Paper 102963). World Bank Group.

[28] Ranjbari, M., G. Morales-Alonso, and R. Carrasco-Gallego. 2018. "Conceptualizing the Sharing Economy through Presenting a Comprehensive Framework." *Sustainability* 10, no. 7, p. 2336.

[29] Hill, S. 2015. "Raw Deal: How the 'Uber Economy' and Runaway Capitalism Are Screwing American Workers." St. Martin's Press.

[30] Scholz, T. 2017. "Uberworked and Underpaid: How Workers are Disrupting the Digital Economy." John Wiley & Sons.

[31] Bernhardt, A. 2014. "Labor Standards and the Reorganization of Work: Gaps in Data and Research."

[32] Christensen, C. 2016. "Disruptive Innovation." *Key Concepts.* http://claytonchristensen.com/key-concepts/

[33] Kamenetz, A. 2013. "Does the Sharing Economy Have a Shadow Side." *Fast Company* [Online]. Available at http://fastcompany.com/3013272/does-the-sharing-economy-have-a-shadowside (accessed April 01, 2015).

[34] Ramasastry, A. 2015. "Too Much Sharing in the Sharing Economy? Uber's Use of Our Passenger Data Highlights the Perils of Data Collection via Geolocation." *Verdict.* https://verdict.justia.com/2015/02/10/much-sharing-sharing-economy

[35] Ravenelle, A. 2015. "A Return to Gemeinschaft: Digital Impression Management and the Sharing Economy." Unpublished paper, City University of New York.

[36] Fraiberger, S.P., and A. Sundararajan. 2015. "Peer-to-Peer Rental Markets in the Sharing Economy." NYU Stern School of Business Research Paper. http://ssrn.com/abstract=2574337

CHAPTER 12

The Fourth Industrial Revolution

The Making of the Fourth Industrial Revolution

According to Klaus Schwab, we are currently witnessing the emergence of an all-inclusive revolution that is going to essentially change the way we live, work, and relate to one another [1, 2]. Schwab popularized the term *Forth Industrial Revolution* (4IR) to refer to the confluence of mainly technological innovations, including artificial intelligence (AI) robotics, nanotechnology, biotechnology, quantum computing, blockchain, Internet of Things, and 3D printing. Schwab suggests that the 4IR is expected to affect all aspects of our lives "unlike anything humankind has ever experienced" [3]. Schwab maintains that the world has witnessed four industrial revolutions: the First Industrial Revolution allowed the use of steam engines for mechanical production and happened around 1784 or almost 235 years ago. The introduction of the factory system, the development of the railroad, and huge advances in metallurgy and chemistry are some consequences of the First Industrial Revolution [4]. The Second Industrial Revolution happened at the beginning of the 20th century and relied on electricity, mass production, and the division of labor. The Second Industrial Revolution resulted in the development of electricity networks, telephone lines, automobiles, gas turbines, artificial fertilizer, and similar technologies that transformed transport, communication, and consumption [4]. The Third Industrial Revolution took place in the late 1970s and matured sometime around the early 2000s. The Third Industrial Revolution relied mainly on the advances in information technology, production of the integrated circuits, microprocessors, and digital telecommunications. All these technologies were integrated into the Internet and mobile telephony and completely changed our lives.

Currently, we are at the early stages of the 4IR, which is marked by increasing reliance on cyber-physical systems as the basis of intelligent network systems and processes. The 4IR is ushering us to a digital transformation that universally influences all aspects of human civilizations across the globe, including work, energy, production, governance, education, and recreation. In the 4IR, technologies amplify each other across the physical, digital, and biological spheres and revolutionize our lives by disrupting the conventional industries, thus creating new business models, and reformatting production, consumption, transportation, and delivery systems [2]. Hence, the 4IR is not about particular innovative technologies, it is rather about their complex and wide-ranging confluence. The 4IR is a paradigm shift that affects how we produce, how we consume, and how we work, but it goes beyond the economic and business boundaries. The 4IR is unlike anything humankind has experienced in the past. At this time, new businesses are developed based on their capacity to link the physical and virtual worlds. In a near future, by infusion of multiple technologies and transformation, the conventional boundaries of the physical, digital, and biological worlds will be broken.

We may identify three major characteristics of the 4IR as high velocity, systematic impact, and zero marginal cost. First, the 4IR is marked by its high velocity because it is mounting at an exponential, rather than a linear pace, breath, and depth. It took almost 120 years for the First Industrial Revolution to spread outside the European continent, but it took only less than a decade for the Internet to pervade across the globe. In the case of the 4IR, we may expect drastic changes across the globe in a few years. More and more, we are living in an accelerated and interconnected world, so each powerful technology generates technologies that are even faster and more powerful. The second characteristic of the 4IR is its systematic impact. While the previous industrial revolutions initially influenced particular aspects of the human economy in certain countries, the 4IR involves the transformation of entire systems across and within societies, markets, industries, and the whole planet. Third, the 4IR bridges the gap between virtual and physical spheres on both production and consumption sides and leads to the zero marginal costs. Many businesses and consumers will produce and consume informational goods that imply zero cost of storage, transportation, and replication [4].

The main pillars of the 4IR are cyber-physical systems, intelligent data gathering, and data storage and distribution systems [1]. The new digital technologies such as blockchain will revolutionize the collaboration and engagement of organizations, workers, and consumers. Developments in information technologies, combined with robotization, automation of tasks, Internet of Things, advanced manufacturing, driverless cars, cyber weapons, sensors, biotechnology, and surveillance, will fuel the economic growth and wealth creation [5]. The electronic devices will become an inevitable part of consumers' lives, as they can anticipate the consumers' needs. Due to the availability of data, production and consumption will be highly precise, and the amount of waste will decrease substantially [1]. The main beneficiaries of the 4IR are the providers of intellectual capital, innovators, and shareholders of new business entities. Consequently, the gap in wealth and power between the workers and capitalists may deepen even more [1]. To deal with speed and impacts of the 4IR, the businesses have to stay agile and competitive by offering innovative products and services. Indeed, in the 4IR, the competitiveness of businesses will depend much more on their innovative capacity than on their cost-effectiveness. Established companies will constantly come under extreme pressure by emerging disruptors and innovators from other industries and countries [1].

The Implications of the Fourth Industrial Revolution

Implications for Businesses

The most important implications of new technologies so far have been related to the consumption experience. In recent years, consumers around the world have greatly benefited from lower prices, abundance of products, and associated improved quality of life. With the advent of the 4IR, there will be significant transformations in the supply side and long-term achievements in productivity. Consequently, transportation, communication, trade, logistics, and global supply chains costs will decline drastically [1]. While the cost of doing business tends to decline in the future, the economic inequality is expected to rise because labor markets may be disrupted, and automation could sweep across the global economy. It is too difficult to predict the implications of the new economic setting on the labor, but consistent with the existing trends, the importance of talent as a critical factor of production will continue to grow. Consequently, the job market may be divided into two opposite poles as low-skill or low-pay versus high-skill or high-pay [1]. This cleavage in the workforce, and thus in income, could lead to greater levels of economic inequality across the world. The income inequality might be transformed into a winner-takes-all economy that offers only limited opportunities to the majority of the population. Due to its peculiar nature, the main winners of the 4IR are expected to be the providers of intellectual and physical capital, including the innovators, shareholders, and investors. In the evolving economic system, there will be more demand for educated and highly skilled workers. The ordinary workers will be surprised by the extent of stagnation of their income levels over the course of the next few years.

The existing value chains in many industries will be disrupted by a combination of technological and competitive factors. The agile and innovative competitors who have access to global digital platforms may beat the conventional incumbents by improving the quality, speed, and price [1]. Similarly, the demand and consumption behavior are expected to undergo major transformations, as new technologies will result in more transparency and consumer interaction. As a result, many businesses will have to customize not only their products and services but also their marketing campaigns. The advances of smart platforms will be matching the supply and demand so efficiently that the conventional business structures could be extremely disrupted [1]. Therefore, it is possible to suggest that the 4IR may have major business effects on customer expectations, product enhancement, collaborative innovation, and organizational forms. According to Schwab, the Third Industrial Revolution was focusing on digitization, but the 4IR offers a complex confluence of multiple technologies in all industries [1]. The 4IR will enable businesses to exploit the interaction of digital, physical, and human realms and create economic value by offering services, rather than products.

The Second Industrial Revolution popularized the hierarchical organizational structure, unity of command, and strict managerial controls. By contrast, the competitiveness of the organization in the era of the 4IR will depend increasingly on the extent of their organizational flexibility. Organizations will move from hierarchical and centralized structures to more networked and collective models [1]. Such flexible structures will help organizations deal with the uncertainty and disruption of emerging technological transformations.

Implications for Governments

The existing systems of public administration have been built around the social structure of the Second Industrial Revolution with centralized, linear, and rigid decision-making organizations in which the administrators and policy makers could take time to study, deliberate, and develop the appropriate regulations. With the advent of the 4IR, the socio-technological innovations will push the governments to change their traditional administration systems by adopting less centralized and more open approaches to policy making. The adaptation of public administration will necessitate more agility, innovation, and collaboration with the private sector, businesses, and civil society. Those governments that cannot adapt their structures to these new trends may experience disruption and dysfunctionality. Because of the 4IR, the demarcation between physical and digital spaces will continue to erode, and new hybrid interfaces will be created. Under these circumstances, state power will be shared with nonstate actors, and its institutional influence will be shared with nebulous networks. The citizens will be able to express their opinions, get involved in governments, and direct their collective efforts. At the same time, the confluence of physical and digital spaces will enable governments to increase their control over populations, monitor their activities, and track their movements. The 4IR may have serious consequences for national security, as new technologies and the confluence of virtual and physical spaces will result in the occurrence of cyberattacks, and hybrid and asymmetrical confrontation. The modern conflicts will be less conventional and more complex than ever. This implies that the demarcation between war and peace will be more blurry, and future conflicts could involve the widespread use of autonomous and sophisticated weaponry.

Implications for Citizens

The 4IR is expected to affect many aspects of our lives including the perceptions of communication, socialization, consumption, ownership, leisure, and time. The integration of new technologies into our lives will result in human augmentation that may drastically change our identity as human beings [1]. The integration of technology into human lives could deprive them of many essential human capacities such as emotion, conversation, interaction, and reflection. For example, the technological innovations in biotechnology and AI may change the essential human characteristics associated with health, cognition, and emotions.

The Second Industrial Revolution and the division of work created long-lasting patterns in our collective psyche, including the linear perception of time, protection of privacy, and commitment to one task at a time. With the advent of the 4IR, temporal circularity shared privacy, and increasing levels of multitasking will replace these behavioral and cultural traits. In the 4IR, customers are at the focus of the digital economy, as the new technologies will enable businesses to serve their customers more effectively. Customers can be identified based on their previous experience. Thanks to further advances in data analytics, customer service is expected to become even more personalized and faster than ever [6].

The conventional education system is deeply rooted in the Second Industrial Revolution and even in the European traditions of the middle ages. It is marked by a slow pace of change, distinct disciplines, formal lectures, structured programs, and devotion to some particular professions. The ultimate goal of many schools is still to train ideal employees. Education is expected to become more student-oriented and technologically intensive to keep up with the major business and technological transformations of the 4IR. This will necessitate new skills and qualifications for teachers and faster adaptation to the world of work [7].

The Industrial Internet

The digitization of the economy means that many tasks in our life can be reduced to a few sequences of the human-to-machine, machine-to-machine, and machine-to-human chains. The digital technologies are creating new combinations of mental, physical, and mechanical work. The integration of information technology and operational technology in many industries will lead to cost reduction, improved quality, and efficiency [1]. According to Siegfried Dasch from Bosch [1], in future manufacturing, everything will be linked to everything else so that the virtual-real processes will improve productivity. In other words, the future of manufacturing will be an interplay between the real and digital. General Electric has used the term *Industrial Internet* to refer to the addition of digital technology to all machines and all devices. For instance, General Electric is adding sensors in the engines of planes, trains, and MRI scanners to make aviation, railway services, and health care, respectively, more efficient. According to the General Electric's estimates, the Industrial Internet could save the aviation sector $2 billion a year [1]. This kind of smart manufacturing can be used in many industries from food to consumer goods and the high-tech sector. The addition of networked software to products and machines will enable businesses to gain in several areas. For example, by enabling machine-to-machine communication without human intervention, the need for human work is reduced, and important contributions to efficiency and security are made. Machine-to-machine applications rely on microelectronics and wireless technology to gather and distribute real-time data in a network. For example, the Parker Water and Sanitation District in Colorado is linking pumps and pipes in the systems via a software-controlled water system to optimize the use of mechanical, human, and natural sources [1]. Businesses can use the Industrial Internet to conveniently conduct their upgrades and maintenance tasks and improve the reliability and speed of their operations. The Internet of Things will be used to interact with customers in real time via all kinds of domestic appliances, such as refrigerators, toothbrushes, televisions, and vacuum cleaners. The users' data can be collected in order to create business value and to offer services more efficiently. According to the Cisco estimates, the total market value of the Internet of Things will be worth $14 trillion in 2022 [1]. Most of the Internet of Things market will be dedicated to manufacturing that will be valued about $3.88 trillion.

Managing the Fourth Industrial Revolution

Most of the industrial countries have experienced a steady and significant rate of economic growth (GDP per capita) since the First Industrial Revolution in the 1800s. Before the First Industrial Revolution, much of

Europe was suffering from low or zero economic growth accompanied by social stagnation [8]. After the First Industrial Revolution, new technologies combined with mechanization, automation, and specialization stimulated the Western European economies and resulted in the creation of unprecedented wealth and higher standards of living [9]. For instance, real income per person in the Organization for Economic Co-operation and Development (OECD) economies has risen almost 2,900 percent since 1800 [10]. According to the World Economic Forum [4], in the recent decades, many advanced economies are showing signs of decline as they are failing to preserve the rate of economic growth and living standards for their citizens [6].

As the world is entering the 4IR, the introduction of emerging technologies is expected to alter the relationships and power dynamics between governments, companies, communities, and citizens. It is plausible to believe that, in the new era, economic crises will be no longer linear, rather they will occur simultaneously, side by side, and due to their velocity, they will not leave us enough time to react, contemplate, plan, and strategize. Indeed, emerging crises will be various in nature; they will range from geopolitical, ecological, and political to technological, financial, and economic factors. Due to much uncertainty and ambiguity surrounding the 4IR, many observers remain cautious and even pessimistic about the future socioeconomic conditions. The growing power of tech giants and the subsequent concerns such as the elimination of jobs, loss of privacy, transformation of identity, and dominance of AI are some scary outcomes associated with the 4IR [11]. The 4IR can eliminate not only the low-wage and low-skilled jobs but also those jobs that bring prodigious benefits. Furthermore, the 4IR may aggravate a harmful cleavage, which already exists in the distribution of wealth. A small number of talented people take on the majority of complex tasks, and a large number of citizens lose their jobs and remain unemployed or underemployed.

In the past three decades, many developing countries have taken advantage of the global business environment to achieve rapid rates of economic growth. Some emerging economies, notably China, have adopted technological sophistication and reached higher standards of living and productivity. Similarly, some developing countries benefited from this environment and achieved rapid rates of economic growth and poverty reduction. Consequently, the world as a whole has enriched, and the number of the abject poor has fallen significantly, but the advanced economies of the West have grown much more slowly [12]. The Third Industrial Revolution has resulted in lower labor and capital costs and easier access to global markets. At the same time, many countries, notably the developed Western economies, have experienced economic pressure from dislocation, skills mismatches, long-term unemployment, and wage stagnation. The rising levels of income inequality and prospects of growth preoccupy many developed economies. Consequently, there is a mounting pressure on social and political institutions to find solutions. By promising quick fixes, the right-wing parties, demagogues, and populist politicians are gaining popularity in the Western nations from Europe to North America. Currently, there are major concerns about emerging technologies among populations. These concerns are related to the impacts of new technologies on employment, security, privacy, food, and income inequality, among others [8]. Many advanced countries are incapable of upholding the rate of increase in living standards for their citizens. For instance, over the course of the past five years, annual median incomes have declined by 2.4 percent in the OECD economies, while the wage gaps have increased [13].

With all its radical transformations, the 4IR is expected to exacerbate the existing socioeconomic drifts, threatening large segments of both developed and emerging countries [4]. While the waves of the 4IR could destroy the structure of the current economies, the ensuing innovative technologies and business models could generate exciting opportunities for improving employment, productivity, and quality of life. The 4IR may result in new levels of affluence as an enhanced quality of life, shorter working days, and increased family time [13]. The technologies such as machine learning, AI, and automated vehicles could significantly enhance the quality of life of citizens. The 4IR relies on the idea that a confluence of technological systems should serve human beings in sustainable and inclusive ways [4]. To deal with the adverse effects of the 4IR, a new human-centered economic model is required, in which the emphasis is put on social inclusion, wealth distribution, and social justice. Considering the paradigmatic shifts of the 4IR, the policy makers should rely on a more wide-ranging approach by prioritizing their citizens and their welfare instead of stimulating the short-term economic growth. In preparation for the 4IR, first, policy makers should take adequate measures to address the problems caused by the Third Industrial Revolution and globalization. Then, they should plan to capitalize on the opportunities and technologies of the 4IR. The G20 countries have highlighted three main strategies to deal with the challenges of the 4IR: management of aggregate demand through macroeconomic policy, export-led growth through trade and industrial policy, and regional integration combined with domestic deregulation [13]. Facing the enormous challenges of the 4IR, the governments should reinstate their confidence in the capacity of the liberal political and economic order to embrace new technologies and achieve a comprehensive and sustainable growth.

References

[1] Schwab, K. 2017. *The Fourth Industrial Revolution.* Crown Business.

[2] Bloem, J., M. Van Doorn, S. Duivestein, D. Excoffier, R. Maas, and E. Van Ommeren. 2014. *The Fourth Industrial Revolution.* Things Tighten.

[3] Effoduh, J.O. 2016. "The Fourth Industrial Revolution by Klaus Schwab." *The Transnational Human Rights Review* 3. http://digitalcommons.osgoode. yorku.ca/thr/vol3/iss1/4

[4] Samans, R., and N. Davis. 2017. "Advancing Human-Centred Economic Progress in the Fourth Industrial Revolution." *Recuperado de.* http:// www3.weforum.org/docs/WEF_Advancing_Human-Centred_Economic_ Progress_WP_2017. pdf

[5] McKenzie, F. 2017. The Fourth Industrial Revolution and International Migration.

[6] Centers for Disease Control and Prevention analysis for the United States, which found life expectancy for the US population in 2015 was 78.8 years, a decrease of 0.1 year from 2014. CDC. December 2016. "Mortality in the United States, 2015." Available at https://cdc.gov/nchs/products/databriefs/ db267.htm

[7] "Lisbon International Trade Fair, Learning, Working, and Competing in the Horizon of the 4th Industrial Revolution." March 2017. *Social Dialogue on the Emergence of the Fourth Industrial Revolution: Education, Employment and Youth,* pp. 30–31. | Lisbon Futuralia-http://medsocialdialogue.org/sites/ default/files/A_1.2.3_Report_SOLID.pdf

[8] Historical Data on Economic Activity Prior to 1800 are Patchy but Have Benefitted from Innovative Work by a Range of Scholars. See, for example,

Fouquet, R., and S.N. Broadberry. 2015. "Seven Centuries of European Economic Growth and Decline." In *Journal of Economic Perspectives* 29, no. 4. Available at http://lse.ac.uk/GranthamInstitute/wp-content/uploads/2015/09/Working-Paper-206-Fouquet-and-Broadberry.pdf

[9] "The Maddison Project Database Indicates that Average Yearly Per Capita Growth in the United Kingdom Rose from 0.1% Between 1400–1700 to 0.3% from 1700-1800, to 0.7% from 1800–1900 and 1.6% from 19002000." 2013. Available at http://ggdc.net/maddison/maddison-project/data.htm, 2013 version

[10] McCloskey, D.N. 2016. *Bourgeois Equality.* University of Chicago Press.

[11] Briscoe, D., I. Tarique, and R. Schuler. 2012. "International Human Resource Management: Policies and Practices for Multinational Enterprises." Routledge.

[12] "G20 Enhanced Structural Reform Agenda." September 2016. *Prepared by the G20 Framework Working Group,* Available at http://mofa.go.jp/files/000185875.pdf

[13] Samans, R., and N. Davis. 2017. "Advancing Human-Centred Economic Progress in the Fourth Industrial Revolution." *Recuperado de.* http://www3.weforum.org/docs/WEF_Advancing_Human-Centred_Economic_Progress_WP_2017.pdf

CHAPTER 13

The Gig Economy

The Rise of the Gig Economy

The gig economy is a popular term referring to various forms of work and employment marked by short-term, on-demand, and unpredictable arrangements. The gig economy is above all a technology-influenced development of labor that is transforming the conventional norms and beliefs about the place of work in society and the respective responsibilities of workers, businesses, and governments [1]. In the gig economy, workers no longer choose between working either as an employee or as a business owner. They may take a third path. While they are not subject to the restrictions and control of their employer, they do not have to start and run their own businesses. By using mobile applications, gig workers can tap into the existing infrastructure and customer network of an online platform company while maintaining the freedom of setting their own hours and choosing which jobs to take [2]. In contrast to a typical business owner, the average gig workers are generally younger and less financially sophisticated and tend to work fewer hours and make less money [3].

The gig economy may include two forms of work: crowdwork and work on-demand [4]. Crowdwork is about completing some tasks through online platforms that put in contact an indefinite number of organizations and individuals [5]. By contrast, work on-demand implies the execution of some activities such as transport, cleaning, and clerical work via applications managed by firms that also intervene in setting the minimum quality standards of service and in the selection and management of the workforce [6]. Both types of gig work rely on the Internet and new technologies to match demand and supply of work and services at an extremely high speed. Because of their reliance on advanced technologies, both types of gig work are highly efficient, minimize transaction costs, and streamline frictions on markets [7]. By relying on digital platforms, freelancers may quickly connect with customers or employers to offer their products, services, or skills and secure payments. Very often, the gig work is a means of generating additional income outside of regular employment or a full-time job [8]. A gig worker can be defined as an independent contractor who freely contracts via an app or web-based platform [1]. In a gig economy, the term employer refers to those who are responsible to pay the gig worker directly or indirectly. Under such circumstances, it is difficult to distinguish between employees of a company and its contractors or service providers. Consequently, the demarcation between employment and entrepreneurship becomes so blurred that the two terms may be considered as interchangeable. Indeed, the term employer could be misleading in a gig economy because the so-called employer does not hire gig workers. For instance, in the case of Uber and many other electronic platforms, the riders and beneficiaries hire the driver, and the platforms simply connect them and manage payments [1]. While the platforms such as Uber do not hire drivers, they are fully involved in the processes, as they are responsible for providing services and equipment, making decisions, setting the rates, and activating or deactivating drivers.

While much of the debate about the gig economy and alternative employment has focused on the sharing economy platforms such as Uber and Airbnb, it is important to mention that such platforms account for only a small share of the gig workers [9]. According to the Freelancers Union, there are almost 54 million independent workers comprising 34 percent of workers [10]. Of course, many of these independent workers may have more than one job, and depending on their employment, they can be categorized as an employee or independent contractor. The number of gig workers who rely only on digital platforms is estimated around 600,000, of which 400,000 work for Uber [11]. By any measure, we can say that the number of gig workers is already huge and is rapidly rising.

This quick rise in the number and share of gig workers is transforming the American economy. It is widely expected that the economy of tomorrow will not consist of employments, but rather gigs. People will not have an employer, rather they will perform tasks, coordinated through faceless online platforms and compensated through digital transfers [12].

We are in the midst of a fundamental shift in the U.S. economy. Only a few decades ago, the average worker could remain with the same employer and job for the total duration of their career. The employees used to profit from a wide range of benefits, including job security, unemployment insurance, and retirement plans. Things have changed, as conventional employment is not the norm anymore, and a growing number of people work autonomously and combine income from multiple sources [13]. According to the Federal Reserve, the share of workers earning income from multiple jobs increased from 15 to 22 percent between 2014 and 2015 [14]. Similarly, Katz and Krueger [15] report that there was an increase of 9.4 million workers in alternative work arrangements in the past decade.

Some surveys and estimates show that most of the employment growth in the U.S. economy from 2005 to 2015 is attributed to the gig workers [16]. Based on a recent survey, currently, there are 3.2 million gig workers, growing at an 18.5 percent to reach 7.6 million by 2020 [17]. Despite the occurrence of the global financial crisis, gig workers in the United States grew at a rapid pace between 8.8 and 14.4 percent from 2002 to 2014 [18]. Self-employed and on-demand workers are expected to exceed 40 percent of the American workforce by 2020 [19]. These transformations have been happening for many years, and the nature of work is changing drastically.

Context of the Gig Economy

The Motivations

Flexibility is recognized as the main reason why people prefer gig work. Above all, workers appreciate the fact that they can choose their work environment and their work schedule [16]. The youth are particularly interested in autonomous and flexible employment. In recent years, an increasing number of workers are using new information technologies to carry out their tasks remotely. Some studies indicate that, because of such flexibility, most of the gig workers have shown higher levels of engagement and satisfaction with their work [20]. For instance, according to one recent study, more than 80 percent of the independent contractors and freelance workers indicated their preference for flexible work arrangement to being an employee [16]. Interestingly, gig workers may prefer flexibility to benefits in a usual schedule. For example, another recent study revealed that 55 percent of the Australians would take a 20 percent salary cut in order to work from home [18].

After the great financial crisis of 2007 to 2008, unemployment rates surged, and in the post-Great Recession era, the unemployment for many years stayed high. The increasing difficulty in finding decent employment opportunities led many job seekers to the gig work [21]. Another motivation behind the rise of gig work resides in a growing financial disparity in America and the stagnating wage levels over the course of the past three decades. Since the 1970s, American purchasing power, as a whole, has been stagnant, and low-income workers have experienced more financial hardship. This increasing financial pressure has led many to seek additional income in the gig economy. It is estimated that more than 31 percent of Uber drivers have sought additional income in undertaking a gig work [22].

Another important driver of the gig economy is the value creation in businesses and their commitment to shareholders. In the past decade, many businesses have relied on optimization of their workforce to increase productivity and profitability. Accordingly, the gig workers are on-demand personnel who can create value without the cost and inconvenience of permanency, bonuses, and benefits [23]. Conventional employees can be much more expensive than on-demand contractors or contingent workers. Federal and state unemployment taxes, social security and Medicare, pensions, health insurance, training, and workers' compensation premiums are examples of costs associated with conventional employment. Furthermore, employers may face other hurdles such as employment regulations, minimum wage requirements, and collective bargaining [1].

One major driver of the gig economy is the efficiency of the labor market that is done mainly via electronic platforms. On the one hand, online platforms connect workers and employers and enable them to efficiently exchange work and compensation. On the other hand, the gig economy enables businesses to find the right specialization and economies of scale of contractors [24]. Moreover, the gig economy enables businesses to scale according to demand, so they will be able to search, interview, hire, and terminate their contractors more effectively [25].

The Profile of Gig Workers

Gig workers are diverse; they come in all ages, education levels, incomes brackets, occupations, and nationalities. The gig economy is an emerging trend associated with advanced technologies, and naturally, it remains popular among the younger generations. At the global level, between 46 and 60 percent of the young people participate in the gig economy. The youth account for a quarter of gig workers [26]. Other age groups show significant interest in the gig economy as well. Women make up around 50 percent of the gig workforce. While age and gender are not issues in the gig economy, it seems that the household income level has some important effects on the degree of participation in the gig economy. It is found that people from low-income groups are more likely to participate in the gig workforce [26]. Gig workers are found in a wide range of industries from construction trades, household and personal services, and transportation to professional services such as accounting, interior design, and writing and editing. According to the McKinsey Global Institute, those gig workers with lower levels of education and skills are more likely to work out of necessity [26]. Therefore, we can categorize gig workers as primary or supplemental earners depending on whether they work by choice or out of economic necessity [27]. A large number of gig workers choose this working style because they value its independence and flexibility. Many gig workers choose their work as a matter of preference, not a necessity [26]. Generally, gig workers are more involved in their tasks, show more interest in what they do, and enjoy the freedom and flexibility of their job. Therefore, in comparison with conventional workers, gig workers seem more satisfied with their occupations and are happier with their overall level of income. Even those working out of obligation typically appreciate the flexibility of the gig work. Even with regard to income security and benefits, it seems that gig workers are as satisfied as traditional workers are [27].

The Rise of the Gig Economy in Developing Countries

Gig economy and on-demand platforms are becoming gradually dominant across the world, particularly in developing countries, because of the rapid growth in digital connectivity [28]. According to the International

Telecommunications Union (ITU), in 2016, there were about 898 million more Internet users than those in 2013 [29]. It is estimated that, currently, around 48 percent of the global population is using the Internet. The number of people subscribed to mobile services is constantly increasing in Africa, particularly in countries such as Egypt, Nigeria, and South Africa. The substantial increase in the Internet connectivity predicts the promising future of the gig economy in developing countries. In many developing countries, unemployment and poor working conditions may offer incentives for workers to switch from formal employment to the on-demand economy [29]. The growth of middle-income earners with significant disposable incomes is another driver of the gig economy in developing countries [30]. On-demand platforms devoted to serving domestic workers are evolving in many developing countries such as India, Mexico, and South Africa. While the share of such services is still negligible, the recent studies suggest promising growth potentials [31].

The Dark Side of the Gig Economy

The gig work is part of a larger trend toward the casualization of labor in modern economies. Consistent with this trend, corporations are seeking more efficiency and less commitment to managing their human resources. They are developing work arrangements such as zero-hour contracts and on-call labor that bring about the possibility to hire-and-fire a significant portion of the workforce on an on-demand basis [32].

The gig economy creates numerous opportunities for workers, but it attracts a large number of contractors and gradually creates more competition among independent workers. Like any other labor market, the average income of gig workers is determined by the makeup of the pool of workers. Consequently, the increased competition among independent workers necessarily reduces workers' income levels, worsens work conditions, and raises the likelihood of their joblessness. Due to the high levels of flexibility, the gig workers are more likely to change their jobs, fill the vacant positions, or compete with the conventional workers or their gig counterparts. Therefore, the level of competition in a gig labor market tends to be even higher than that of a conventional economy. What makes the gig workers very vulnerable is that the technological advancement of digital platforms and their rising popularity are expected to increase the level of pressure on them.

Another major concern for gig workers is their vulnerability to the abuse of large corporations because they are not protected by state and federal regulations such as minimum wage requirements or unemployment insurance, workers' compensation, and disability insurance [1]. It is widely known that gig workers do not have access to sick pay, maternity pay, holiday pay, employer pension contributions, and many other benefits of employees. Furthermore, gig workers face many difficulties such as reduced access to credit, the risk of not being paid for work that is already performed, complex tax filings, licensing, and regulatory compliance requirements [26]. In general, a full-time employee with regular and steady paycheck has better access to home financing and credit than a gig worker does. Gig workers often face financial instability, as they do not have access to steady employment income, they do not save enough for their retirement and do not benefit from health and disability insurance [33]. In some cases, gig workers face abuse or nonpayment of clients and may suffer from substantial financial losses. Another concern is that gig workers often suffer from higher levels of risk associated with their tasks and are not subject to strict safety regulations. They often remain unprotected and unsupported against the work-related hazards. In the absence of effective regulation, gig workers are subject to discrimination from clients and colleagues. The flexibility of gig work remains very attractive to both workers and organizations, but this flexibility should not be considered as an absolute advantage. Indeed, the flexibility of gig work may not be necessary for a large portion of workers and could reduce the competence of some professions [34]. The rise of the gig work is a potentially disruptive phenomenon [35]. For instance, it is not clear that existing federal and state tax regulations can be applied to gig workers. In many cases, the rationale behind the formation of gig work is the evasion of conventional regulations, including tax codes [12].

Due to the confusion regarding the definition of employment, there are many cases of litigation over worker misclassification lawsuits in various U.S. jurisdictions. Some argue that to resolve these issues, a hybrid category of employment should be created positioned between employee and independent contractor [36]. The proponents of the third category argue that

the novelty of the gig work causes social and organizational transformations, and thus requires novel treatment and regulation [36]. Indeed, the
Internet platforms and customers could not be considered employers [36].
Therefore, instead of litigating the issue of whether a particular worker
merits employee status, gig workers may be put under a different umbrella.

Implications of the Gig Economy for Businesses

The gig economy increases the fluidity of the workforce and consequently
impacts on organizations' structure and their hiring systems. Businesses,
in general, view nontraditional staffing as a vital facet of their overall
corporate strategy that provides fresh and various skills [37]. The main
beneficiaries of the gig workers are those businesses that take advantage
of fluid human capital to scale up and down on a project basis [38].
For example, it takes on average 2.7 days to hire a freelancer in contrast
to more than 34 days to hire a conventional full-time worker [39]. The
promptness and flexibility of companies in hiring and dismissing the
gig workers mean that they can quickly start additional projects without
significant investment and preparation [39]. Furthermore, the global
reach of new technologies means that businesses have access to the best
reservoir of talent around the world. The globalization of contingent
workers has opened the door to a broader pool of talented and hardworking
professionals at competitive rates [40]. Incorporating freelancers into
the conventional workforce is seen as a smart move that often causes
higher levels of productivity [41]. The gig economy could be particularly
beneficial to small and medium businesses, as they are marked by serious
limitations in their financial, technological, and human resources and do
not afford to hire and retain full-time talented employees. The gig work
allows many corporations to keep core operations focused on what they
do best and call in independent service providers on demand. Because
of this flexibility, they can add new capabilities without disrupting their
regular operations. [26]. The gig economy is structured around networks,
rather than traditional institutions [42], and because of its flexibility,
it can disrupt the conventional societal and organizational norms. In
the gig economy, organizations and businesses rely on provisional and
independent contractors to operate efficiently and deliver their on-demand

services [43]. The flexible management of workers enables organizations to utilize the commercial value in underused personal assets according to the demand conditions [44]. In other words, the gig economy applies the notion of just-in-time management to the workforce to attain at the lowest levels of cost and the highest levels of profitability. For that reason, companies in the gig economy do not have to spend money on benefits, training, and development of their personnel [45].

As businesses increasingly rely on freelancers, they have to develop systems to manage them effectively. Indeed, gig workers are highly moveable and can easily switch their jobs. As the gig economy continues to grow, companies will adjust their structures to this labor trend. For example, they have to acquire new technology, tools, and processes to benefit from the increasing number of gig workers. Many businesses need to adapt their organizational structure to the presence of gig workers. Some businesses may choose a mixed hiring method by recruiting generalists for in-house and using freelancers for some specialist knowledge and skills [46].

The gig work has been beneficial to many gig corporations that take advantage of a global workforce. While many corporations maintain control over the Internet applications they create, they distance themselves from their responsibilities. The result is net profit for these corporations on the back of competitors, nations, governments, municipalities, and communities, and above all, gig workers. On the one hand, they control the apportionment of work, working conditions, prices, work standards, and disciplinary actions. On the other hand, these companies dodge their fair commitments, reject ownership of merchandise bought or sold via their apps, and deny their duties toward workers [47].

At the macroeconomic level, the gig work may increase labor force participation and the number of hours worked in the economy. According to the McKinsey Global Institute studies, the gig economy has increased the labor participation in the United States [18]. The gig work can be beneficial to unemployed, retirees, and students who are seeking some additional sources of income and can ultimately lead them to permanent jobs. Some gig workers can specialize in doing what they do best [26]. Therefore, one may suggest that, by increasing the workers' efficiency, the gig economy may lead to the creation of more productive and satisfying jobs across the globe [18].

References

[1] Brumm, F. 2016. *Making Gigs Work: The New Economy in Context.* University of Illinois—Urbana Champaign, Master of Human Resources and Industrial Relations.

[2] Donovan, S.A., D.H. Bradley, and J.O. Shimabukuru. 2016. "What Does the Gig Economy Mean for Workers?" *CONG. RES. SERV. R44365.* Available at https://fas.org/sgp/crs/misc/R44365.pdf

[3] Thomas, K.D. 2018. "Taxing the Gig Economy (June 08, 2017)." *166 University of Pennsylvania Law Review* 1415. UNC Legal Studies Research Paper. Available at SSRN: https://ssrn.com/abstract=2894394 or http://dx.doi.org/10.2139/ssrn.2894394

[4] Cardon, D., and A. Casilli. 2015. "Qu'est-ce que le Digital Labor ?" *Bry-sur-Marne.* INA Editions.

[5] Eurofound. 2013. "Self-Employed or Not Self-Employed?" *Working Conditions of Economically Dependent Workers.'* Background Paper, Dublin, Eurofound.

[6] Aloisi, A. July 08–10, 2015. "The Rising of On-Demand Work, A Case Study Research on a Set of Online Platforms and Apps." *Paper Presented at the IV Regulating for Decent Work Conference.* ILO, Geneva. Available at http://rdw2015.org/download (accessed October 26, 2015).

[7] De Stefano, V. 2015. "The Rise of the Just-In-Time Workforce: On-Demand Work, Crowdwork, and Labor Protection in the Gig-Economy." *Comp. Lab. L. & Poly J.* 37, p. 471.

[8] Manyika J., S. Lund, K. Robinson, J. Valentino, and R. Dobbs. June 2015. *A Labour Market that Works: Connecting Talent with Opportunity in the Digital Age.* McKinsey & Company.

[9] Kennedy, J.V. 2016. "Three Paths to Update labor law for the Gig Economy." *Information Technology and Innovation Foundation* 18.

[10] Horowitz, S.R. October 01, 2015."Freelancing in America 2015 Report." *Freelancers Union.* https://freelancersunion.org/blog/dispatches/2015/10/01/freelancing-america-2015/

[11] Harris, S.D., and A.B. Krueger. December 2015. "A Proposal for Modernizing Labor Laws for Twenty-First-Century Work: The 'Independent Worker.'" *Discussion Paper 2015-10, The Hamilton Project, The Brookings Institution.* http://hamiltonproject.org/assets/files/modernizing_labor_laws_for_twenty_first_century_work_krueger_harris.pdf

[12] Stewart, A., and J. Stanford. 2017. "Regulating Work in the Gig Economy: What are the Options?" *The Economic and Labour Relations Review* 28, no. 3, pp. 420–437.

[13] ESTY. 2016. "Economic Security for the Gig Economy: A Social Safety Net that Works for Everyone Who Works." *Fall.* https://extfiles.etsy.com/advocacy/Etsy_EconomicSecurity_2016.pdf

[14] Federal Reserve Board. 2015. "Report on the Economic Well-Being of U.S. Households in 2014." https://federalreserve.gov/econresdata/2014-report-economic-well-being-us-households-201505.pdf

[15] Katz, L.F., and A.B. Krueger. 2016. "The Rise and Nature of Alternative Work Arrangements in the United States, 1995–2015." http://scholar.harvard.edu/files/lkatz/files/katz_krueger_cws_v3.pdf

[16] Katz, L.F., and A.B. Krueger. 2016. *The Rise and Nature of Alternative Work Arrangements in the United States,* 1995–2015, no. w22667. National Bureau of Economic Research.

[17] Intuit. 2015. "Intuit Forecast: 7.6 Million People in On-Demand Economy by 2020." August 13 [Online], available at http://investors.intuit.com/press-releases/press-release-details/2015/Intuit-Forecast-76-Million-People-in-On-Demand-Economy-by-2020/default.aspx

[18] Australian Industry Group. 2016. "The Emergence of the Gig Economy." http://cdn.aigroup.com.au/Reports/2016/Gig_Economy_August_2016.pdf

[19] Intuit. October 2010. "Intuit 2020 Report: Twenty Trends that Will Shape the Next Decade."

[20] Gallup. 2013. *Remote Workers Log More Hours and Are Slightly More Engaged.*

[21] Ghayad, R., and W.T. Dickens. 2012. "What Can We Learn by Disaggregating the Unemployment-Vacancy Relationship?"

[22] Krueger, A.B., and J.V. Hall. 2015. *An Analysis of the Labor Market for Uber's Driver-Partners in the United States,* 587. Princeton University Industrial Relations Section Working Paper.

[23] Davis, G.F. 2009. "The Rise and Fall of Finance and the End of the Society of Organizations." *Academy of Management Perspectives* 23, no. 3, pp. 27–44.

[24] Abraham, K.G., and S.K. Taylor. 1996. "Firms' Use of Outside Contractors: Theory and Evidence." *Journal of Labor Economics* 14, no. 3, pp. 394–424.

[25] Cohen, S., and W.B. Eimicke. 2013. *Independent Contracting Policy and Management Analysis.* New York, NY: Columbia University.

[26] Manyika, J., S. Lund, J. Bughin, K. Robinson, J. Mischke, and D. Mahajan. 2016. *Independent Work: Choice, Necessity, and the Gig Economy.* McKinsey & Company.

[27] Etsy. July 2015. "Building an Etsy Economy: The New Face of Creative Entrepreneurship."

[28] Rudram, B., B. Faith, P. Prieto Martin, and B. Ramalingam. 2016. "Ten Frontier Technologies for International Development." Brighton: Institute of Development Studies.

[29] Hunt, A., and F. Machingura. 2016. "A Good Gig?" *The Rise of On-Demand Domestic Work.* London, UK: Overseas Development Institute.

[30] Birdsall, N. 2010. "The Middle Class in Developing Countries." In *Equity and Growth in a Globalizing World*, eds. K. Kanbur. and M. Spence, pp. 157–189. Washington: World Bank.

[31] Hindustan Times. 2016. http://hindustantimes.com/more-lifestyle/bai-on-call-how-home-service-apps-changing-the-maids-market/story-s6zz6kmWw1a EamZ1yLxjaL.html. First Published: February 21, 2016 14:15 1ST

[32] Freedland, M., and N. Kountouris. 2011. *The Legal Construction of Personal Work Relations*. Oxford: Oxford University Press.

[33] Freelancers Union. 2009. "Independent, Innovative, and Unprotected: How the Old Safety Net is Failing America's New Workforce." [Online]. Available: https://fu-res.org/pdfs/advocacy/surveyreport_overview.pdf

[34] Codagnone, C., F. Abadie, and F. Biagi. 2016. "The Future of Work in the 'Sharing Economy.'" *Market Efficiency and Equitable Opportunities or Unfair Precarisation?*

[35] "The New Work Order: Ensuring young Australians have Skills and Experience for the Jobs of the Future, not the Past, Foundation for Young Australians." August 2015.

[36] Cherry, M.A., and A. Aloisi. 2016. "Dependent Contractors in the Gig Economy: A Comparative Approach." *Am. UL Rev.* 66, p. 635. "The State of Contingent Workforce Management: The 2014–2015 Guidebook." October 2014. *Ardent.*

[37] "The Future, Employees Won't Exist." June 13, 2015. *Tad Milbourn, Tech Crunch.* http://techcrunch.com/2015/06/13/in-the-future-employees-wont- exist/

[38] Online Work Report. Upwork. http://elance-odesk.com/online-work-report-global

[39] "How Hiring International Freelancers Opens The Door To Untapped Talent, Scott Galit, CEO World Magazine." http://ceoworld.biz/2015/07/08/how-hiring-international-freelancers-opens-the-door-to-untapped-talent

[40] "Freelancers are the Future of Hyper-Specialised Teams, Xenios Thrasyvoulou, Wallblog." November 12, 2015. http://wallblog.co.uk/2014/11/12/freelancers-are-the-future-of-hyper-specialised-teams/

[41] Sundararajan, A. 2016. *The Sharing Economy: The End of Employment and the Rise of Crowd-Based Capitalism*. MIT Press.

[42] Friedman, G. 2014. "Workers Without Employers: Shadow Corporations and the Rise of the Gig Economy." *Review of Keynesian Economics* 2, pp. 171–188.

[43] Kenney, M., and J. Zysman. 2016. "The Rise of the Platform Economy." *Issues in Science and Technology* 32, no. 3, pp. 61–69.

[44] Moran, J.A. 2009. "Independent Contractor or Employee-Misclassification of Workers and Its Effect on the State." *Buff. Pub. Int. LJ* 28, p. 105.

[45] "The Rise of the Freelancer: What It Means for Employers and Workers, Sue Barrett, Smart Company." November 2015. http://smartcompany.com.au/ marketing/sales/49198-the-rise-of-the-freelancer-what-it-means-for-bosses-and-workers/72 http://www.truelancer.com/

[46] Healy, J., D. Nicholson, and A. Pekarek. 2017. "Should We Take the Gig Economy Seriously?" *Labour & Industry: A Journal of the Social and Economic Relations of Work* 27, no. 3, pp. 232–248.

CHAPTER 14

Consumers and Consumption

Surge in the Global Middle Class and the Shift of Consumption From West to East

Behind the economic performance of the developed countries, their significant consumers' markets are sizeable middle classes. The middle-class citizens usually enjoy a decent level of financial security, and as a result, they conduct a comfortable life marked by access to stable housing, decent health care and educational opportunities, reasonable retirement, and discretionary income that can be spent on vacation and leisure pursuits [1]. The middle class is an ambiguous social classification and may involve different meanings across the world, but we may simply suggest that the middle-class citizens are those who can have a relatively comfortable life. The importance of middle class resides particularly in its consumerism and in its constant desire for acquiring high-quality and differentiated products. The middle-class consumers often are willing to pay for quality and differentiation [2]. In the 20th century and the early decades of the 21st century, the middle-class consumers of North America and Europe have been responsible for generating demand, while low- and middle-income citizens in Asia have been the main source of supply.

Currently, 1.8 billion people or 28 percent of the world's population are categorized as middle-class citizens. Half of the middle-class people live in developed economies. The middle-class citizens are concentrated in North America (338 million), Europe (664 million), and Asia (525 million) [1]. The United States, the EU, and Japan with, respectively, 230, 450, and 125 million middle-class consumers are at the top of the list. By contrast, there are very few middle-class consumers, approximately 32 million, in sub-Saharan Africa. Obviously, the middle class is a broad category, and there are significant differences between the purchasing power of middle-class consumers in the United States, Europe, Africa, and China. For instance, the United States is home to 12 percent of the world's middle-class people, but it accounts for 21 percent or $4.4 trillion of the global spending by middle-class consumers [1].

Currently, the vast majority of the world's population or almost 70 percent are categorized as poor. Over the next 20 years, this pattern is expected to change, as the world's population will become richer and the share of the middle class will increase substantially. For instance, by 2022, more people in the world will be middle class than the poor, and by 2030, five billion people or two-thirds of the global population could be categorized as middle class. According to the World Bank's Global Economic Prospects, the global middle class would expand from 7.6 percent of the world's population in 2000 to between 16.1 and 19.4 percent of the world's population by 2030 [3]. Goldman Sachs estimated that the global middle class is expected to increase from 29 percent of the world population in 2008 to 50 percent in 2030 [4]. In the same way, the global spending of the middle class could increase from $21 trillion in 2009 to $56 trillion by 2030.

Due to the accelerated economic growth in Asia, and particularly in China, the center of gravity of global output is expected to shift from the West to Asia involving that the Asian countries, notably China, India, Indonesia, and Vietnam, will account for a larger share of the world economy [5]. Therefore, there will be a major shift in the distribution of wealth from the Western developed countries to Asia (see Figures 14.1 and 14.2). Some studies suggest that almost all of the new members of the global middle class will live in Asia [1]. In the next 20 years, the number of middle-class consumers may increase sixfold from the current 500 million to more than 3.2 billion. The share of Asian middle-class consumers will increase from one-quarter to two-thirds by 2030. By contrast, the share of North America and Europe can drop from 54 to 17 percent for the same period (see Tables 14.1–14.3).

The Asian middle-class growth is remarkably rapid. By 2030, Asia will be home to three billion middle-class people, which are 10 times more than North America and five times more than Europe. Asia's share of the global middle class' spending may increase from 23 percent in 2009 to

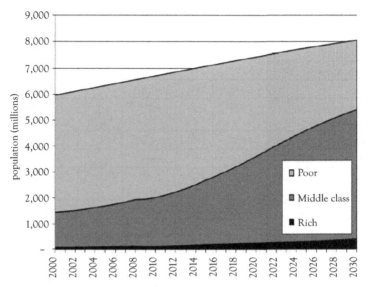

Figure 14.1 A surge in the global middle class
Source: [1].

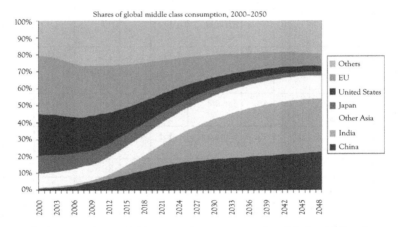

Figure 14.2 India and China make waves in the global middle class
Source: [5].

59 percent by 2030 [1]. By 2020 and 2030, China and India could be ranked among the top three countries with regard to the middle-class spending surpassing the United States [1]. Thus, the global consumer market is changing fast. For example, as of 2000, the United States accounted for 37 percent of global car sales, while China accounted for

Table 14.1 Total middle-class consumption, regions (2005 PPP$, billions and global share)

	2009		2020		2030	
North America	5,602	26%	5,863	17%	5,837	10%
Europe	8,138	38%	10,301	29%	11,337	20%
Central and South America	1,534	7%	2,315	7%	3,117	6%
Asia Pacific	4,952	23%	14,798	42%	32,596	59%
Sub-Saharan Africa	256	1%	448	1%	827	1%
Middle East and North Africa	796	4%	1,321	4%	1,966	4%
World	21,278	100%	35,045	100%	55,680	100%

Source: [1].

Table 14.2 Total middle-class consumption, top 10 countries (2005 PPP$, billions and global share)

	2009			2020			2030		
1	The United States	4,377	21%	China	4,468	13%	India	12,777	23%
2	Japan	1,800	8%	The United States	4,270	12%	China	9,985	18%
3	Germany	1,219	6%	India	3,733	11%	The United States	3,969	7%
4	France	927	4%	Japan	2,203	6%	Indonesia	2,474	4%
5	The United Kingdom	889	4%	Germany	1,361	4%	Japan	2,286	4%
6	Russia	870	4%	Russia	1,189	3%	Russia	1,448	3%
7	China	859	4%	France	1,077	3%	Germany	1,335	2%
8	Italy	740	3%	Indonesia	1,020	3%	Mexico	1,239	2%
9	Mexico	715	3%	Mexico	992	3%	Brazil	1,225	2%
10	Brazil	623	3%	The United Kingdom	976	3%	France	1,119	2%

Source: [1].

barely 1 percent. By 2020, China is expected to account for 25 percent of the global car market [6]. This phenomenon is not limited to China, as other developing economies are on the same path. In the next decade,

Table 14.3 Spending by the global middle class, 2009 to 2030 (millions of 2005 PPP dollars)

	2009		2020		2030	
North America	5,602	26%	5,863	17%	5,837	10%
Europe	8,138	38%	10,301	29%	11,337	20%
Central and South America	1,534	7%	2,315	7%	3,117	6%
Asia Pacific	4,952	23%	14,798	42%	32,596	59%
Sub-Saharan Africa	256	1%	448	1%	827	1%
Middle East and North Africa	796	4%	1,321	4%	1,966	4%
World	21,278	100%	35,045	100%	55,680	100%

Source: [1].

the share of developing economies in the global middle class will surpass the share of advanced countries. For instance, the middle class in Latin America is expected to grow from 181 to 313 million by 2030. In Africa and the Middle East, the middle class is expected to more than double, from 137 to 341 million [7]. In the past decade, private consumption in developing economies has been growing at about three times the rate of advanced countries, and this surge in consumption is expected to increase even further [8]. Developing economies are showing the rapid growth of demand for all discretionary products from cars, electronics, and cell phones to toothpaste and air conditioners. Consequently, there will be a tectonic consumption shift from the West to the East, and the products, fashions, tastes, and designs are expected to be adapted to the new global middle class' preferences. A large number of middle-class consumers in the East will shape global consumption.

The Growing Importance of Cities as Centers of Consumption

Over the course of the past three decades, the world has experienced a wave of fast urbanization. The world's population is becoming more urbanized than ever, and big cities are attracting a large number of inhabitants. For the first time in 2007, the world's urban population surpassed the world's rural population. According to the World Bank reports, the share of the world's urban population has risen from 30 percent in 1950 to more than 54 percent in 2015. The ongoing urbanization in conjunction with the growth of the global population will add 2.5 billion people to the urban population by 2050, with nearly 90 percent of the increase concentrated in Asia and Africa [9]. In the age of globalization, the economic activity is becoming highly clustered around urban centers. Almost all manufacturing, logistics, distribution, employment, health care, financial and business services, and by extension, demand and spending are located in urban places. A few cities are becoming responsible for much of the national economic activity. Within every country, we find out significant disparities between urban and regional economies, in terms of their specialization, growth rates, and future prospects. In some countries, one or two major cities dominate the national economies. In some others, a few large and mid-sized cities determine the dynamism of the national economies. Some cities are so integrated into the global economy that transcends their respective national borders and acts as quasi-independent economic players [10]. By 2030, the world is expected to have 41 megacities with more than 10 million inhabitants [11]. Currently, 29 megacities are home to 471 million people, an equivalent of 6 percent of the world's total population [12] (see Figure 14.5). Furthermore, the number of cities with populations over 20 million is increasing fast. As shown in Figure 14.3, a relatively small number of cities are dominating the global economic arena because of their active involvement in business occupations such as financial and business services, and corporate control and coordination functions (see Figure 14.4) [13]. In the developed economies of the West, urbanization is a well-established phenomenon that experienced much of its growth in the 1950s and 1960s [14]. By contrast, urbanization in developing economies is a new phenomenon that accelerated only after the 1990s. Currently, more than 75 percent of the populations in developing economies still live in rural areas, suggesting that the sharpest increase in the urban centers will happen in such countries [15]. Based on the United Nations estimates, almost 2.5 billion people will be added to the global urban population between 2014 and 2050. Of these 2.5 billion new urban dwellers, almost 90 percent will live in Africa and Asia. Only three countries, namely India, China, and Nigeria, are expected to account for more than one-third of the global urban population growth [16].

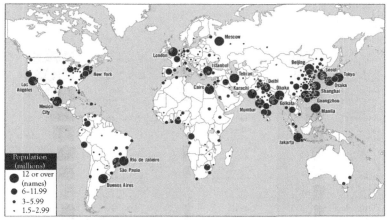

Figure 14.3 The world's major cities by size of population

Source: citypopulation.de.

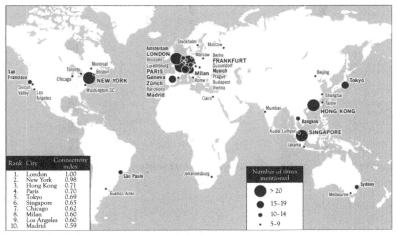

Figure 14.4 Key cities in the global economy

Source: [13].

The recent population movement from rural areas to cities in China, India, and other developing or emerging economies creates huge opportunities for marketers. By 2030, consumers in large cities will account for half of the global population and will generate 81 percent of the global consumption [17]. From a marketing perspective, we may suggest that the urban world is where consumption takes place. Consumers in large cities will account for 81 percent of the global consumption by

Figure 14.5 *Top cities by absolute consumption and consumption growth*

Source: [17].

2030 and 91 percent of consumption growth between 2015 and 2030. What is more interesting is that global urban consumption is highly concentrated. Only 100 cities will account for 45 percent of consumption growth, and 32 of them will account for a quarter of the global total ($23 trillion) between 2015 and 2030 [18]. The growth in urban consumption is related to the consumption of services and amenities in cities, including growing expenditures for entertainment, restaurants, and travel. Many multinational corporations (MNCs) are developing strategies to serve the world's new urban consumers more effectively. According to the Deloitte's Globalization Survey (2013), around 50 percent of the companies have already developed customized strategies for specific cities [19]. Underlying their business strategies is the financial power of urban centers and the affluence of their residents. Large cities in emerging countries are rapidly claiming their place alongside the long-established cities of the developed world. From a marketing standpoint, the urban centers in emerging or developing economies are more attractive as they are growing faster than their counterparts in developed economies are (see Figures 14.3 and 14.4).

Table 14.4 lists the cities with the highest consumption and the consumption growth between 2015 and 2030. As shown in the figure, the top five cities with the largest projected growth in consumption are London ($367 billion), Tokyo ($354 billion), New York ($351 billion), Beijing ($300 billion), and Shanghai ($277 billion). As shown in Figure 14.4, of the 20 cities with the largest predicted increase in consumption between 2015 and 2030, seven are located in the United States, six are in China, and two are in Japan. The following cities will have the largest consumption by 2030: Tokyo (Japan), New York (the United States), London (the United Kingdom), Los Angeles (the United States), Osaka (Japan), Houston (the United States), Chicago (the United States), Dallas (the United States), Washington, DC (the United States), Rhein-Ruhr (Germany), Beijing (China), Shanghai (China), Nagoya (Japan), Mexico City (Mexico), Paris (France), Sao Paulo (Brazil), Boston (the United States), San Francisco (the United States), Atlanta (the United States), and Philadelphia (the United States).

The Shortening Product Life Cycles

The product life cycle is a useful concept that describes the sales history of the product over its lifetime. Generally, the product life cycle is presented as a bell-shaped curve and is divided into some major stages, including introduction, growth, maturity, and decline. During the last stage or decline stage, the more innovative and competitive products replace the old ones. In recent decades, businesses have come under growing pressure from investors and consumers to innovate and introduce their products faster. As a result, the pace of innovation has substantially accelerated, and product life cycles have continued to shorten. We are witnessing a growing temporal acceleration in production, purchase, and consumption processes. On the one hand, the temporal acceleration pushes manufacturers to create more innovative and performing products because there is only a narrow opportunity to earn profits before the competition catches up. On the other hand, the temporal acceleration pushes the consumers to rush and buy the latest products to fulfill their lives by consuming faster than ever. The temporal acceleration destroys stability by making the items such as electronic devices obsolete shortly after their introduction. The average lifespan of a computer has shrunk from four or five years to two years in the past decade. That is why a large proportion of sales in electronic devices happen soon after the introduction of the product. As trade becomes more global, new products and technologies have the potential to reach a larger number of users in shorter periods. For example, while it took the telephone almost 70 years to reach 80 percent penetration in the U.S. households, it would take only 12 to 15 years for smartphones to reach the same level of penetration [20]. The shortening product life cycle pushes companies to keep low inventory levels and minimize investments at every point in their value chain [21]. The speedy manufacturing is expected at all stages of production, including supply chains and technological development. As the product life cycles shorten, the introduction and growth stages of the product life cycle are merged and are followed immediately by a steep decline. In other words, the shortening product life cycles indicate the lack of a maturity stage. In other words, a narrow space of opportunity exists to make profits on a new product before the competition catches up and margins decline. The sharp decline in the product life cycle and sudden shift of users to the next-generation products means that businesses may lack time and resources to reach out to all their potential users. Hence, businesses are often caught in a situation where a new product replaces the old ones before they are able to conduct their marketing campaign [22]. To deal with the effects of the shortening product life cycle, firms can consider three marketing strategies: extensive marketing effort, simultaneous appeal to various segments, and intensive marketing effort. Shortening product life cycle means that firms have a small amount of time to conduct their marketing campaigns and reach potential customers [23]. When selling products with shorter life cycles, businesses should collect and process information for various segments quickly and simultaneously. Finally, firms should conduct more intensive and high-quality marketing campaigns to increase the number of customers [23].

Digitization of Consumption

In the past decade, we have been witnessing a significant intersection between consumption and advanced information technologies. Because of technological advances, physical and virtual environments are rapidly converging, and companies are required to satisfy customers' needs and desires more quickly. Customers are benefiting from an infinite number of online and offline options for researching and buying new products and services at their fingertips, and digital devices have become indispensable for executing promotions, stimulating sales, and increasing market share [24]. Thanks to new information technologies, the consumers are gaining control of their interactions with businesses [25]. At the same time, customers are demanding instantaneous and continuous digital experience from businesses. We witness that both business-to-consumer and business-to-business customers are developing their expectations of product or service quality around the speed, convenience, and ease of use [26]. Customers are raising their expectations by referring to companies such as Amazon and Apple. They expect that any other business delivers products and services with rapidity, convenience, and ease of use compared to the tech giants. In dealing with the increasing pressure of consumption digitization, businesses focus on three main areas to attract and retain their customers: customer experience, personalization, and ownership to access [26]. First, customer experience is becoming an important variable in addition to the quality of products and services. For that reason, businesses are figuring out that offering only products and services is not enough to attract customers. Rather, they are relying on digital interfaces to offer their customers unique and impressive experiences. Second, digitization is enabling companies to deliver personalized and highly customized products and services. Businesses are capitalizing on new technologies to offer their customers the freedoms they seek based on the data that they collect. Third, because of the sharing economy, across the world and more particularly in North America, the concept of ownership is being replaced by access and utility [27]. More than 110 million people are participating in the collaborative economy in North America alone [26]. More and more, customers are attracted to businesses models based on sharing and access, convenience, and affordability, rather than ownership. As the prospects of sharing economy rise, businesses are facing new challenges to change the way they track and respond to customer expectations. Businesses collect and use data to create digitally enabled revenue models by tailoring products and services to their consumers' needs and preferences. Conversely, customers desire to take more control of their own product, service, or brand experience; they expect to have access to transparent information about the features of products and services. In the new age of consumption digitization, peer review and advocacy are gaining importance, and customers rely on peer recommendations to make their decisions [26]. Therefore, it is important for the businesses how to engage customers in the new digital channels not only to make short-term profits but also to create lasting pleasant digital experiences. Many businesses, particularly those operating in traditional industries, are required to invest heavily in the digitization of their business processes to meet the lofty expectations of their customers.

Consumers' Attention as a Precious Commodity

Attention is defined as the allocation of mental resources to visible or conceptual objects and is considered key to marketing management [28]. Indeed, without attention, advertising has no impact on consumers. For that reason, advertising managers always seek to grab consumers' attention in order to convert it to purchase behavior. It is widely accepted that greater attention leads to higher advertising impact, and thus higher sales. Attention is a complex concept, but it can be reduced to two major dimensions: intensity and duration. The intensity is a measure of the quality of attention during an interval, while the duration refers to its quantity [28]. In the past three decades, both the intensity and duration of consumers' attention have been declining. Based on a study conducted by Microsoft, since 2000, the average person's attention span has dropped from 12 to only 8 seconds [29]. Our personal and social lives have been invaded by a plethora of audiovisual information coming from the new media, including the Internet, mobile devices, and traditional media such as radio, television, and newspapers. Most people find an advertising video of 52 seconds too long. The more we are exposed to information, the more we get distracted, and the more we lose our attention.

The success of some Internet platforms such as Twitter, Facebook, and Snapchat is based on quickly catching their consumers' attention by offering short-format content. For example, Snapchat is a highly popular platform among the young mobile generation that is positioning itself by offering short and disposable contents. With over 10 billion daily video views, Snapchat hosts only videos that are 10 seconds or shorter [29]. Along with shortening attention spans, the quality of consumers' attention has been deteriorating in the past decades. Indeed, many indexes confirm that consumers have lost interest in the information content of the advertisement. Consumers do not feel the need of advertisement very much as they can obtain any piece of information on a company's products, prices, and technical features from a wide range of sources, including the company's website or from the peer evaluations. Webpages can be seen as replacements of advertisement that are available, reliable, and often more informative and more customized than advertisements. In short, we may suggest that consumers are attributing less attention to advertisement because of a wide range of factors. They are increasingly exposed to commercial messages, but they do not see any benefits in them as they have extensive information outlets at their disposal [28]. Facing the lack of customers' interest in the advertisement, businesses have reacted by increasing the volume of their advertisement and by grating price promotions. These countermeasures have caused adverse effects on both current profits and future revenues and have resulted in the rising cost of buying customers' attention [28]. For example, it is suggested that the price of high-quality attention has risen as much as ninefold in the last two decades [28]. This trend is expected to continue in the near future, and the market for consumer attention is supposed to become even more crowded and more competitive. As such, the customers' attention may be viewed as a precious commodity that should be managed judiciously. Considering the fierce competition for consumers' attention, marketing managers have to adapt the adequate advertising strategy to the level of attention in order to increase their advertisement campaign's success [28]. Marketing managers may use cautious advertising principles to buy customers' attention at a cheaper price. They may create advertisements that are effective even under low levels of attention. Finally, marketing managers may use advertisement content that causes higher levels of attention, so it can be more effectively converted into persuasion and purchase behavior [28].

References

[1] Kharas, H. 2010. "The Emerging Middle Class in Developing Countries." Brookings Institution.

[2] Murphy, K.M., A. Shleifer, and R. Vishny. 1989. "Income Distribution, Market Size, and Industrialization." *The Quarterly Journal of Economics* 104, no. 3, pp. 537–564.

[3] Collier, P. 2007. "The Bottom Billion." *Economic Review-Deddington* 25, no. 1, p. 17.

[4] Kaufmann, D., A. Kraay, and M. Mastruzzi. 2009. *Governance Matters VIII: Aggregate and Individual Governance Indicators* 1996–2008. The World Bank.

[5] Kharas, H., and G. Gertz. 2010. *The New Global Middle Class: A Cross-Over from West to East,* pp. 1–14. Wolfensohn Center for Development at Brookings.

[6] https://statista.com/statistics/225123/chinas-share-of-the-global-car-market/

[7] Yueh, L. June 18, 2013. "The Rise of the Global Middle Class." *BBC News.*

[8] Dadush, U.B., and S. Ali. 2012. *In Search of the Global Middle Class: A New Index.* Carnegie Endowment for International Peace.

[9] United Nations, Department of Economic and Social Affairs, Population Division. n.d. "World Urbanization Prospects: The 2014 Revision."

[10] Henderson, J.W., and M. Castells. 1987. *Global Restructuring and Territorial Development.* Sage Publications Limited.

[11] United Nations, Department of Economic and Social Affairs, Population Division. 2014. "World Urbanization Prospects: The 2014 Revision, Highlights (ST/ESA/SER.A/352)."

[12] Bloom, D.E. 2016. "Demographic Upheaval." *Finance and Development* 53, no. 1, pp. 6–11.

[13] Dicken, P. 2007. "Global Shift: Mapping the Changing Contours of the World Economy." Sage Publications Ltd.

[14] Guadalupe, M., H. Li, and J. Wulf. 2013. "Who Lives in the C-Suite? Organizational Structure and the Division of Labor in Top Management." *Management Science* 60, no. 4, pp. 824–844.

[15] Winthrop, R., G. Bulloch, P Bhatt, and A. Wood. 2015. "Development Goals in an Era of Demographic Change." *Global Monitoring Report*, 2016.

[16] The United Nations, Department of Economics and Social Affairs. n.d. http://un.org/en/development/desa/population/publications/factsheets/index.shtml

[17] Dobbs, R., J. Remes, J. Manyika, J.R. Woetzel, J. Perrey, G. Kelly, and H. Sharma. 2016. *Urban World: The Global Consumers to Watch*. McKinsey Global Institute.

[18] Khanna, P. 2016. "Connectography: Mapping the Future of Global Civilization." Random House.

[19] Marchese, K., and B. Lam. 2014. "Anticipatory Supply Chains Business Trends 2014: Navigating the Next Wave of Globalization."

[20] Dediu, H. 2012. "When Will Smartphones Reach Saturation in the US?" Retrieved from http://asymco.com/2012/04/11/when-will-smartphones-reach-saturation-in-the-us/

[21] Goyal, T. 2001. "Shortening Product Life Cycles?" *Electronic News (North America)* 47, no. 16, p. 46.

[22] Geyer, R., L.N. Van Wassenhove, and A. Atasu. 2007. "The Economics of Remanufacturing Under Limited Component Durability and Finite Product Life Cycles." *Management Science* 53, no. 1, pp. 88–100.

[23] Goldman, A. 1982. "Short Product Life Cycles: Implications for the Marketing Activities of Small High-Technology Companies." *R & D Management* 12, no. 2, pp. 81–90.

[24] https://mckinsey.com/business-functions/marketing-and-sales/our-insights/digitizing-the-consumer-decision-journey

[25] Accenture. 2015. *Digital Transformation in the Age of the Customer: A Spotlight on B2C*. https://accenture.com/acnmedia/Accenture/Conversion-Assets/DotCom/Documents/Global/PDF/Digital_2/Accenture-Digital-Transformation-B2C-spotlight.pdf

[26] Pilkington, M. 2016. "11 Blockchain Technology: Principles and Applications." *Research Handbook on Digital Transformations*, p. 225.

[27] https://mckinsey.com/business-functions/digital-mckinsey/our-insights/accelerating-the-digitization-of-business-processes

[28] Teixeira, T.S. 2014. *The Rising Cost of Consumer Attention: Why You Should— Care, and What You Can do About It.*

[29] Lindner, E. 2012. "A Dignity Economy: Creating an Economy that Serves Human Dignity and Preserves Our Planet." *Dignity Press*. https://adweek.com/digital/john-stevens-guest-post-decreasing-attention-spans/

CHAPTER 15

Labor, Work Organization, and Education

The Slowdown in Labor Growth and Aging Workforce in the United States

Over the course of the next decades, the world's population will be aging rapidly across the globe, particularly in developed countries. Currently, there are around 962 million people aged 60 years or over in the world, comprising 13 percent of the global population and growing at a rate of about 3 percent per year [1]. By 2050, half of the global population will reside in countries where at least 20 percent of the inhabitants are aged 60 years or over [2]. In the United States, the pace of aging is so significant that, by 2050, the number of Americans aged 65 years and more will reach 90 million [3]. As a result, in the next few decades, we expect a general trend toward the aging workforce and slower labor growth across the United States. Nevertheless, the aging population and slow labor growth problem are much more notable in China, Japan, and many other European countries such as Italy and Germany. In the United States, the workforce growth has declined continually from 2.6 percent in the 1970s to 1.6 percent during the 1980s and 1.1 percent in the 1990s, despite immigration and higher participation of women in the workforce. In the past three decades, the increase in the labor force has been boosted mainly by progressively higher labor force participation by women and large inflows of immigrants. Since the 2000s, the female workforce participation rate has been approaching that of men. Therefore, the decline in the workforce growth is expected to be very significant in the next coming years. By 2025, the rate of workforce growth may decline to as low as 0.3 or 0.4 percent per year [4]. Because of the combined effects of the aging population and slower workforce growth, some businesses may encounter difficulty in finding and recruiting qualified workers, especially in periods of faster economic growth [5]. The reliance of businesses on women and migrants will lead to the formation of a balanced workforce marked by different age cohorts, genders, and visible minorities. An aging workforce necessitates substantial changes to the workplace regulations and atmosphere because older workers have special needs. For example, workers aged 65 years and older have been shown to experience higher rates of permanent disabilities and workplace fatalities than their younger counterparts in the same industries and occupations.

Growing Importance of Cognitive Skills and Education Attainment

The transition from an industrial to a knowledge-based economy is expected to accelerate in the next decades. The global decline in the manufacturing sector, combined with automation technologies, will reduce the demand for labor-intensive and entry-level jobs and will boost job creation in technology, engineering, and computer science [6]. Consequently, the demand for highly skilled and educated workers will continue to accelerate. These trends imply that the economies that can train and maintain a high-skilled workforce are expected to outperform. Businesses will continue to look for the technical workforce capable of operating computer systems, developing and installing software, and managing networks. Organizations, whether for-profit or nonprofit, are expected to favor workers with high-level cognitive skills such as abstract reasoning, problem-solving, communication, and collaboration. Furthermore, those workers who can interact in a global marketplace, participate in cross-national teams, and collaborate in diverse cultural and linguistic settings will have higher chances of recruitment and achievement. The mounting demand has been driving up the salary premium paid to workers with higher skills and education levels since the late 1990s. Closely associated with the demand for a highly skilled workforce is the educational attainment measured as years of schooling. Between 1973 and 2001, the wage premium for a college degree compared with a high school diploma increased 30 percent from 46 to 76 percent [5]. For that reason, the level of education attainment has been increasing in most of the developed and developing economies [7]. In the United States, college graduation rates among young white men and women have been rising, but a substantial fraction of African Americans and Hispanics workers are still lagging behind. Compared to other developed nations, the U.S. students' scores are ranked about the average, despite greater public and private expenditures on education. For example, schooling expenditures amounted to 2.3 percent of the GDP in the United States versus 1.9 percent of the GDP in Canada and around 1 percent of the GDP in other G8 countries [8]. The relatively low ranking of the U.S. students could be because of widespread educational, cognitive, and social disparities among American students. Considering the scale of upcoming technological disruptions, we may expect an extraordinary rate of change in the core curriculum contents of many academic fields. Based on some estimates, nearly 50 percent of subject knowledge acquired during the first year of a four-year technical degree could be outdated by the time students graduate [6]. Technological advances increase the demand for a more skilled workforce, but at the same time, new technologies provide immense opportunities to support the workers' education and training. The knowledge economy necessitates continuous learning and training throughout the working life, and many organizations are gradually relying on technology and the use of computers and other information technologies to enhance their workers' skills. The technology-mediated learning has the potential to offer efficient, individualized, and affordable education to a large number of students and employees and is becoming an integral part of workforce training.

The Move Toward Flattened, Fluid, and Flexible Organizations of Work

Technological forces and their subsequent social transformations are making organizations less vertical, more decentralized, and more specialized. To adapt themselves to the new conditions, the organizations shift from the rigid pyramidal structures to participatory management. The increasing importance of knowledge and intellectual property is pushing many organizations to empower their employees at all the organizational levels. Under the new circumstances, offering employees with higher levels of authority and decision making can result in higher levels of productivity. More specialization is pushing many organizations to rely more and more on outsourcing, even for crucial activities such as industrial design, manufacturing processes, business processing tasks, and human resources. Globalization is creating opportunities for outsourcing on a global scale, and organizations will continue to exploit the cost advantages across borders. In search of efficiency, organizations may scatter their value chain activities across the globe or break up their structures into semiautonomous units. The new telecommunication technologies provide opportunities for firms to manage or coordinate their decentralized structures. Consistent with these transformations, there will be an increase in the portion of workers in flexible arrangements such as self-employment, contract work, temporary help, and lease agreements. Undeniably, transient work arrangements are expected to become more widespread in the face of rapid technological change and competitive market pressures. The new forms of organizations could be based on electronically connected networks of contractors, freelancers, and semiautonomous entities. The focus of work is gradually shifting from the solid organizational structures to flexible and project-based operations. Under the fierce competition from globalization and outsourcing, employers are increasingly turning to part-time, contingent, and contract workers to meet their business goals. According to one estimate, the freelance workforce may grow to 40 percent of the U.S. workforce or nearly 60 million workers in the next five years [9]. Those employees who stay with their organizations may have to work under part-time and other flexible work arrangements [10]. These transformations may have significant implications for the current employment laws and regulations, tax systems, employees' benefits such as health care, life or disability insurance, and pensions that are generally defined for regular and traditional organizations [11]. Because of all these socioeconomic transformations, the organization of work is moving toward a flattened, fluid, and flexible configuration [12].

In tandem with the move toward a flexible organization of work, innovative technologies are changing the very concept of the workplace. Unlike the traditional workplace, the new workplace arrangements are not reliant on a physical space. While many salary jobs, particularly those involving manufacturing, will continue to be tied to a designated physical space, a growing portion of the workforce will move toward distance work when tasks can be done off-site [13]. These work arrangements are beneficial as teleworking allows employers to accommodate the needs of workers who care for children at home or for a sick family member. The new concept of workplace implies that a geographic place gradually may become even less relevant, and cities may lose their importance as the centers of economic activity [14]. For instance, high-tech centers are forming on the fringes of major metropolitan areas or in such smaller urban areas such as Austin, Texas, and Raleigh, North Carolina [5]. In other words, technology is flattening the structure of geographic space into smaller horizontal regions with specialized agglomeration.

The flexibility and fluidity of work arrangements do not equate with the employee's freedom, as many employers can rely on new data-driven tools to control and monitor their off-site workers. For example, the software firm Sociometrics Solutions has developed badges that can track tone, mood, and stress during employee conversations [15]. Obviously, wearing a mood-sensing badge makes monitoring obvious to workers, but there are other data-driven techniques that can be used covertly by employers. Future analytics tools may use Big Data approaches to match jobs and workers and appraise or manage them more effectively. There are some software and tools that can be used across social media and other online sources to identify potentially qualified workers [16]. In a conventional way, workers have to demonstrate their skills and capabilities during the job interview by relying on their credentials, degrees, and other pieces. In the future, some new evaluation metrics will enable employers to measure the candidates' skills much more accurately. These kinds of workforce analytics need ethical considerations to secure workers' privacy and to protect them from potential employment discrimination [15].

Growing Diversity of the Workforce

In the past decades, immigration has substantially influenced the U.S. population and workforce composition. While relative to the population size, immigration was biggest in the early part of the 20th century; in the past three decades, the absolute number of immigrants has been the largest. According to the Bureau of Labor Statistics, in 2017, there were 27.4 million foreign-born persons in the U.S. labor force, comprising 17.1 percent of the total workforce. Hispanics and Asians, respectively, accounted for 47.9 and 25.2 percent of the foreign-born labor force in 2017. That is the highest proportion in records going back to 1996 when immigrants accounted for just 10.8 percent of the workforce [17]. Hispanics and Asians are the fastest-growing racial and ethnic groups in the population. The number of Hispanics in the American workforce is expected to grow because of high birth rates, as well as ongoing immigration. Consistent with the current trends, much of the growth in the U.S. workforce will be fueled by immigration and the growing work participation of socio-ethnic minorities. The population aging and higher participation of women in the workforce are other emerging trends that will affect the composition of the workforce. The American labor force is becoming more balanced with regard to genders as the labor force participation for women and men are, respectively, increasing and declining. Therefore, the U.S. workforce is expected to become older, more feminine, and more ethnic-racially diverse in the next three decades.

Automation Is Expected to Displace a Huge Number of Jobs in the Short- and Mid-Term

Automation is the outcome of various technologies such as AI, digitization, robotics, and connectivity and is expected to involve massive social and economic disruption. The upcoming revolution will enable the computerization of a wide range of simple and complex, cognitive and physical, or routine and changing tasks. Automation remains an emerging and complex phenomenon and is almost impossible to predict its consequences. Generally, there are two major views on the consequences of automation for the future of work. The optimistic view is to see automation as the source of entirely new industries that can attract the displaced workers. The pessimistic view implies that automation will eliminate a large number of jobs permanently, but it will not create opportunities for the displaced or unemployed workers. The optimistic view relies on the premise that human and machine will develop a collaborative relation, so work will be done by both humans and automated systems. The proponents of this perspective argue that human and machine collaboration will lead to highly positive outcomes for the economy. The more meaningful and rewarding tasks will be done by human beings, while menial and routine tasks are done by machines. Consequently, humans will increasingly be supported by automation in the workplace, improving productivity and developing new opportunities. Accordingly, human–machine cooperation may lead to the creation of new kinds of jobs because humans will need to develop new skills and ways of thinking in order to collaborate with automated systems. In other words, in the long term, automation will not reduce the amount of work available to workers, but rather will reorder it. In the short term, automation may reduce the amount of work available to human workers, as it takes time for the economic systems to adapt to new technologies. The risk of job elimination due to automation is particularly serious in the case of lower skill and lower entry positions that are characterized by low education attainment [15]. The other perspective about automation is more pessimistic and involves a general take over by machines that permanently eliminates a large number of jobs. The advocates of this perspective forecast that automation will reduce the need for physical and mental labor in the 21st century and will replace millions of workers from all sectors. The important point is that the disruption from automation will be so pervasive and permanent that new jobs will not suffice to replace the lost jobs. Accordingly, the automation process is considered as a continuous phenomenon that will ultimately move up the skill ladder by eliminating a large number of middle- to high-skill jobs in various sectors and industries [15].

Whether we subscribe to the optimistic or pessimistic perspective, it is credible to say that, in the short- and mid-term, the automation process is expected to significantly affect the labor market and eliminate a large number of jobs. The disagreement between the optimists and pessimists is essentially about the long-term outcomes. Therefore, it is crucial to identify effective ways to manage automation's impacts on workers' lives. The effects of automation will be particularly painful for the senior workers who are in the last stages of their careers and are either reluctant to or incapable of upgrading their professional skills.

References

[1] United Nations, Department of Economic and Social Affairs, Population Division. n.d. "World Urbanization Prospects: The 2017 Revision."

[2] Nations, U. 2013. "World Population Aging 2013." Department of Economic and Social Affairs PD.

[3] Lam, D. 2011. "How the World Survived the Population Bomb: Lessons from 50 Years of Extraordinary Demographic History." *Demography* 48, no. 4, pp. 1231–1262.

[4] Fullerton, H.N., and M. Toossi. November 2001. "Labor Force Projections to 2010: Steady Growth and Changing Composition." *Monthly Labor Review*, pp. 21–38.

[5] Karoly, L.A., and C.W. Panis. 2004. *The 21st Century at Work: Forces Shaping the Future Workforce and Workplace in the United States* 64. Rand Corporation.

[6] World Economic Forum. January 2016. "The Future of Jobs: Employment, Skills and Workforce Strategy for the Fourth Industrial Revolution." In World Economic Forum.

[7] Day, J.C., and K. Bauman. 2000. "Have We Reached the Top?: Educational Attainment Projections of the US Population." *Population Division*. US Census Bureau.

[8] Organisation for Economic Co-operation and Development (OECD). 2001. *Education at a Glance*. Paris: OECD.

[9] Neuner, J. March 20, 2013. "40% of America's Workforce Will Be Freelancers by 2020." *Quartz*. http://qz.com/65279/40-of-americas-workforce-will-be-freelancers-by-2020

[10] Kantor, J. August 13, 2014. "Working Anything but 9 to 5." *New York Times*. nytimes.com/interactive/2014/08/13/us/starbucks-workers-scheduling-hours.html

[11] Thomas, W.M., and J.L. Robert. 1998. "The Dawn of the E-Lance Economy." *Harvard Business Review*, pp. 145–152.

[12] Anton, P.S., R. Silberglitt, and J. Schneider. 2001. "The Global Technology Revolution: bio/nano/Materials Trends and their Synergies with Information Technology by 2015." Rand Corporation.

[13] Hecker, D.E. November 2001. "Occupational Employment Projections to 2010." *Monthly Labor Review* 124, no. 11, pp. 57–84.

[14] Kotkin, J., and F.F. Siegel. 2000. *Digital Geography: The Remaking of City and Countryside in the New Economy*. Indianapolis, Ind: The Hudson Institute.

[15] Foresight Alliance LLC. 2016. "The Futures of Work." http://foresightalliance.com/wp-content/uploads/2010/03/The-Futures-of-Work-1.12.2016.pdf

[16] Richtel, M. April 27, 2013. "How Big Data Is Playing Recruiter for Specialized Workers." *New York Times.* www.nytimes.com/2013/04/28/technology/how-big-data-is-playing-recruiter-for-specialized-workers.html

[17] https://bls.gov/news.release/pdf/forbrn.pdf

CHAPTER 16

Innovation and Research

The Shifting Landscape of Global Innovation

The global investment in research and development has been rising fast across the world and has reached $1 trillion in 2015. The Group of Seven (G7) consisting of Canada, France, Germany, Italy, Japan, the United Kingdom, and the United States accounts for more than $615 billion of this investment in research and development. The United States with $325 billion and Japan with $123 billion are still front-runners in all areas of innovation investment [1]. Nevertheless, consistent with other changes on the world stage, the landscape of global innovation is rapidly undergoing significant transformations. The shares of the United States and Japan in the global research and development spending have declined since the late-1990s, because of gains in China and other growth markets in Asia. In the past decade, Asia has surpassed the EU in the research and development investment, and if the trend maintains, Asia could overtake the United States in a near future (see Figures 16.1 and 16.2). Multiple indicators reveal that the G7 countries are facing fierce rivalry from many emerging countries, particularly from China. As a matter of fact, the research and development spending is growing much faster in Asian countries than that in G7 countries [1]. For example, in the past decade, the research and development spending has grown more than 20 percent per year in China and more than 8 percent per year in Korea. For the same period, the growth in the research and development investment has been hovering around 3 percent in G7 countries. Comparing the research and development spending to the GDP (measuring the R&D intensity) indicates that Asian countries such as China and South Korea have grown even at a faster pace than their Western counterparts have. As emerging countries continue to increase the size of their economies, they are motivated to increase their research and development budgets even more aggressively.

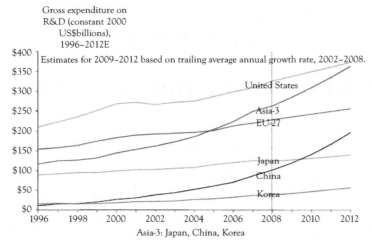

Figure 16.1 Steady rise in global research and development investment (Asia outspends Europe and continues to converge to U.S. levels)

Source: [2].

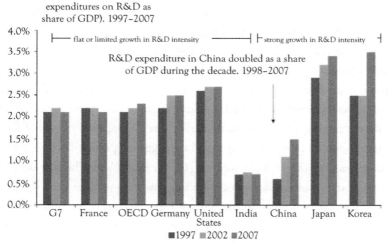

Figure 16.2 Greatest research and development intensity gains are in Asia

Source: [2].

China's government has the ambitious objective of spending 2.5 percent of the GDP on R&D by 2020, which means $300 billion investment per year [1]. Obviously, the growth in research and development spending is only a part of the story, because, in addition to the increased spending, Asian countries are training a large number of researchers and scientists. In the past two decades, higher education has been growing fast outside the major developed countries. This has resulted in a steep rise in the number of researchers and innovators in developing countries. For example, the United States' share of the global university student population has declined from 20 percent in 1990 to less than 13 percent [1]. By contrast, for the same period, China's share of the global university students has more than doubled to 15 percent. Likewise, in recent years, Asian countries have become the origins of a growing number of patents and innovations, significantly improved high-tech trade balances, and experienced strong labor productivity growth. All these signs are indicative of a promising innovation in Asia.

The Dependence of Innovation on Higher Education and Immigration

Certainly, innovation is primarily about training qualified scientists and researchers who can conduct research and develop new products and services. The G7 advanced economies, particularly the United States, face major challenges in training qualified workers to stimulate or at least to maintain their technological edge. The basic data suggest that local students in G7 countries show insufficient interest in science and engineering education. For instance, science and engineering programs include less than 25 percent of the university degrees awarded in G7 countries, and only 15 percent of all new degrees awarded in the United States [1]. The United States enjoys an unmatched position in scientific innovation, and most of the top universities are located in the United States, but surprisingly, American secondary students are generally ranked lower in science and mathematics aptitude than their counterparts in other developed countries. The explanation is the American top universities and research institutions attract a large number of talented people from all over the globe. For example, most engineering PhD degrees at American universities are granted to people born abroad. The short supply of local scientists and researchers in the G7 countries and particularly in the United States is a major reason that businesses try to attract qualified immigrants. Consequently, a notable trend is that innovation in developed economies is becoming increasingly dependent on immigration. In the United States, more than 20 percent of the science and engineering workers are immigrants born in developing countries and high-skilled immigrants account for roughly a quarter of the U.S. patents [3]. In the United States, immigrants account for a disproportionate share of innovation superstars and are overpresented among most-cited authors, scholars, researchers, and among members of the National Academy of Sciences [4]. It has been found that American winners of the Nobel Prize are disproportionately from immigrants [5]. Other G7 countries are similar to the United States in this respect. For example, a study in Canada suggested that more than 35 percent of Canada Research Chairs are foreign-born, while immigrants are just one-fifth of the Canadian population [2]. In addition to talent and education, many immigrants are equipped with high levels of motivation, risk-taking capacity, and persistence that turn them to innovators par excellence. Inventors tend to be more mobile than the rest of the population. For example, 10 percent of the inventors worldwide showed a migratory background in 2005. The United States is the most popular destination for migrant inventors, hosting 57 percent of the world's inventors who reside outside their home countries. Almost 75 percent of the migrant inventors from low- and middle-income countries reside in the United States. China and India are the two largest origins of high-value migrants followed by Russia, Turkey, Iran, Romania, and Mexico (see Figure 16.3). After the United

Figure 16.3 The origins of migrant inventors to the Unites States
Source: [6].

States, Switzerland, Germany, and the United Kingdom are attractive destinations to inventors [6]. Among the larger European countries, the United Kingdom enjoys a relatively high share of immigrant inventors, while Germany, France, Italy, and Spain have a lower percentage of foreign-born citizens among their inventors. Considering the importance of immigration for innovation, public policies in G7 should aim at attracting highly skilled and educated migrant workers [1].

The Increasing Importance of Corporate Innovation

In the age of global capitalism, large multinational corporations (MNCs) are becoming the main producers, users, and disseminators of knowledge and innovation. For instance, MNCs are estimated to account for the majority of total global spending on research and development in the United States and Japan, as well as across many growth markets [7]. Based on some assessments, the research and development investment by American multinationals doubled between 1997 and 2007 [8]. In addition to huge investments in research and development, large multinationals play an important role in the dissemination of knowledge through their operations in different countries across the world. Multinationals apply the technical knowledge to build, introduce, and sell new products and processes across the globe. Multinationals and their affiliates are responsible for one-third of the world exports that ultimately circulate their innovative products throughout the world [9]. In addition to trade, MNCs disseminate innovation through competition and forward and backward integration strategies such as cross-national mergers and acquisitions. In order to maintain their competitive advantages, large multinationals continuously focus on research and development. Many of these multinationals see innovative advantages in acquiring small and entrepreneurial companies when building competencies themselves would simply take too long [10]. Because of concerns about the cost of innovation and infringement of intellectual property rights, many U.S.-based MNCs are focusing on incremental innovation or creative imitation. The global race toward innovation has led to a proliferation of innovation centers. Innovation centers represent enterprise investments that aim at understanding new market dynamics, acquiring new expertise and resources, and cooperating with entrepreneurs, startups, investors, academic institutions, and related ecosystems [11]. Innovation centers are located outside the traditional operational landscape with the goal of accelerating digital innovation, rethinking customer experience, improving operational efficiency, and testing new business models. Silicon Valley' region as the epicenter of innovation hosts 65 innovation centers [11].

Frugal and Reverse Innovation Models

In tandem with the growth of emerging economies and their multinational corporations, the new tendencies such as frugal innovation and reverse innovation are becoming widespread. Frugal innovation is a broad concept that is described by characteristics such as affordability, low-cost manufacturing, low-cost materials, and focus on basic functionality [12]. Frugal innovation is essentially about the needs and circumstances of citizens in the developing economies in order to develop appropriate, adaptable, affordable, and accessible services and products [13]. Frugal innovation is encouraged by low-income consumers and resource scarcity [14]. Frugally innovative organizations rely on more cost-effective products, services, processes, and business models [15]. Simply put, frugal innovation is primarily the ability to create significantly more value by minimizing the use of resources such as energy, capital, and time [16].

Frugal innovation surmounts financial, technological, material, or other resource constraints, in order to offer the final product, which is much cheaper than competitive alternatives. Frugal innovation is particularly popular and effective in the context of developing economies where a significant number of people live on low levels of income [17]. The mass markets in the bottom of the pyramid have attracted multinational companies from around the world to frugal innovation. While multinational companies from advanced economies initially aimed at exploiting the low-cost manufacturing in developing economies, they gradually created centers for investing in R&D in their host countries and took advantage of frugal innovation [18]. As an increasing number of MNCs from developed economies are targeting the low-income customer base in developing or low-income countries, the strategic importance of frugal innovation continues to grow. More recently, we have been witnessing imitations and innovations led by MNCs based in emerging or developing economies. Emerging markets multinationals are not big innovators; rather, they are recognized as imitators that duplicate intellectual property from their rivals in advanced economies and adapt it to local consumers. As emerging markets are maturing, they are keen on moving away from imitations to innovations. Features such as improvisation, adjustment to the local markets, and organizational novelty mark such innovations. These types of innovation are more adapted to developing economies' needs, constraints, culture, and customs. Because of shortages of capital, technology, and talent, the entrepreneurs in developing economies need to find solutions to their problems with rare resources. These frugal innovations are low-cost solutions for low-income customers. For example, much of Haier's success is attributed to developing products adapted to Chinese customers.

Some frugal innovations, labeled as reverse innovations, are exported from developing and low-income countries to developed and high-income economies. Frugal innovation involves designing solutions specifically for low-income market segments, but reverse innovation involves new products developed in emerging markets, which are then modified for sale in developed economies [19]. In other words, reverse innovation denotes low-cost innovations, which are first adopted in emerging economies and then *trickle up* to developed countries [20]. Reverse innovation is about developing new products in emerging markets first and modify them for sale in developed countries later. The reverse innovation has become an important part of the global innovation, implying that developing countries are not merely recipients of innovations from developed countries. Sometimes, the Western MNCs use the reverse innovation models in order to reduce their costs and enhance their competitiveness in their home countries. For instance, companies such as Siemens and General Electric have been developing such unique products, which are developed specially for the emerging and developing countries consumers and also have potential to succeed in the developed markets [21].

Innovation as Competitive Advantage

Traditionally, countries and companies have been labeled competitive on the basis of their static comparative advantages, including natural and physical endowments, the cost of factors of production, or specific technological advantages. More recently, the competitiveness at the national and organizational levels is defined as a complex concept that depends on the capacity of continuous innovation, high skills, learning, efficient communications, transport infrastructures, and supportive environments [22]. In the rapidly changing global business context, firms have to constantly innovate to keep their competitive edge over their rivals. We may consider five areas of innovation, including generation of new or improved products, introduction of the new production process, development of new sales market, development of new supply market, and reorganization of the company [23]. Therefore, innovation includes the process of creating a new product or service, new technologic process, a new organization, and enhancement of existing product, technologic process, or organization [24]. The innovation process can be radical or incremental. A radical innovation is about developing products, processes, or services with unprecedented features, while incremental innovation involves improvements in cost or existing processes, products, and services [25]. Thus, innovation has many dimensions and goes beyond technological advances. For instance, innovation may include more efficient managerial techniques and flexible organizational models [25]. Many giant firms such as Dell, Uber, Amazon, and Netflix owe their success to innovative business models, rather than to their technological innovations. For example, Dell developed an innovative business model by subcontracting production to third parties, eliminating distributors, and selling directly to the final consumer. Likewise, Wal-Mart took advantage of an innovative business model by monitoring consumer demand and linking that information via central ordering directly to producers all around the world in order to eliminate intermediaries in production and distribution [8]. A company's innovative capacity is the result of relationships between its organizational culture, resources, competencies, and relationships with other organizations. The need for innovation is translated into higher investment in research and development and in the education and training programs. Currently, we are witnessing an extraordinary wave of acceleration in the creation and dissemination of knowledge. The lapses between basic scientific discovery and commercial application are declining fast, and as a result, innovation is becoming a tough race [20].

The Global Map of Innovation

The Global Innovation Index report (2020) ranks more than 130 countries by relying on six key pillars, including infrastructure, human capital and research, institutions, market sophistication, business sophistication, knowledge and technology outputs, and creative outputs. Based on this comprehensive approach, there are significant disparities across the world with regard to innovation [26]. North America, Europe, and South East Asia are ranked as the innovation leaders, while Latin America, sub-Saharan Africa, and Central and Southern Asia are considered as the innovation laggards. In the 2020 Global Innovation Index report, the United States is placed at the third rank. Indeed, the United States has increased its innovation ranking since 2012, mainly because of the advancement in information technologies, Internet, and financial sector. In absolute terms, the United States is the top contributor in key innovation inputs and outputs, including investment in research and development, and second after China in the volume of researchers, patents, and scientific and technical publications. Canada, another North American economy, is ranked the 17th position overall, with advantages in ease of starting a business and venture capital deals.

The top 11 innovating economies are European, including Switzerland, the Netherlands, and Sweden. While the EU is among the most innovative areas, there are significant levels of disparity among the European countries. For example, many European countries are included in the top 10, while some are in the top 30 and 40, or even in the top 50 [26]. All countries in South East Asia, East Asia, and Oceania region are ranked within the top 100 innovators. In this region, Singapore, the Republic of Korea, and Japan are ranked as highly innovative. Singapore keeps its first place in government effectiveness, regulatory quality, and foreign direct investment outflows. Japan ranks first in gross domestic expenditure on research and development financed by businesses. The

Republic of Korea maintains its top rankings in patent applications by origin and various indicators measuring research and development efforts. In the Central and Southern Asia region, India, Iran, and Kazakhstan are on the top of the list. India is categorized as a low-income economy and ranks well in a number of important indicators, including productivity growth, exports of information, and communication technology and services. Considering its large and rapidly growing population, India could make a big difference to the global innovation landscape in a near future. Iran maintains the second place in the Central and Southern Asia region and earns top ranks in productivity growth and graduates in science and engineering. In the Northern Africa and Western Asia, Israel, Cyprus, and the United Arab Emirates are ranked at the top of the list. Israel leads in many indicators, including a number of researchers, research and development expenditures, venture capital deals, research talent in business enterprise, and exports of information and communications technology. In Latin America and the Caribbean, Chile, Costa Rica, Mexico, and Brazil rank high. Brazil, as the largest economy of the region, has strength in many areas, including research and development expenditures, high-tech net imports and exports, and quality of scientific publications and universities. In sub-Saharan Africa, South Africa is on the top of the list followed by Mauritius and Kenya. South Africa shows strengths in its sophisticated market and business sector, access to credit, market capitalization, university and industry research collaborations, cluster development, and intellectual property payments.

Table 16.1 depicts the top/bottom innovative countries based on the Global Innovation Index. It is noticeable that there is a positive link between innovation performance and an economy's level of development as measured by the GDP per capita. This means that high-income countries are more likely to innovate, especially when their economic structures, and thus their industry portfolios are more diverse. All countries, regardless of their level of development, are likely to be more innovative when they have a more diversified export portfolio. The other findings of the Global Innovation Index report show that a country's size or population is not correlated with the level of innovation. Indeed, some small countries such as Switzerland, the Netherlands, Sweden, and Singapore are ranked among the top innovative nations [26]. According to the

Table 16.1 Top and bottom of list: Global innovation index rankings in 2020

The most innovative			The least innovative		
Rank	Economy	Score	Rank	Economy	Score
1	Switzerland	66.1	111	Malawi	21.4
2	Sweden	62.5	112	Cote d'Ivoire	21.2
3	The United States of America	60.6	113	Lao People's Democratic Republic (the)	20.6
4	The United Kingdom	59.8	114	Uganda	20.5
5	The Netherlands	58.8	115	Madagascar	20.4
6	Denmark	57.5	116	Bangladesh	20.4
7	Finland	57	117	Nigeria	20.1
8	Singapore	56.6	118	Burkina Faso	20
9	Germany	56.5	119	Cameroon	20
10	The Republic of Korea	56.1	120	Zimbabwe	20
11	Hong Kong, China	54.2	121	Algeria	19.5
12	France	53.7	122	Zambia	19.4
13	Israel	53.5	123	Mali	19.2
14	China	53.3	124	Mozambique	18.7
15	Ireland	53	125	Togo	18.5
16	Japan	52.7	126	Benin	18.1
17	Canada	52.3	127	Ethiopia	18.1
18	Luxembourg	50.8	128	The Niger	17.8
19	Austria	50.1	129	Myanmar	17.7
20	Norway	49.3	130	Guinea	17.3

Global Innovation Index report (2020), a number of emerging economies are likely to continue their ascendency in the innovation rankings. China's ranking has been improving in the past decade, and the country is already among the top 25 innovative nations. Other countries, including India, Iran, Mexico, Thailand, and Vietnam, are consistently climbing in the rankings of the most innovative countries [27].

References

[1] Gilman, D. 2010. *The New Geography of Global Innovation*. Global Markets Institute of Goldman Sachs.

[2] The Conference Board of Canada. 2015. "Immigrants Make Significant Contributions to Innovation." https://www.conferenceboard.ca/?gclid=EAIaI QobChMIh561rpGq4AIVS5yzCh3KgQKTEAAYASAAEgIbUvD_ BwE&gclsrc=aw.ds

[3] Kerr, W.R. 2008. "Ethnic Scientific Communities and International Technology Diffusion." *The Review of Economics and Statistics* 90, no. 3, pp. 518–537.

[4] Kerr, W.R. 2015. "International Migration and US Innovation: Insights from the US Experience." In *Routledge Handbook of Immigration and Refugee Studies,* pp. 106–111. Routledge.

[5] Hunt, J. 2012. *Does the United States Admit the Best and Brightest Computer and Engineering Workers.* Rutgers University working paper.

[6] Fink, C., E. Miguelez, and J. Raffo. 2013. *The Global Race for Inventors.* Forthcoming as a WIPO Economic Research Working Paper.

[7] Berger, S. 2006. *How We Compete: What Companies Around the World are Doing to Make it in Today's Global Economy.* New York, NY: Random House.

[8] Dahlman, C. 2007. "Technology, Globalization, and International Competitiveness: Challenges for Developing Countries." *Asdf,* p. 29.

[9] Kaplinsky, R. 2005. *Globalization, Poverty, and Inequality.* Cambridge: Polity Press.

[10] Brondoni, S.M. 2014. "Innovation and Imitation for Global Competitive Strategies." The Corporation Development Models of US, Japan, Korea, and Taiwan. Symphonya. *Emerging Issues in Management* 1, pp. 12–27.

[11] Garrity, T.F. March 2009. "Innovation and Trends for Future Electric Power Systems." In *Power Systems Conference,* PSC'09, pp. 1–8. IEEE.

[12] Hossain, M., H. Simula, and M. Halme. 2016. "Can Frugal Go Global? Diffusion Patterns of Frugal Innovations." *Technology in Society* 46, pp. 132–139.

[13] Basu, R.R., PM. Banerjee, and E.G. Sweeny. 2013. "Frugal Innovation: Core Competencies to Address Global Sustainability." *Journal of Management for Global Sustainability* 2, pp. 63–82.

[14] Sharma, A., and G.R. Iyer. 2012. "Resource-Constrained Product Development: Implications for Green Marketing and Green Supply Chains." *Industrial Marketing Management* 41, no. 4, pp. 599–608

[15] Hossain, M. 2015. "Frugal and Reverse Innovations: What, Where and Why?" *Clarifying the Concepts and Creating a Research Agenda.*

[16] Radjou, N., and J. Prabhu. 2015. "Frugal Innovation: How to do More with Less." *The Economist.*

[17] Walsh, J.P., J.C. Kress, and K.W. Beyerchen. 2005. "CK Prahalad: The Fortune at the Bottom of the Pyramid: Eradicating Poverty through Profits." *Administrative Science Quarterly* 50, no. 3, p. 473.

[18] Singhal, V. 2011. "The Impact of Emerging Economies Innovative New Models of Global Growth and Vitality are Emerging." *Visions* 35, no. 2, pp. 12–14.

[19] Nunes, P.F., and T. Breene. 2011. *Jumping the S-curve: How to Beat the Growth Cycle, Get on Top, and Stay There*. Harvard Business Press.

[20] Govindarajan, V., and C. Trimble. 2009. "How GE Is Disrupting Itself (How General Electric has Switched to Selling Products Originally Aimed at Developing Country Markets to the USA)." *How GE is Disrupting Itself*, eds. J.R. Immelt, V. Govindarajan and C. Trimble. *Harvard Business Review* 87, no. 10, pp. 56–65.

[21] Agarwal, N., and A. Brem. June 2012. "Frugal and Reverse Innovation—Literature Overview and Case Study Insights from a German MNC in India and China." In *Engineering, Technology and Innovation (ICE), 2012 18th International ICE Conference on*, 1–11. IEEE.

[22] Dahlman, C.J., and J.E. Aubert. 2001. *China and the Knowledge Economy: Seizing the 21st Century*. Washington, DC: World Bank.

[23] Reguia, C. 2014. "Product Innovation and the Competitive Advantage." *European Scientific Journal, ESJ* 10, no. 10.

[24] Ramadani, V., and S. Gerguri. 2011. *Theoretical Framework of Innovation: Competitiveness and Innovation Program in Macedonia*.

[25] Sh, G., G. Rexhepi, and V. Ramadani. 2013. "Innovation Strategies and Competitive Advantage." *Modern Economy: Challenges, Trends, Prospects* 8, p. 1.

[26] Asheim, B.T., and M.S. Gertler. 2005. "The Geography of Innovation: Regional Innovation Systems." In *The Oxford Handbook of Innovation*.

[27] Dutta, S., R.E. Reynoso, A. Garanasvili, K. Saxena, B. Lanvin, S. Wunsch-Vincent, and F. Guadagno. 2018. "The Global Innovation Index 2018: Energizing The World with Innovation." *Global Innovation Index 2018*.

CHAPTER 17

Emerging Technologies

Automation and Robotics

Augmented Intelligence

Augmented intelligence involves the use of intelligent tools by human beings in order to enhance their intellectual and cognitive capacities [1]. Augmented intelligence systems rely on machine learning to extend human cognitive abilities such as the brain's capacity to calculate, assess, prioritize, and analyze information. Augmented intelligence systems use natural language processing, spatial navigation, machine vision, logical reasoning, and pattern recognition [1]. In other words, augmented intelligence systems help connect people and computers to jointly analyze, interpret, and process the fast-changing big data in real time. While most AI methods focus on replacing humans, augmented intelligence aims at creating collaboration between machines and humans. The augmented intelligence systems are characterized by five major abilities: (1) understanding, they derive meaning from all forms of multistructured data and user interactions, (2) interpreting, they represent the meaning in a deterministic and probabilistic knowledge graph based on declared, observed, and inferred entities, events, and relationships, (3) reasoning, they reason over the domain-optimized interpretation in business and user context to come up with personalized advice with supporting evidence, (4) learning, they learn continuously based on real-time and historical data, user, and system interactions, and (5) assuring, they ensure ongoing compliance and governance for responsible and risk-managed use of cognitive services [1]. By using these capacities, augmented intelligence will assist users to make more informed and faster decisions in a wide range of areas, including finance, investment, health care, manufacturing, retail, travel and tourism, energy, and agriculture. Augmented intelligence systems can be used by businesses that are facing fast-changing customer behavior, strict security, and regulatory requirements. For instance, augmented intelligence may help patients with chronic diseases get personalized care and avoid medical errors. Augmented intelligence systems can analyze an individual's environment and lifestyle patterns to deliver targeted health-related recommendations. Likewise, financial planners can use augmented intelligence systems to offer personalized financial services to their clients. Augmented intelligence systems can help shoppers in their shopping experience depending on the context, occasion, and location of their purchase [1].

Autonomous Vehicles

In the past two decades, advances in multiple technologies such as robotics, navigation, sensing, computer vision, and high-performance computing have revived interest in autonomous vehicles. Autonomous vehicles are being developed along two streams: (1) vehicle automation, which consists of technologies concerning automation of vehicle control functions without direct driver inputs, and (2) vehicle connectivity, which consists of different vehicular communication technologies such as vehicle-to-vehicle, vehicle-to-infrastructure, and vehicle-to-personal device communication [2]. Indeed, vehicle automation is part of a much larger revolution in automation and connectivity, as multiple technologies are combined to sense and manipulate the physical environment [3].

The National Highway Traffic Safety Administration (NHTSA) proposed a five-level conceptualization of the automated vehicles as the following [4]:

Level 0: No automation, the human driver is in complete control of all functions of the car.

Level 1: Driver assistance, the vehicle can assist the driver or take control of either the vehicle's speed or its lane position.

Level 2: More than one function is automated at the same time, but the driver must remain constantly attentive.

Level 3: Limited self-driving, the driving functions are sufficiently automated that the driver can safely engage in other activities.

Level 4: Full self-driving under certain conditions.

Level 5: Full self-driving under all conditions: the vehicle can operate without a human driver or occupants.

A future with autonomous motor vehicles is not very far away, as currently, various models of autonomous vehicles are being tested in research facilities and on public roads. A growing number of carmakers are showing interest in autonomous vehicles, including Audi, BMW, Ford, GM, Mercedes-Benz, Nissan, Toyota, Volkswagen, Volvo, Tesla, and Local Motors. Even technology companies such as Apple, Google, and Uber are investing in autonomous vehicles technology [2]. There is extensive agreement that Levels 3 to 5 of automated vehicles will be commercially available to some buyers within 5 years or even as early as 2020. In 2016, Ford announced its plans to have a high-volume, fully autonomous SAE Level 4 vehicle in commercial operation in 2021 in a ride-hailing or ride-sharing service [5]. Autonomous vehicles will be probably available for sale across the country in a few years, but all vehicles on the road will not be autonomous and conventional driving will continue to exist for a long time [4]. Most experts believe that Level 4 or 5 of autonomous vehicles will be widely commercialized sometime after 2025 to 2040 [4]. According to a recent study, the Netherlands, Singapore, the United States, Sweden, and the United Kingdom are ranked as the most prepared countries for the commercialization and the widespread use of autonomous vehicles with regard to policy and legislation, technology, infrastructure, and consumer acceptance [6].

The commercialization of autonomous vehicles will have substantial implications for many aspects of our lives including transportation, jobs, urban planning and infrastructure, economic models, and more obviously for roadway rules and regulations. Autonomous vehicles are expected to reduce human error on roadways, improve capacity on the roadways, and increase the utilization of travel time [7]. The market for liability coverage may be impacted significantly for manufacturers, owners, and operators [8]. Autonomous cars are expected to significantly reduce the cost of congestion because drivers could engage in alternative activities. Autonomous vehicles could restructure transportation models that are based on car ownership. Furthermore, autonomous vehicles can increase the mobility of young people, the elderly, the disabled, and other communities underserved by traditional personal and public transportation systems [7]. The commercialization of autonomous cars could lead to more dispersed and low-density patterns of land use surrounding metropolitan regions [9]. Currently, a large portion of space in metropolitan regions is devoted to parking. Naturally, the use of autonomous vehicles and sharing programs necessitate fewer parking spaces, and thus could revolutionize the land use in metropolitan areas. The overall effect of autonomous vehicles on energy and pollution is indeterminate, but it is widely expected that autonomous vehicles will reduce energy use and pollution. Autonomous vehicles require adapted infrastructure, pavements, traffic signals, signs, and street markings. Moreover, the autonomous vehicle needs the installation of various types of sensors and communications technology to allow vehicles to travel more efficiently [10]. Buildings will need to be located and designed to facilitate both pedestrians and autonomous deliveries. The commercialization of the autonomous vehicle technology involves some important impacts on the transportation industry and associated sectors. For instance, truck, bus, taxi, and delivery vehicles are expected to undergo major transformations. Cab and truck drivers and mechanics may lose their jobs, and the revenues derived from selling or renting parking spots may decline or disappear. Likewise, all those workers and institutions involved in car maintenance and insurance may be disrupted [9].

Drones and Unmanned Aerial Vehicles

The U.S. Department of Transportation estimates that the number of drones and unmanned aerial vehicles operations will exceed that of regular or manned aircraft operations by 2035 [11]. The rising popularity of drones and unmanned aerial vehicles is the result of recent developments in a wide range of technologies, including microprocessors, GPS, sensors, batteries, motors, lightweight structural materials, and advanced manufacturing techniques. Drones can be used in many sectors, including agriculture, energy, public safety, security, military, e-commerce, delivery, and transport. In the military sector and defense, drones are already employed, and their application will continue to increase in the next several years. Drones can be used in precision agriculture to enhance farms' productivity. In the energy sector, drones may reduce various risks to personnel performing hazardous tasks, or the risks to the environment and assets. Furthermore, they can be used in inspecting industrial infrastructure, oil refineries, pipelines, tanks, and power lines. In public safety and security, drones can play an essential role by facilitating the assessment and management of hazardous situations. In e-commerce and delivery, the drone may be used to deliver packages and supply materials more efficiently and more quickly. Most of all, drones can replace the present aircraft, railways, buses, and taxis by providing safe, reliable, and fast mobility. Autonomous drones can be used as a mode of transport to carry individuals or small groups of passengers to a destination. Currently, different prototypes are in development for use, particularly in high-density urban environments. Passenger drone is a prototype that is slightly larger than a small car and can change the traditional means of commuter transportation by flying at a speed of 50 miles per hour [12]. Public acceptance for flights with automated drones will require substantial improvements in other technologies such as connectivity and autonomy in ground vehicles, aerial transport and the design of buildings, public spaces and power systems, and transport infrastructure. Dubai has already begun trials of a passenger drone service. The advent of partial and fully autonomous flying vehicles will be sometime after 2025 [13]. Drones will bring about new forms of air traffic, especially at very low levels of airspace with high demand in densely populated areas. The implications of such air traffic will be significant particularly in urban centers.

Data and Connectivity

5G Mobile Internet and the Internet of Things

As the volume of data is growing exponentially, the next generation of the mobile Internet or 5G is expected to handle huge amounts of data, connect more devices, reduce latency, and provide increased network reliability. The 5G networks have a speed of 10 Gb/s per user, which is over 1,000 times that of 4G [14]. 5G is not an extension of 3G and 4G; rather, it is an innovative web that includes a heterogeneous network, including 4G, Wi-Fi, millimeter wave, and other wireless access technologies [15]. The 5G networks offer a fully connected and interactive world with a variety of applications, including enhanced mobile broadband, machine-to-machine communications, AI, and advanced digital services. By 2020, the 5G network will support 50 billion connected devices and 212 billion connected sensors and will enable access to 44 zettabytes (ZB) of data [16]. The huge network of devices connected to the Internet or the *Internet of Things* (IoT) may incorporate sensors to measure different variables in real time, including energy consumption, pressure, temperature, and many other economic, medical, or social indexes. Thanks to 5G, digital networks will connect billions of devices and sensors enabling advances in health care, education, resource management, transportation, agriculture, and many other areas [17]. For example, medical devices can reliably transmit the data about variables such as blood pressure, pulse, and breathing rate in near-real time to a health service provider, which can rapidly intervene in case of need. Road transport, train travel, and flights can become safer and more efficient, as connected vehicles and planes share information in real time with others. Similarly, manufacturing can be revolutionized with connected robots and sharing information about the different activities of the supply chain [18]. Buildings, bridges, and roads can be monitored continuously. Similarly, governments may use air-pollution monitoring data to control emissions.

The 5G systems include heterogeneous devices incorporating both low and high bandwidth. 5G is considered as a transformative system because it moves us from a user-centric world to the one based on machine-to-machine communications. This transformation and the ensuing IoT will connect these devices intelligently and lead to the commodification of information and intelligence [17]. The 5G will provide access to a wide range of services with increased resilience, continuity, and much higher resource efficiency, including a substantial decrease in energy consumption [19].

Blockchain

Blockchain can be defined as a distributed digital ledger that records transactions in a peer-to-peer network. The blockchain technology is a register that notifies and time—stamps and date—stamps each exchange between each node in a block [20]. These characteristics enable several parties to use blockchain to engage in multiple transactions or exchanges without the presence of a third party. In other words, blockchain liberates users and transactions from the company of a trusted third party and creates immense opportunities for a distributed, secured disintermediation organized in a peer-to-peer mode. The blockchain technology has the potential for innovation and the disruption of dominant economic models by creating an Internet of transactions. While the idea of blockchain was appeared by the emergence of bitcoin, it can be used to create transactional highways for any peer-to-peer economic mode [20]. The concept of blockchain is very revolutionary because it can create a system based on trust, but without trusted third parties such as banks, financial institutions, Airbnb, and Uber. Indeed, the alternative models to Uber may use the blockchain technologies to eliminate the intermediaries. The blockchain technologies allow the traceability, security, and transparency of each transaction. For example, cryptocurrencies such as bitcoin incorporate into the source code access to the past transactions relating to the unit of value, and at the same time, they protect the identity of the individuals associated with the transaction. As a result, the theft of a person's identity during the execution of a transaction becomes impossible [20]. Another advantage of the blockchain technology is its high speed of execution. The world of finance is currently testing the use of blockchain with a view to facilitating intermediation between banks, clearing houses, and central banks. The blockchain technology can be applied in various areas such as financial systems, sharing economy, smart contracts, including self-executing and autonomous algorithms, the digital vote, and the management of the logistics chain. The blockchain technology can transform the organization of transport, supply chain, advertising, energy production, distribution sector, real estate market, insurance industry, and many other sectors by uniting the digital and physical worlds. Blockchain may help give objects an identity and full autonomy, thus creating opportunities for driverless cars and the IoT. In the field of Internet security, a startup called oneName is using the blockchain technology to make a unique digital identity, so the user can use this identity in multiple web-based platforms without memorizing different usernames and passwords. In the health care sector, another company BlockRX is using blockchain to digitize medical records and information about the patient that can be transferred more easily from one health care professional to another. The peer-to-peer insurance may create a revolution in the insurance industry by abolishing the current standards and the tripartite relationship between payers, insured parties, and insurers. Blockchain can be used in smart contracts where an agreement between two parties is digitalized, automated, and therefore self-executed. Ethereum, the second most popular cryptocurrency after bitcoin, is relying on smart contracts to give the various parties the assurance that, once the conditions have been fulfilled, the contract will be honored, with no possibility for fraud or interference with a third party [20].

Bluetooth 5.0

Bluetooth is a relatively old technology that has been developed more than two decades ago and is used for data transmission through radio waves. Bluetooth is a flexible technology, as it does not have any constraints to the type of the transmitted data, including photos, documents, music, and videos. However, one major limitation with Bluetooth has been the short range of data transmission that generally did not exceed 100 meters. Bluetooth 5.0 is the latest version of the Bluetooth wireless communication standard that offers significant improvements regarding the range, speed, and broadcasting capacity of data [21]. Bluetooth 5.0 offers 800 percent increase in data broadcasting capacity by doubling the speed and quadrupling the range of previous versions and maintains a very low power consumption. Therefore, the latest version of Bluetooth known as Bluetooth 5.0 can be used for wireless communication between various machine-to-machine communication and IoT devices [22]. Bluetooth technology will support the consumer adoption of the IoT, industrial automation, and the proliferation of dense sensor networks. By 2022, more than 50 billion connected devices worldwide will rely on Bluetooth 5.0 to connect and communicate [22].

Li-Fi

Li-Fi or light fidelity is a form of visible light communication that uses the visible light portion of the electromagnetic spectrum to provide local wireless communications at very high speeds. In other words, Li-Fi is a visible light communication system capable of transmitting data at high speeds over the visible light spectrum. As the visible light spectrum is 10,000 times larger than the radio waves, the Li-Fi technology can achieve Internet speeds of up to 224 GB per second that are much faster than the current standard Wi-Fi. The Li-Fi technology offers many advantages and peculiarities. For instance, while Wi-Fi works close to full capacity, Li-Fi has almost no limitations on capacity. As light cannot pass through walls, Li-Fi makes the transfer of data more secure than Wi-Fi and reduces the interference between multiple devices, and as a result, the transmitted data via Li-Fi cannot be hacked. Li-Fi offers many advantages, including working across higher bandwidth and working in areas susceptible to electromagnetic interference such as aircraft cabins and nuclear power plants. The Li-Fi technology may be applied in several areas such as the IoT, retail, construction, aviation, transportation, traffic management, and urban environments. Furthermore, future home and building automation are expected to be highly dependent on the Li-Fi technology for being secure and fast.

Quantum Computing

Quantum computing uses subatomic particles and quantum-mechanical phenomena such as superposition and entanglement to store data [23]. The current digital computing encodes data into binary digits (bits) that are always in one of two definite states (0 or 1), but quantum computation uses quantum bits that can hold much more complex information or even negative values [24]. In a conventional computer, bits are processed sequentially, but in quantum computation, qubits are entangled together, so changing the state of one qubit influences the state of others [24]. Unlike classical computing, quantum answers are probabilistic, and because of superposition and entanglement, multiple possible answers are considered in a given computation [24]. Therefore, quantum computers have a superior processing power than the current computers based on binary logic. Quantum computers are able to compute complex problems and offer novel possibilities. While classical or binary computers take more time for each variable added, quantum computers can rely on quantum bits to solve complex problems. Currently, quantum computing is more suitable for solving problems using three types of algorithms: optimization, sampling, and machine learning [24]. Full-scale quantum computers have not been developed yet, but the first basic systems threading together tens of quantum bits have been made available. Several national governments and military agencies are funding research to develop quantum computers for civilian, business, trade, environmental, and national security purposes. Many companies, including D-Wave, Google, Microsoft, MIT Lincoln Laboratory, and Intelligence Advanced Research Projects Activity, are working on developing quantum hardware [24].

The applications of quantum computers are gaining acceptance in health care, manufacturing, supply chain management, purchasing, and procurement, production, and distribution. In investment and financial services, quantum computing could help determine attractive portfolios, given thousands of correlated assets [24]. Furthermore, quantum computing could be used to effectively identify fraud indicators. In health care, quantum computing can be used to predict the effects of potential therapeutic approaches and to optimize nonadverse effects. Lockheed Martin, one of the largest defense companies in the world, is using quantum computing to verify and validate aeronautics systems, design lifesaving drugs, and debug millions of lines of code [25]. In manufacturing, quantum computing could improve supply chain optimization problems in procurement, production, and distribution. Quantum computing can be useful in product optimization, advertising scheduling, and revenue maximization systems where hundreds of attributes about a consumer's preferences are collected. Quantum computing may strengthen the next generation of transport or logistics automation and remote sensor management.

Smart Dust

Smart dust is a network of micro-electro-mechanical devices, which includes a processing unit, some memory, and a radio chip, allowing them to communicate wirelessly with other smart dust devices within range [26]. Smart dust incorporates sensing, computing, wireless communication capabilities, and autonomous power supply at low cost.

Furthermore, these smart dust devices are expected to be so small and light that they can remain suspended in the environment like ordinary dust particles [27]. Because of these features, smart dust can be used to scrutinize the environment without affecting the natural processes. By collecting data in real time via miniaturized low-power sensors and wireless networks, smart dust will transform our understanding of the environment. Currently, the size of smart dust particles is about five cubic millimeters, but the size will continue to become smaller. The University of California at Berkeley's Smart Dust research team estimates that they can fit in the necessary sensing, communication, and computing hardware, with a power supply, in a volume no more than a few cubic millimeters [27]. Therefore, the future models of smart dust are expected to be small enough to remain suspended in air and communicate for a long period, sometimes for many years. The smart dust technology is in its infancy, but it has the potential to be applied in different areas, including security, military, traffic management, construction, mining, agriculture, and urban planning. The smart dust technology can allow continuous real-time monitoring of industrial and urban projects and structures. The data gathered on environmental, biological, and structural variables may help to improve the efficiency of global resource use. The experiments in California showed that the smart dust technology can be used by military and law enforcement personnel to monitor movement in the region [27]. Some examples of the smart dust technology include arranging defense networks by unmanned aerial vehicles; tracking the movements of birds, small animals, and insects; monitoring environmental conditions; managing inventory; and monitoring product quality [28].

The development of smart dust technology increases some concerns about privacy and security issues. The minuscule smart dust sensors could be used for mischievous, illegal, or unethical purposes. For example, the smart dust technology can be used for industrial espionage or for monitoring people without their knowledge. As smart dust technology becomes smaller, cheaper, and more powerful, the risks and concerns associated with the misuse of this technology will grow exponentially. One major concern is that once the smart dust networks are scattered, they are not easily retrieved, and they may involve serious environmental polluting effects.

Interfaces and Visualization

Deep Mapping

Deep mapping is an emerging technology that refers to a map incorporating various types of data within a geographic information system (GIS) environment [29]. Thus, deep mapping investigates the spatial location and systematizes different levels of information into conceptions using three-dimensional scenes. Deep mapping collects data from many sources, including remote sensor networks, aerial and satellite imagery, crowdsourcing, smartphones, and on-site mapping vehicles. The deep maps may contain rich and valuable information about a location regarding health, education, demographics, physical variables, air pollution, driving conditions, commercial and business issues, and many other factors. Deep mapping can be combined with surveillance devices to provide a richer visualization of a location. By offering both historical and real-time information about each particular location in one single interface, deep mapping can facilitate planning and decision making in many areas such as construction, traffic control, agriculture, and business activities. For instance, Google's Ground Truth is an ongoing project that combines data from governments and other organizations with the data it gathers itself through satellite imagery [30].

Mixed Reality

The concept of mixed reality is an emerging trend in information technology and refers to the integration of the physical and digital worlds. Mixed reality is the result of recent progress in computer vision, graphical processing power, sensors, display technology, mobile network capacity, and input systems. Unlike virtual reality and augmented reality, mixed reality does not immerse any content onto the real world; rather, it uses transparent lenses to make virtual objects both appear and interact with real ones. The mixed reality technological features provide virtual objects with a realistic sense of touch and change how people access information, share experiences, and provide feedback. Therefore, the mixed reality is expected to drastically change the relationships between human, computer, and physical environment. The combination of computer processing, human input, and environmental input creates mixed reality experiences. For instance, movement in the physical space can be translated into movement in the digital world and vice versa. Indeed, mixed reality can be positioned between augmented reality and virtual reality. The current augmented reality and virtual reality offerings represent a very small part of this spectrum and do not allow blending digital representations of people, places, and things with the real world. The windows mixed reality devices are either holographic or immersive. The holographic devices can place digital content in the real world as if it were there, whereas the immersive devices can hide or change the physical world and replace it with a digital experience. Fragments and RoboRaid are immersive devices that use the user's physical environment such as walls, floors, and furniture to place digital content in the world. Mixed reality can unleash unbelievable possibilities beyond our imagination. Due to its spatial technology, mixed reality will have major applications and implications in the areas such as design, architecture, and construction. For example, Microsoft's HoloLens enables users to view and interact with scalable, photorealistic, and responsive 3D holograms overlaid on the user's visual field. Some businesses are using mixed reality technology to inspect three-dimensional renderings of site plans prior to construction.

Multisensory Interfaces

Multisensory interfaces are emerging technologies that allow communication between humans and machines through a wide range of senses, eye or body movements, speech, and gestures. Due to their ease of use, multisensory interfaces are expected to replace conventional computer control systems such as keyboard and mouse. The integration of speech and other forms of conversational interfaces may allow real-time cross-language communications in a near future. Developments in mixed reality and virtual reality will require a new generation of user interfaces and experiences. Multisensory interfaces process multiple inputs across multiple devices to deliver contextual, connected, and viral experiences; they use all senses to capture information; and they do not ask for any information they should already know. They can rely on the previous data, and they continue to learn from their user's behaviors [31]. For instance, Samsung Inc. is developing a blink-detecting contact lens equipped with a display, camera, antenna, and movement sensors that can project an image directly onto the eye's retina.

Materials

Nanomaterials

Nanotechnology is a fast-growing area that is concerned with the production of very small particles or nanomaterials. A nanometer is one billionth of a meter, and nanomaterials are less than 100 nanometers.

Nanotechnology relies on microscopic processing techniques to produce various materials and components. Generally, there are two methods to produce nanomaterials. In the top-down method, small components are produced using larger parts of the material. In the bottom-up method, nanomaterials are produced from molecules or atoms. In nanotechnology, normal rules of physics and chemistry no longer apply, and many materials may show unique properties. For instance, they may become very much stronger, more conductive, or reactive [32]. One substantial property of nanoparticles is the massive surface area that makes them different from other materials [33]. Because of their essential characteristics, such as strength, lightweight, and insulating properties, nanomaterials have widespread applications in many industries, including agriculture and food, energy production and efficiency, automotive industry, cosmetics, medical appliances and drugs, household appliances, computers, and weapons [34]. There are many possible applications of nanomaterials in building corrosion-free steel, low-energy LEDs, and ultra-thin PV cells. Nanomaterials such as graphene could be used in water purification technology to improve access to clean drinking water. Nontechnology has various applications in the field of electronics. For instance, nontechnology is used in the miniaturized products to make high-purity materials with better thermal conductivity. Furthermore, nanomaterials are used to produce long-lasting and durable interconnections. Because of their physical characteristics, nanomaterials are used in developing supercapacitors that have a large capacity compared with normal capacitors.

Nanotechnology can be used to produce effective insulation materials for homes and offices. High-energy density batteries, heating and cooling bills, and cutting tools are other areas of nanomaterial applications. Nanoparticles can be used in medicine to selectively deliver drugs to specific cells. This method reduces the overall drug consumption and side-effects by placing the active agent in the morbid region [35]. Nanotechnology may be applied in all stages of food preparation, including production, processing, safety, and packaging. Currently, nanoparticles are used to create new food products. By adding nanoparticles to a polymer, a nanocomposite is formed that is much more transparent than a polymer containing micron particles, which is opaque. In energy production, nanotechnology offers a practical alternative to nonrenewable fossil-fuel consumption by producing cheaper, cleaner, and more efficient and renewable energies. Nanotechnology is still in its infancy, and many of its applications are under development.

Programmable Materials

Programmable materials can change their physical properties such as shape, density, conductivity, and optical properties in a programmable way depending on user input or self-sufficient sensing [35]. In other words, programmable materials refer to a form of controlled and shape-shifting matter that can transition from their current shape into the desired shape with complete reversibility [36]. There are two primary approaches to programmable matter: bottom-up attempts to change the behavior of materials at the atomic or molecular level and top-down approaches to creating miniature robotic systems to form a larger item [37]. Programmable materials could drastically change our understanding of the matter, and naturally, could have major implications for all aspects of our lives. The idea of programmable materials implies that the matter can be reused infinitely for different purposes. Programmed materials could bring a new generation of structures that respond dynamically and automatically to their environment. Applications of programmable materials could include architecture, infrastructure, production lines, construction, and operation. Programmable materials can be used in paintable displays, shape-changing robots and tools, rapid prototyping, and sculpture-based haptic interfaces. For instance, researchers at the MIT are working on a project to build shape-shifting carbon fiber in a racing car spoiler. The spoiler reacts to environmental change, morphing into its most efficient shape and improving the car's performance. The MIT Media Lab recently showed the latest version of Transform, which is a form of dynamic furniture that can turn digital information into three-dimensional shapes. The Transform dynamic furniture responds to hand movements to change its shape.

Bio-Based Materials

The term *bio-based material* refers to a wide range of substances such as chemicals, natural fibers, plastics, concrete, wood, composites, and final products. Bio-based materials are substances derived from living organisms. The production of bio-based materials does not rely on the extraction and emission of fossil carbon; instead, it uses feedstock that contains biogenic carbon. The feedstock may include agricultural crops, residues, and organic waste streams, wood, microorganisms, and animal products [38]. Bio-based materials offer sustainable alternatives to fossil-based materials, as they are often biodegradable and use low-energy production routes. The production of bio-based materials smartly uses biomass and contributes positively to savings in greenhouse gas emissions, toxicity, and waste reduction [39]. Therefore, the bio-based materials industry is attractive to policy makers, as it is associated with sustainable development, environmental protection, and the circular economy [38]. Furthermore, the bio-based materials industry offers exciting opportunities to rural areas in terms of economic development and job creation [40]. Due to their environmental benefits, bio-based materials have various applications. The bio-based materials industry may grow by 300 percent in the next four years. Construction, furniture, packaging, and manufacturing industries are likely to adopt bio-based materials. The attractiveness of bio-based materials will encourage researchers and engineers to accelerate innovation. For instance, researchers at the Wageningen Institute in the Netherlands have developed bioplastics for packaging, casings for consumer electronics, textiles, and parts for the automotive industry. Furthermore, they are developing inks, coatings, paper, cardboard, and construction materials from biomasses [41].

Energy and Resources

Foam Batteries

Batteries are big businesses, as they are used in various devices from computers and tablets to cars and wearables. The conventional batteries are made up of two-dimensional surfaces that limit the direction and speed at which energy can flow. As a result, the existing batteries take a long time to charge, lose energy rapidly, and require frequent replacement. Prieto, an innovative startup, is introducing the new batteries produced with a copper foam substrate that is approximately 98 percent air or void space [28]. Due to an increase in the surface area of approximately 60 times, the foam battery is expected to have much higher power densities. The foam battery will be customizable and can be optimized for either power density or energy density [42]. Furthermore, the foam battery technology promises to be cost-effective to manufacture and fast to charge. In addition, the foam batteries are smaller, lighter, safer, and less toxic than traditional 2D batteries. Some large companies in the consumer electronics sector, such as Apple, LG, and Nokia, have shown a growing interest in the new battery technology [28]. The foam batteries can be shaped to fit spaces that are inaccessible to traditional batteries in a safer and less expensive way. Because of its unique design, the foam battery can be used in wearables and tablets without compromising energy and power [42]. Furthermore, the foam battery technology can be used to build novel devices with military and industrial applications. In the transport sector, the foam battery technology is expected to be a viable option by offering improved efficiency, higher safety, and lower cost. Over time, the foam technology could provide energy storage solutions for grid-scale applications [28].

Fusion Reactors

In a fusion process, power is generated by using nuclear fusion reactions. During the process, two lighter atomic nuclei combine to form a heavier nucleus, and at the same time, they release large amounts of energy that can be harnessed to produce electricity. The fusion process in reactors is similar to what happens in stars like the sun. The fusion releases massive amounts of energy about one million times more power-ful than a chemical reaction, and it is three to four times more powerful than a conventional fission nuclear reaction. Fusion seems more advan-tageous than fission because it is safer and produces more energy and less waste and radioactivity. Fusion reactors could provide clean energy with no long-lasting radioactive waste. The vast amount of energy produced by fusion reactors can change the transport and other energy-intensive industries and replace fossil fuels. The major barriers to fusion power are fuel and a highly confined environment with a high temperature and pressure. Lockheed Martin, a giant defense firm, is working on the use of magnetic field pressure to make a fusion reactor that is 10 times smaller than other prototypes. The use of magnetic field pressure may be effective in managing extremely high temperatures during the fusion process [27].

Transparent Solar Panels

Researchers at Michigan State University invented a transparent luminescent solar panel in 2014 [43]. Transparent solar panels use organic materials to absorb light wavelengths that are invisible to the human eye. Currently, the main obstacle to the widespread use of conventional photovoltaic panels is their appearance [44]. Therefore, the transparency of solar panels is a significant game-changer because the transparent panels could replace conventional window glasses. Urban areas that do not have enough rooftop space will be able to transform their glass windows into energy-producing panels. Commercial buildings have many windows, which means huge energy generation with solar panels [44]. In addition, the new solar panels can come in colorful semitransparent devices, which designers and architects can use to design or decorate building [28]. In addition, transparent materials can be used on car windows, cell phones, or other devices with a clear surface and transform any surface into an energy-producing system. It is estimated that, by using invisible solar panels, a skyscraper could provide more than a quarter of the building's energy needs [45]. The widespread adoption of such panels can meet U.S. electricity demand and significantly reduce the use of other energy resources like fossil fuels. Transparent solar technologies could supply some 40 percent of energy demand in the United States in the next decade. Although the cost of developing transparent panels remains high and their energy output is still limited, their prospective extensive application is appealing to scientists and investors.

Pollution Digesters

With increasing levels of environmental pollution, the reduction of pollutants is becoming a serious challenge for many countries across the world. The pollution digestion technologies have been considered as solutions to the deteriorating air quality and environmental pollution, particularly in urban areas. Pollution digesters could include a wide range of methods, including anaerobic, large-scale air ionizers, and photocatalytically active substances. In the anaerobic digestion, organic matter is broken down into smaller particles by reactions in the absence of oxygen [46]. An anaerobic digester can be designed to treat different waste flows, for example, municipal solid waste, municipal organic waste, industrial waste, or sludge from a wastewater treatment plant [47]. The pollution digestion technologies can be used to remove, filter, and transform airborne pollutants, and thus improve air quality. Pollution digesters may be installed in building facades or across the urban areas to improve air pollution. As the quality of air, particularly in Asia and South America, continues to deteriorate, there is a growing interest from business and scientific communities in developing more efficient pollution digesters. For instance, Photoment is a powder-like substance that is photocatalytically active and reacts with sunlight to transform toxic airborne nitrous oxide into nontoxic nitrates that are not harmful to the environment or human health and is washed away by rain. Photoment can be added to the concrete paving surfaces in urban areas to reduce the number of airborne pollutants.

References

[1] Sabhikhi, A. 2018. "10 Questions about Augmented Intelligence." *Cognitive Scale*. https://cognitivescale.com/augmented-intelligence-you-can-trust/
[2] Kockelman, K. 2017. "An Assessment of Autonomous Vehicles: Traffic Impacts and Infrastructure Needs--Final Report." *Center for Transportation Research*. The University of Texas at Austin.

[3] Smith, B.W., and J. Svensson. 2015. Automated and Autonomous Driving: Regulation under Uncertainty.

[4] Hedlund, J. 2017. "Autonomous Vehicles Meet Human Drivers: Traffic Safety Issues for States." *Spotlight on Highway Safety.* Governors Highway Safety Association.

[5] Ford. 2016. "Ford Targets Fully Autonomous Vehicle for Ride Sharing in 2021; Invests in New Tech Companies, Doubles Silicon Valley Team." Press release August 16, 2016. https://media.ford.com/content/fordmedia/fna/us/en/news/2016/08/16/ford-targets-fullyautonomous-vehicle-for-ride-sharing-in-2021.html

[6] Autonomous Vehicles Readiness Index, Assessing countries' openness and preparedness for autonomous vehicles. https://assets.kpmg.com/content/dam/kpmg/nl/pdf/2018/sector/automotive/autonomous-vehicles-readiness-index.pdf

[7] Angerholzer III, M., D. Mahaffee, M. Vale, J. Kitfield, and H. Renner. 2017. *The Autonomous Vehicle Revolution: Fostering Innovation with Smart Regulation.*

[8] Autonomous Vehicles Considerations for Personal and Commercial Lines Insurers. 2016. https://munichre.com/site/mram-mobile/get/documents_E706434935/mram/assetpool.mr_america/PDFs/3_Publications/Autonomous_Vehicles.pdf

[9] Anderson, J.M., K. Nidhi, K.D. Stanley, P Sorensen, C. Samaras, and O.A. Oluwatola. 2014. *Autonomous Vehicle Technology: A Guide for Policymakers.* Rand Corporation.

[10] Henaghan, J. 2018. "Preparing Communities for Autonomous Vehicles." https://planning-org-uploaded-media.s3.amazonaws.com/document/Autonomous-Vehicles-Symposium-Report.pdf

[11] Kuzma, J., S. O'Sullivan, T.W. Philippe, J.W. Koehler, and R.S. Coronel. 2017. "Commercialization Strategy in Managing Online Presence in the Unmanned Aerial Vehicle Industry." *International Journal of Business Strategy* 17, no. 1, pp. 59–68.

[12] www.PassengerDrone.com

[13] Undertaking, S.J. 2016. European Drones Outlook Study-Unlocking the Value for Europe. *SESAR, Brussels.*

[14] Starkloff, E. 2015. "The Future of 5G: The Internet for Everyone and Everything." *Business 2 Community Magazine* 21.

[15] West, D.M. 2016. "How 5G Technology Enables the Health Internet of Things." *Brookings Center for Technology Innovation* 3, pp. 1–20.

[16] Numbers cited in MacGillivray, C. October 03, 2013. "The Internet of Things Is Poised to Change Everything, Says IDC." *Business Wire*; and McLellan, C. March 02, 2015. "The Internet of Things and Big Data." *ZDNet.*

[17] King, I. May 02, 2016. "5G Networks Will Do Much More Than Stream Better Cat Videos." *Bloomberg News.*

[18] Davies, R. 2016. "5G Network Technology: Putting Europe at the Leading Edge." *EPRS, European Parliamentary Research Service, Members' Research Service.*

[19] 5G Infrastructure Association. 2015. "The 5G Infrastructure Public Private Partnership: The Next Generation of Communication Networks and Services."

[20] Peters, G.W., and E. Panayi. 2016. "Understanding Modern Banking Ledgers through Blockchain Technologies: Future of Transaction Processing and Smart Contracts on the Internet of Money." In *Banking Beyond Banks and Money,* pp. 239–278. Springer, Cham.

[21] Collotta, M., G. Pau, T. Talty, and O.K. Tonguz. 2017. *Bluetooth 5: A Concrete Step Forward Towards the IoT.* ArXiv preprint arXiv: 1711.00257.

[22] Chang, K.H. 2014. "Bluetooth: A Viable Solution for IoT? [Industry Perspectives]." *IEEE Wireless Communications* 21, no. 6, pp. 6–7.

[23] Gershenfeld, N., and I.L. Chuang. June 1998. "Quantum Computing with Molecules (PDF)." *Scientific American.*

[24] Accenture. 2018. "Innovating with Quantum Computing Enterprise Experimentation Provides View into Future of Computing." https://accenture.com/t00010101T000000w/br-pt/_acnmedia/PDF-45/Accenture-Innovating-Quantum-Computing-Novo.pdf

[25] Srivastava, R., I. Choi, T. Cook, and N.U.E. Team. 2016. "The Commercial Prospects for Quantum Computing." *Networked Quantum Information Technologies.*

[26] Arief, B., P. Blythe, and A. Tully. 2013. *Using Smart Dust in Transport Domain.*

[27] Azodolmolky, S., P. Wieder, and R. Yahyapour. 2013. "Cloud computing Networking: Challenges and Opportunities for Innovations." *IEEE Communications Magazine* 51, no. 7, pp. 54–62.

[28] Chen, C.C., L. Dou, R. Zhu, C.H. Chung, T.B. Song, Y.B. Zheng, and Y. Yang. 2012. "Visibly Transparent Polymer Solar Cells Produced by Solution Processing." *Acs Nano* 6, no. 8, pp. 7185–7190.

[29] Bodenhamer, D.J., J. Corrigan, and T.M. Harris, eds. 2015. "Deep Maps and Spatial Narratives." *Indiana University Press.*

[30] https://techcrunch.com/2014/09/03/googles-ground-truth-initiative-for-building-more-accurate-maps-now-covers-50-countries/

[31] Coenraets, C., and J. Ward. 2015. "Principles of Multi-Sensory Applications." Available at: https://multisensory.github.io/

[32] Roco, M.C., C.A. Mirkin, and M.C. Hersam. 2011. "Nanotechnology Research Directions for Societal Needs in 2020: Summary of International Study."

[33] Shaffer, M.S., and A.H. Windle. 1999. *Advanced Materials* 11, p. 937.

[34] Varma, R.S., R.K. Saini, and R. Dahiya. 1997. "Active Manganese Dioxide on Silica: Oxidation of Alcohols under Solvent-Free Conditions Using Microwaves." *Tetrahedron letters* 38, no. 45, pp. 7823–7824.

[35] Knaian, A.N. 2008. *Design of Programmable Matter.* Doctoral [dissertation], Massachusetts Institute of Technology.

[36] Amend, J.R., and H. Lipson. 2009. "Shape-Shifting Materials for Programmable Structures." In *International Conference on Ubiquitous Computing: Workshop on Architectural Robotics.*

[37] Kirby, B.T., B. Aksak, J.D. Campbell, J.F. Hoburg, T.C. Mowry, P. Pillai, and S.C. Goldstein. 2007. "A Modular Robotic System Using Magnetic Force Effectors." *Proc. IROS* 2007, *IEEE Comp. Soc. Press,* pp. 2787–2793.

[38] Broeren, M.L.M. 2018. "Sustainable Bio-Based Materials-Application and Evaluation of Environmental Impact Assessment Methods." *Utrecht University.*

[39] Schmidt, O., S. Padel, and L. Levidow. 2012. "The Bio-Economy Concept and Knowledge Base in Public Goods and Farmer Perspective." *Bio-Based and Applied Economics* 1, no. 1, pp. 47–63.

[40] van der Meer, Y. 2017. Sustainable Bio-Based Materials: Opportunities and Challenges.

[41] https://wur.nl/en/About-Wageningen.htm

[42] https://prietobattery.com

[43] "This Full Transparent Solar Cell Could Make Every Screen a Power Source." *Extreme Tech.* April 20, 2015. http://extremetech.com/extreme/188667-a-fully-transparent-solar-cell-that-could-make-every-window-and-screen-a-power-source (accessed December 31, 2016).

[44] "Solar Energy That Doesn't Block the View." Michigan State University, August 19, 2014. (accessed October 29, 2016)

[45] Chang, S.Y., P. Cheng, G. Li, and Y. Yang. 2018. "Transparent Polymer Photovoltaics for Solar Energy Harvesting and Beyond." *Joule* 2, no. 6, pp. 1039–1054.

[46] Adekunle, K.F., and J.A. Okolie. 2015. "A Review of Biochemical Process of Anaerobic Digestion." *Advances in Bioscience and Biotechnology* 6, no. 6, pp. 205–212. http://doi.org/10.4236/abb.2015.63020

[47] Arivalagan, K., S. Ravichandran, K. Rangasamy, and E. Karthikeyan. 2011. "Nanomaterials and Its Potential Applications." *Int. J. ChemTech Res* 3, no. 2, pp. 534–538.

About the Author

Dr. Yeganeh is a professor of business and international management at Winona State University in Minnesota. Professor Yeganeh is a multidisciplinary scholar who has earned his MSc, MBA, and PhD from Université Laval in Québec, Canada. His research has appeared in various journals such as *Journal of International Management, International Journal of Conflict Management, Critical Perspectives on International Business, International Journal of Sociology and Social Policy, European Business Review, Personnel Review*, and *Competitiveness Review*.

Index

OTHER TITLES IN THE INTERNATIONAL BUSINESS COLLECTION

S. Tamer Cavusgil, Manchester Business School;
Michael Czinkota, Georgetown; and
Gary Knight, Willamette University, Editors

- *Adjusting to the New World Economy* by Michael Czinkota
- *The Chinese Market Series* by Danai Krokou
- *Trading With China* by Danai Krokou
- *The Chinese e-Merging Market* by Danai Krokou
- *The Chinese Market* by Danai Krokou
- *Creative Solutions to Global Business Negotiations, Third Edition* by Claude Cellich
- *Exporting* by Laurent Houlier and John Blaskey
- *Global Trade Strategies* by Michel Borgeon and Claude Cellich
- *Doing Business in Germany* by Andra Riemhofer
- *Major Business and Technology Trends Shaping the Contemporary World* by Hamid Yeganeh

Concise and Applied Business Books

The Collection listed above is one of 30 business subject collections that Business Expert Press has grown to make BEP a premiere publisher of print and digital books. Our concise and applied books are for...

- Professionals and Practitioners
- Faculty who adopt our books for courses
- Librarians who know that BEP's Digital Libraries are a unique way to offer students ebooks to download, not restricted with any digital rights management
- Executive Training Course Leaders
- Business Seminar Organizers

Business Expert Press books are for anyone who needs to dig deeper on business ideas, goals, and solutions to everyday problems. Whether one print book, one ebook, or buying a digital library of 110 ebooks, we remain the affordable and smart way to be business smart. For more information, please visit www.businessexpertpress.com, or contact sales@businessexpertpress.com.

Made in the USA
Middletown, DE
27 August 2024

59819058R00186